MW01037483

Confessions of an American Doctor:    A true

story of greed, ego and loss of ethics

by Max Kepler, M.D.

# FOREWORD

This is a true story.

I wrote it, in part, to assuage my own guilt. In that sense, it is self-serving. But I also wrote it because I thought it might benefit others. To me, that would be far more rewarding. Something good should come from what I've done.

The twelve years that have passed since my arrest have only deepened my sense of responsibility for all that transpired. Let there be no doubt: I am wholly to blame. But in telling the story, I wanted to tell the entire, non-sanitized version. That meant including my innermost thoughts and feelings that I didn't share with others, including my rationalizations that allowed my illegal behavior to continue. Embarrassing things, for sure, but I felt that if I was going to be true to the process, I had to tell everything. So, if sometimes it sounds like I'm engaging in self-apologist ruminations, it's because I was. That's what facilitated the fraud.

For legal reasons, I have changed some of the names, including my own. I have also altered details of the patient stories, due to confidentiality rules.

*The discipline of the written word punishes both stupidity and dishonesty.*    -John Steinbeck

# CHAPTER ONE

Wednesday, October 12, 2005, was a typical gleaming fall day in San Francisco. I had taken the week off, with plans to visit my best friend Greg and his family in Maryland, the perfect get away from my stressful job at the hospital. My flight left in several hours, and I needed to get my three-year old daughter to preschool. Jessica, however, wasn't having any of it, making a big fuss about missing her mother. I tried rubbing her back, holding her, even filling her favorite sippy cup with milk and poking it into her mouth. In the end, my suggestion that we stop by to see mommy on the way to school did the trick, and, with that, we were off.

Upon returning home, I quickly moved to finish packing for the trip. I was just grabbing some last-minute essentials—camera, my favorite watch, and a book and medical journals to read on the flight—when the doorbell rang just before 9:30. I assumed that the cabbie had arrived a few minutes early. Then the bell rang again, then again and again in rapid sequence.

"What's going on?" I thought as I stuffed the last remaining items into my bag. I left the back bedroom, walked to the top of the stairs, then down to the upper landing, where there was a large metal lever, a simple pull of which would open the front door via cables that ran inside the wall. Just outside the front door was a wrought-iron gate which provided additional security by preventing access to the door. I gave the lever a big heave, and with a groan, the front door swung open. Standing, I could not see who was outside the gate on the sidewalk, and so I knelt to have a look.

Peering back at me were six men, all dressed in black, eyes wide open, fidgeting nervously. They looked like a revved-up football team before a big game, being held back by their coach until just the right moment for them to be released onto the football field. My mind raced as I tried to figure out why these men were at my front door, when suddenly a loud voice called up to me.

"Are you Dr. Kepler?" one of the men asked.

"Yes," I replied, completely confused.

"Come down here immediately and keep your hands where we can see them," he commanded.

Stunned, I reached for the railing, and held onto it tightly for a few seconds, trying to collect my thoughts while I began moving slowly down the stairs.

"Open this gate immediately," a voice commanded.

Hand shaking, I released the gate's lock.

"Step out onto the sidewalk, please."

Robotically, I did as I was told.

"Are you Dr. Kepler, Dr. Max Kepler?"

"Yes."

"I am Special Agent Jurgenson from the US Postal Service. You're under arrest. Place your hands behind your back," he commanded.

I stared at him for a few moments, looking for an answer in his poker face. Finding none, I slowly rotated clockwise towards my front door.

"You have the right to remain silent. Anything you say can and will be used against you in a court of law..."

A strong hand grabbed my right wrist, and then I felt the cool, no-nonsense of metal slipping over my skin, followed by a clicking sound as the cuff was tightened against me.

"You have the right to speak to an attorney, and to have an attorney present during any questioning..."

My other hand was cuffed.

"If you cannot afford a lawyer, one will be provided for you at government expense."

I stared back into my apartment at one of Jessica's socks sitting on the second stair. It seemed so far away. I was flooded with relief that she was not there to witness this.

# CHAPTER TWO

*Two Years Earlier*

We had tried intensive marriage counseling, five months of it, but ultimately, we couldn't mend the fracture. When it became obvious resolution was not possible, the therapist brought our last session to a close with, "I'm sorry it didn't work out."

"Yeah," I said, standing to leave, painfully aware that I had failed in one of the most important undertakings of my life.

Alice remained seated, blankly staring at the carpet, while I made a break for the door and waited for her outside. A few moments later, the therapist guided her out, his hand on her shoulder.

"Take care," he said as we left.

We walked silently to our car, the one we had purchased together shortly after our wedding a year earlier. As we drove along the undulations of Gough Street in San Francisco, I finally broke the silence.

"I guess I'll move out."

"It's so sad," she replied.

"I never thought it'd come to this," I replied. "We were so in love, such a short time ago."

Alice looked away from me, cleared her throat, and then said, seemingly to herself, "We just couldn't seem to stop arguing."

She was right, of course. Our relationship had turned into one big semantic competition involving two over-educated and stubborn doctors. Pathetically, we couldn't subjugate our own egos for the sake of our precious one-year-old daughter. But, then again, maybe it was much more than that. Maybe we simply weren't as compatible as we first thought. The hastiness by which we got married and had had a child blurred the analysis. And now, the whole mess was unequivocally over, and my thoughts turned to our daughter.

"What about Jessica?" I asked.

With that, Alice put her head in her hands and began sobbing. I reached over and touched her on the shoulder, but she pulled away. And I understood why. The sadness we felt in letting down our daughter was disabling.

I was relieved when we finally arrived at our apartment at the corner of Noe and 24th Street. I got out of the car, while Alice went to pick up Jessica. Once inside, I paced the floors of our apartment, trying to regain my composure, before eventually settling into a chair in our home office. As I sat there, I could feel the failure of the marriage coursing through my entire body. I took a deep breath, to calm myself, but the enormous sense of emptiness and regret was overwhelming. The family I had so desperately longed for was dissolving.

I looked up at the bulletin board where photographs of Jessica were displayed, along with images from the wedding and of friends and family. As I did, it occurred to me for a moment that perhaps nothing I had accomplished or experienced in my life had been good enough. Or, possibly, *I* had never been good enough.

Too disturbed by those thoughts and already emotionally spent, I closed my eyes and tried to relax my mind. I rubbed a hand over my bald head.

*Maybe I'd feel better if I had more hair.*

I chuckled at the silliness of my thought as opened my eyes, rolled my chair close to the computer and Googled "hair loss treatment." Within minutes, I had found an interesting article.

"*Synthetic Peptide for Baldness Holds Promise,*" it trumpeted. Researchers at a company called Follicle Research had evidently discovered a new drug that was regrowing hair in early clinical studies. The drug was so effective, in fact, that it worked even on completely bald areas of the scalp by literally "turning on" dormant hair follicles. And since the peptide was formulated in a special solution that could be applied directly to the scalp, it was supposedly safe.

The story was impressive and seemed scientifically sound. Perhaps this magical tincture really could cure some of my life's ills. Within minutes, I fired off an email to the company, telling them I was a physician interested in trying their drug.

"Is there any way for me to use your formula, perhaps as a research subject?" I asked.

As I hit the "send" button, I could never imagine that I had taken the first step in a process that would culminate in my arrest.

# CHAPTER THREE

The day after our last couples' counseling session, I awoke several hours earlier than usual and drove to my job at Cade County Hospital, a public institution outside of San Francisco for the indigent and underserved. At Cade, I was both a rheumatologist and a hospitalist (a specialist in inpatient medicine), an unusual hybrid position I had accepted after finishing my post-graduate medical training two years earlier at the University of California, San Francisco (UCSF).

As I settled into my office at Cade, I looked at my watch and realized it was only 6 AM. That gave me a full two hours to obsess about the failure of my marriage. I was quite certain that was enough time to make me adequately fucked up for the day.

So, I started right into it, going back to our first date three years earlier in San Francisco while we both were in medical training at the University of California. I was a third-year resident in internal medicine and had not been in a serious relationship in nearly two years. Alice was an intern in radiology who had broken-up with her boyfriend six months before. A mutual friend had given me her phone number, and I called her that same night while I was doing laundry.

The conversation flowed from the beginning. She told me she was the youngest child of first-generation Korean immigrants who had eventually settled down in Darien, Connecticut, an affluent town located forty-five minutes outside of New York City. She had attended a high school that was perennially ranked as one of the best in the country. Her mother was a partner in a hedge fund, her father a real estate investor, and her three siblings, attorneys.

My background, I told her, was quite different. I grew up in Boon, Ohio, a small, socioeconomically depressed town with a population of fewer than twelve-thousand where "corning" (throwing hardened and shucked corn at passing cars in the middle of the night) and cow-tipping were legitimate ways of passing time (no kidding). And dating, let alone marrying, an Asian girl never crossed our radar screens (I didn't tell her that part—thought it might not come across right). Furthermore, the student test scores at my high school were among the lowest in the state. No one in my family had graduated from college. Dad was a restaurant manager, while Mom was a housewife, and my brother Danny had dropped out of college to become an airline pilot.

Despite our differences, I felt a strong connection with her right away. And I loved just listening to her voice and how articulate she was. Before I knew it, we had been talking for close to an hour, and I began to wonder whether I had carried on for too long. I didn't want to sound desperate to keep the conversation going.

A woman like this probably had guys falling all over her. I know I was.

"I'd love to get together some time," I suggested, resting the phone against my shoulder as I pulled my clothes from the dryer.

"I'd like that too. Can you call me in a month, after this rotation ends?"

I felt the energy drain from the conversation. I pushed the clothes back in, took the phone off my shoulder, and stood up.

"It's just a really busy time," she clarified.

"I understand. No problem. I'll give you a call."

I hung up and stood there dumbfounded. A month? Was she really that busy? Or was she not that interested?

Hoping it was the former, I made a mental note of when the thirty days would be up and called her on exactly that day, wondering if she would notice and be impressed. She sounded excited to hear from me, which was a relief.

Shortly into the conversation, I asked, "Would you like to have dinner sometime?"

"Why don't we try coffee?"

"I mean, that's fine, but why not dinner?"

"Coffee might be a better idea."

"Come on, let me take you out for dinner," I insisted.

"Okay," she replied, laughing.

"How does next Friday sound?"

"I think I'm on that night."

"Saturday?"

"That doesn't work either."

I paused, drumming my fingers impatiently on my knee.

"How about the following weekend?"

"That should be okay, but why don't you give me a call next Monday or Tuesday so we can figure it out?"

I agreed, while wondering why we couldn't figure it out then. Nonetheless, I called on Monday, pacing in my apartment while the phone rang.

"How about I pick you up at seven on Saturday?" I suggested after she answered.

"Thanks, but we can just meet at the restaurant."

"No, I'd really like to pick you up."

"Really?"

"Yes."

"Well, okay."

"What's your address?"

"I'm not sure."

Frustrated, I kicked one of my roommate's shoes against the wall. A medical degree from Penn and couldn't remember her own address? Was she playing a game or had she really forgotten? This woman was hard to pin down. Little did I know that these first two conversations would be accurate indicators of the eventual tension in our relationship. But at that point, I was too intrigued to give up. Or too challenged.

"Really?"

"I know it sounds ridiculous, but I actually don't. I can look it up but I don't have time right now. Do you think you can call me tomorrow night at the hospital?"

"Sure," I answered, tossing the phone onto the couch after I hung up.

I called the emergency room where
᠎ overnight shift.   After a five-minute
᠎᠎᠎ came to phone, breathless.

"Hello?"

"Alice, it's Max.   Just calling to get your address."

"Oh.   Can you hold a minute?"

"Sure," I said, shaking my head.   She returned with her address several minutes later.

Logistics finally arranged, I picked her up at her apartment on Saturday night and took her to Rose Pistola, an Italian restaurant in the North Beach section of San Francisco.   Once again, our conversation was effortless.   Even when dinner was over, neither of us was ready for the night to end.

We made our way over to Vesuvio, a beatnik bar several blocks away, and nestled into a cozy space upstairs, the windows affording a great view of City Lights Bookstore next door and the busy scene on Columbus Avenue below.   I ordered a beer, and she a tea, and we continued our conversation.   She was funny, and every time she laughed, I couldn't help but join in.   I had hoped for another hour or two from the night, but it was getting late, and we both had to be at the hospital early in the morning.

After I dropped her off, I watched her walk up to her outer Sunset district apartment, her baggy pants and loose-fitting top far from flattering, but it didn't matter. She tucked her black hair behind her ear and smiled back at me just as she closed the door, and in that instant, I was certain that she'd be my girl.

I'd later discover she'd also be a tremendous pain in the ass, but then again, I was far from an angel.

12

The sound of my beeper jolted me from my thoughts. It was the ER doctor, asking if I could admit a patient to the hospital.

The orange, almost fluorescent, glow of the standard-issue jail garb he wore was the first thing I noticed about Shon. At the time, he was lying in a gurney, ankles shackled to the bed, carrying on a conversation with a deputy sheriff sitting close by. It turned out that Shon had developed a serious hand infection after being bitten by another inmate. I ordered antibiotics and called the plastic surgeon, who took him to the OR to clean out the infection. By the following day, Shon was feeling a little better when I visited him on morning rounds.

As I left his room, I wanted to ask the deputies sitting outside what crime Shon had committed, but I knew they weren't permitted to disclose such information. I thought it was probably serious, though, because the sheriffs seemed particularly cautious with him, always making sure that his legs were never free. Even when he made the five-foot walk to the bathroom, the deputies took the time to shackle his two legs together, the metal chain making a distinctive dragging noise against the hospital floor. It seemed like an inordinate amount of caution for such a small, seemingly harmless man, a man I found funny and grew to like over the next few visits I had with him.

One day when I got back to the nurses' station, I decided to do my own research on Shon. A Google search quickly returned a large number of results. The first to come up was a headline from a newspaper: "Local man charged with sexually abusing five children," it read.

I quickly clicked on the story to verify the name. It was indeed my patient. More reading revealed the offenses had taken place over the previous four years while Shon worked as a karate instructor at a local gym. Furthermore, Shon had already served seven years in prison for molestation committed twenty years previously.

I sat there silently, trying to reconcile my perception of Shon with his crimes against children. My patient, the man I was caring for and whose company I had come to enjoy, was a pedophile.

The next day, as usual, I swiped my hospital ID card across the security pad next to the door of his room and a beep sounded, followed by the loud unlocking of the door, which startled me, even though I had heard it many times before. Without a word, I went to his bedside, picked up his bandaged hand, and began removing the gauze wrappings. Out of my peripheral vision, I could see him looking at me curiously, waiting for the greeting that I didn't give him. The procedure seemed interminable, and I tried hard to focus on the details of it, so as to not think of his crimes. But I found thoughts of his victims intrusive and unavoidable, and I hated that I had to care so meticulously for such a man. I looked at the details of his hands—their length and shape, the fingernails—and I thought about what those hands had done to those children. I wanted to inflict my own brand of vigilante justice, by withholding pain medications and letting him suffer. But I was a physician and he was my patient. I could not provide anything less than standard of care for his condition.

Shon remained in the hospital for another ten days before returning to jail. Each day, I performed the same dressing change and evaluated the hand for improvement. In my mind, I cared for a hand, and just a hand. I found it easier that way.

The day he was discharged, I heard Shon shuffling down the hallway on his way back to jail. As he passed the nurses' station where I was busy writing a note in the chart, he paused for a moment to thank me. I looked up at him, standing there in his oversized orange clothes, and nodded. There was nothing left for me to give him.

The dragging chain noise was fading and I was just starting to feel bad for myself for having to deal with sick sexual deviant bastards when I got a page to admit an ex-heroin addict named Willie for hemodialysis.

"Another day at the lovely county hospital," I muttered to myself as I walked down to the ER. By this point, I could measure my growing bitterness about my job in obvious daily increments.

My first impression of the patient was that he looked pretty young for his age, given the self-inflicted abuse and neglect he had apparently put himself through over many years. He made it clear right away that my questions and physical examination of him were an imposition, snarling, "Jesus Christ, could I just get a goddamn sandwich before you talk to me." Unfortunately, as much as I wanted to, I couldn't say that taking care of him was definitely not my first choice of activities, either. With as much patience as I could muster, I completed my evaluation, informing him of my plan, which included dialysis later that day.

"Do what you have to do," he said with a dismissive wave.

When I returned to the nurses' station, I reviewed Willie's medical history, finding a large volume of information, including the fact that he had contracted HIV years before from drug use.   He had also spent time in prison, but fortunately, there was health care in prison.  Good, free health care with state-of-the-art medications for his HIV disease, which had been brought under control.   After being released from prison, and to his credit, Willie did not return to drug dealing or using.  He stayed in construction, getting paid under the table and never paying insurance premiums or income tax.  Hiding his income and living with his auntie, Willie was able to obtain medical coverage through a county-based health insurance plan for the indigent.  Despite this, he did not regularly attend the doctor appointments they made for him or take the medications they prescribed over next decade.   As a consequence, his kidneys failed and he was started on dialysis, which automatically qualified him for Medicaid for the rest of his life.

But patients have to fill out applications to receive the benefits.  Willie didn't feel like doing that.   So, he didn't receive the benefits, and without those, outpatient hemodialysis centers would not dialyze him.   Instead, Willie was admitted to the hospital every four days for two consecutive days of hemodialysis.  This had been going on for three months, incurring a significant financial cost to the hospital and taxpayers, and now it was my turn to take care of him.

After I finished writing admission orders for Willie, I walked unenthusiastically to the medical wards for morning rounds.   I was dealing far too frequently with

16

patients like Willie, and I was starting to become resentful that I had to care for people who refused to take care of themselves.

I took my patient list out of my coat pocket and began reviewing the names there. After a minute or so, I realized I didn't have the energy, so I put it back. I wasn't in the mood for doctoring.

In fact, for the past six months or so, I was slowly losing interest in my job, particularly the paradigmatic thinking and lack of creativity of clinical medicine. The patients started to run together, a generic assembly line of uninteresting cases. I felt as if I had been dropped into the middle of a computer algorithm. Sighing, I took out the list and began reviewing my patient plans:

"Forty-five-year-old woman with pneumonia: Prescribe antibiotics, oxygen, Tylenol and a cough suppressant."

"Fifty-four-year-old man with asthma attack: Prescribe steroids, antibiotics, inhalers, and oxygen."

"Twenty-three-year-old woman with diabetic coma: Prescribe intravenous fluids, insulin, potassium replacement."

"Sixty-two-year-old man with a skin infection: Prescribe antibiotics, leg elevation, Tylenol."

Who cared? It was like following a cookbook. Couldn't anyone could do that? I felt stuck. I no longer had goals to achieve or challenges to overcome. I wasn't getting enough out of being a doctor. I missed the excitement and intellectual stimulation of academic medicine. Perhaps I had made a big mistake in coming to Cade, and then caused the self-questioning to resume.

*Is this what I signed up for? Is this the best use of my talent? Couldn't just about anyone do this job?*

At UCSF, we saw patients who had been referred from all areas of northern California for unusual and fascinating diseases. The academic center was the bastion of up-to-date knowledge on human illness and treatment, and our expertise was in great demand. In addition, I had conducted clinical research at UCSF that had the potential to help patients all over the world. Now that I was at Cade County, my job description included caring for ungrateful, disrespectful, irresponsible addicts and the infected hand of a child rapist. I started to wonder if these patients deserved to be cared for someone like me, and whether I deserved a lot better than them. Hadn't I transcended my humble beginnings to become extraordinary? And since I was extraordinary, didn't I deserve extraordinary circumstances?

As I bathed in the warm, reassuring waters of self-congratulation and ego inflation, a thought occurred to me:

*You might just want to check that ego at the door, Mr. All-World-doctor-blessing-the-county-hospital-with-his-amazing-talents stud. You're lucky to have such a privilege.*

Embarrassing as it was it admit, it wasn't the first or last time I had or would engage in such self-admiration. But that ego would eventually get checked—oh, would it get checked—courtesy of the United States Government. That would come later, however. For now, I was just starting the process of full flame-out.

The chirp of my Blackberry relieved me of my ruminations. The email was from one Lance Starling,

18

founder and CEO of Follicle Research, telling me his scientific advisory board was busy in the midst of their yearly meeting in Seattle, but he was interested in talking further about their hair growth product, which he called FR-1.    I called him immediately.

After brief introductions, Lance described his company using highly technical terminology and demonstrating an advanced knowledge of hair loss.    He further impressed me by citing their encouraging clinical results from studies performed in collaboration with a doctor in Seattle.    The company's immediate goal was to treat additional patients with FR-1 in order to further validate its effectiveness, after which they planned to bring the product to market.

The treatment was topical—applied directly to the scalp—which Lance felt made it a safe medication.    I didn't necessarily agree with him about that but continued to listen intently.    The challenge, Lance emphasized, was in getting the medication to pass through the outer skin barrier and into the middle layer of the skin where the hair follicles were.    To accomplish this, Lance was adding DMSO, an industrial solvent often used as an ingredient in various horse liniments.    However, adding DMSO would require a doctor's prescription and that prevented it from being sold over-the-counter, which would make it harder to bring to market.    Consequently, Follicle Research needed to establish a network of prescribing physicians that could also help with distribution of the product.    Lance wondered if I might be interested in this opportunity.

Suddenly, my interest shifted from personal hair growth to making money.    If the medication was effective, the demand would be phenomenal.    By the end of our ten-minute conversation, I was convinced I had stumbled into a potential financial windfall. Since Lance had not yet established the proposed network of doctors, I would be entering on the ground floor.

Nonetheless, I had certain ethical obligations as a physician, and so I informed Lance I needed more information to decide, but he was understandably reticent to share any further details.

"I'm in the middle of filing a patent for the peptide," he said. "Let me think about this a little more."

When I arrived home that night, I met Alice at the top of the stairs and gently took Jessica from her. With Asian eyes, dark skin, and dimples, Jessica was a delightful mixture of Alice and me. Alice had put a cute knit cap on her head, and I lifted it to kiss her forehead.

Jessica had been a miracle baby, conceived with sperm I had collected ten years earlier at a facility in Massachusetts and then later shipped to San Francisco. I had done this because my doctor at the time told me that the treatment I needed for a rare autoimmune disease called Wegener's Granulomatosis that I had contracted could cause infertility. The disease came when I was twenty-five years old, causing bleeding in my lungs and failure of my kidneys (they would later recover with treatment), and I would end up missing six months of graduate school due to the illness. Although it was the worst thing that had happened in my life to that point, it was also the best thing, because ultimately it was the reason I had decided to go to medical school.

I had told Alice about my possible infertility soon after our relationship turned serious, but she had been

20

undeterred by it. "You have millions of sperm stored. I'll just go through *in vitro* fertilization if I have to," she told me at the time. Her response gave me a great measure of relief, as I had half expected her to end the relationship. As it turned out, to become pregnant, Alice did have to go through IVF, a procedure that took about three weeks and required injections of high doses of hormones, frequent ultrasounds and various uncomfortable procedures. Alice went through the process without a single complaint, and that, for me, was the single most meaningful act anyone has ever done for me, even if she was doing it for herself as well.

We had arranged for the IVF process to be completed the day before a scheduled trip to Florida. We thought the relaxing nature of the beach would increase our chances of success. After a week, we returned home, and several days later, Alice went for a pregnancy test. We waited several hours and then I called the doctor. Alice sat next to me as I received the great news.

"It's positive? It's positive?" Alice asked, when I broke into a broad smile.

We jumped up and down for a minute, yelling like maniacs, before collapsing into each other's arms.

When Alice was five months pregnant, we married in a lovely ceremony at her brother's house, with the sun setting behind the Golden Gate Bridge serving as a backdrop. We had arranged the entire wedding in less than a month. Despite the rapid decision, we received nothing but support from both our families.

Jessica came four months later, after a lot of trepidation due to her slow growth during pregnancy. Weighing just five pounds, fifteen ounces, she looked like an elongated

21

wet rat when they pulled her out. Although I was a doctor and had witnessed many births during medical school, my hands shook as I cut the umbilical cord. Afraid I might do some damage, the doctor quickly took the scissors out of my hand when I finished. Later, after she had been cleaned and bundled, I cried with gratitude as I held her tight against my chest.

Soon after Jessica's birth, our arguments began again, this time with more vehemence. I had poo-poo'ed Mom's earlier admonition that, "If you have differences before the baby, they're only exaggerated after," but now I knew exactly what she meant. It seemed we couldn't agree on anything about Jessica. I felt she was overly attentive to the baby; she felt I didn't understand the difficulties faced by a first-time mother and wasn't supportive enough. She wanted to wrap the baby in fifteen layers of clothes for a short trip to the pharmacy around the corner; I thought a warm jacket would do the trick. I thought waking the baby up to feed her was a bad idea; she thought we should adhere to a strict schedule. She told me I needed to support the baby's head more when I held her; I told her I doubted the baby's neck would snap off.

And then there were the issues of control that, in my mind, seemed to worsen once Jessica was born. If I felt I had less of an outside life before, now I had none whatsoever. I even had to give up my occasional round of golf on Monday afternoons, despite not having any work or parental responsibilities during that time, because I grew tired of hearing Alice complain about it. I always thought she was unhappy that I was having fun while she was at work.

Things reached a crescendo five months before our eventual break-up.   While Jessica napped in the back bedroom, we stood toe-to-toe in the front of the apartment, arguing about a proposed two-day golf weekend I wanted to take with friends.

"You're not in college anymore, frat boy!" she yelled at me.

"You don't like it because you won't be able to control me for a weekend," I replied.

"You need to grow up."

"Fuck you!   You need to shut up," I replied.

"Don't tell me to shut up.   And you're not going!"

I started stomping around the room like a petulant child, screaming obscenities at her, completely overreacting.   She followed me, yelling right back. After a few minutes, I had had enough and decided to go into the garage to cool off, but I was still livid and hurling invectives as I walked down the two flights of back stairs, my bad temper once again getting the best of me.   I sat on the washing machine for about twenty minutes until I had mostly calmed down, and then returned to our apartment.   Alice was still in the front room and as I turned to walk to the back of the apartment, I heard the doorbell ring.   Alice immediately jumped off the couch and ran down the stairs to open the door.   I walked over for a look and saw two San Francisco police officers coming up the stairs ahead of her.

"Sir, your wife called us about a disturbance here," the taller one said.

I looked for Alice, but she was blocked by the officers, so I yelled, "What the hell are you doing, Alice?"

The police officer put up his hands. "Sir, settle down now." By this time, he had reached the top, and I moved back a few steps to allow him and his partner into the apartment. Alice stayed halfway down the stairs. I looked over the railing at her but her head was down. The police officer pulled me away from the railing and stepped in front of me.

"I think it'd be a good idea if you stayed somewhere else tonight," he said firmly. "Okay? Let things blow over a little. You can come back tomorrow."

I hesitated, looking at his face, and realized I had no choice.

After I finished packing a bag, I walked past the officers and started down the stairs. They quickly turned to follow me. As I passed Alice, I looked at her, jabbed my finger in her face, and said, "I'll remember this."

"Keep moving," the officer said, his hand now on my shoulder.

That night, I found a hotel near the airport. I didn't try to call Alice, and I was too angry to even sleep. By the end of the night, I resolved that I would never allow Alice to do this to me again, whatever it took. That thought process took me to some scary places, and after a while, I pushed those things out of my mind.

The next day, I waited until noon to return home. As it was Saturday, Alice was there when I arrived, and she came out from the bedroom to greet me.

"We need therapy," she said, firmly. "And now."

I walked past her without a word. One week later, we started the process that would ultimately prove futile.

# CHAPTER FOUR

I awoke very early two days after our    last couples session and dragged myself out of bed.    The apartment seemed very quiet, and I felt an enormous emptiness.    I wandered over to our home office and sat down.    I didn't want to cry—maybe couldn't cry—because it all seemed too unreal.    But I could feel the failure of the marriage coursing through my entire body.    I took a deep breath, so as to calm myself down.

I looked around the familiar room I would soon be leaving.    In front of me, perched on the desk, was an old baseball in a plastic display case.    It had been autographed by Sparky Anderson, the Cincinnati Reds manager during the Big Red Machine era of the seventies. He had given it to me before a game at Riverfront Stadium when I was ten, and it remained one of my most prized possessions.

As I stared at the faded writing on the yellowing leather, I remembered the time during that same summer of '76 when I had entered the local Pitch, Hit and Run competition being held in neighboring Middletown, a city five times bigger than Boon. Mom drove me there in our rusty Oldsmobile Cutlass, a whale of a car that was completely white and completely broken, inside and out. That included the driver's seat, so Mom had to sit with her torso twisted halfway to the right, an awkward position whose only advantage was that it afforded her a better view of me sitting next to her, staring intently at the passing neighborhoods of small houses and big trees.

We arrived at Smith Field just as the stifling heat and humidity seemed to peak. The organizers placed the competitors into three groups of about forty each. I ended up in the same group as my best friend Tim Barker, and his presence eased some of my anxiety. Plus, it would allow me to keep an eye on how he was doing. Best friend or not, I wasn't about to let him beat me.

The competition started with a test of our pitching skill. The organizers had set up a square steel frame with netting behind. The object was to toss the baseball into the netting from sixty feet away, the usual distance from the pitching mound to home plate. I was confident I would do well, for Dad had set up a similar contraption in our backyard, hanging an old carpet from a large metal frame and then taping a square box in the middle. I spent many hours all year throwing buckets of old baseballs into that target. The practice paid off; when my name was called, I proceeded to throw all three baseballs into the net.

Next was the running event, where competitors were timed rounding the bases. Running was my specialty; I did it all the time. I ran to school each day. I ran to Tim's house. I ran laps around my own house. Mom and Dad would watch in bewilderment with each pass I made by the kitchen window.

"What are you doing, Max?" Dad would ask when I finished.

"Just running," I'd tell them, as if it were obvious.

"Yeah, but why?"

"Because it's fun," I'd say, leaving them shaking their heads.

I walked to home plate when they called my name. I crouched down and dug my baseball cleats into the dirt. I was wearing my shoes from the previous year, despite the fact my feet had grown more than one size. To make them fit, I had gone into Dad's closet, found a set of shoehorns, and used them to stretch my shoes. I never told my parents; I didn't want to burden them financially, as I knew Dad didn't make much money.

The starter counted down to "go!", and I was off. My long legs chewed up the distance from home to first base more quickly than I anticipated, and I nearly lost my balance. I righted myself and motored past second. By the time I rounded third, I was certain it was the fastest I had ever run. After I crossed home plate, Tim came over to me.

"You were really booking!" he said.

"Was I really?" I asked wide-eyed, trying to appear humble.

I was, indeed. In fact, I was clocked with the second fastest time of the competition. Things were going well, but I still had the hitting event.

For this one, competitors were allowed to hit five balls off a tee. The furthest ball was scored. I had been swinging a bat for as long as I could remember. Dad had built me a tee when I was six, and I had spent a lot of time hitting balls against netting. There were nights when I would spend so much time practicing that our next-door neighbor would come over in his pajamas and plead with me to go to bed and let him sleep.

With my first two swings, I nearly missed the ball. But then I found a rhythm, and my last ball was the longest of the competition.

For my efforts, I won first place for the highest overall score and received a medal and an invitation to compete at the sectional competition the following month, where local competition winners from all over the state would be present. I felt sorry for Tim as he stood watching me receive the award, and I wished he could accompany me to the sectional.

In the weeks leading up to the event, I could barely contain my excitement, and I would lie awake in bed dreaming of the fame and recognition that would surely be mine when I won. I practiced constantly, and when the day finally arrived, my parents drove me the thirty-five miles to Cincinnati. My hands were shaking when I got out of the car, and I nearly missed my turn at the first event: pitching. I ended up getting just one ball in the target, and things seemed to only get worse in the subsequent two events.

This time when the awards were presented, I was the one standing on the sidelines watching others receive their medals. After climbing into the car, I began to cry. Mom let it go on for a bit before turning around from the passenger seat to face me.

"Max, it's going to be okay. It's just one competition," she said softly.

"I know, but I wanted to go to the state championship," I managed.

"You tried your best.   That's all that matters."

"But I only got one pitch in the target."

"It's better than none.   Plus, I thought you had the strongest arm there," she said, smiling.

"But I could have run faster, too."

"I thought you ran like the wind," she said, waving her hand in a swooping motion.

Reaching back, she rubbed my knee until my tears stopped, and then turned back around.   Dad winked at me through the rear-view mirror and then switched on the radio.   The scenery was becoming increasingly rural as we sped north on Interstate 75, and I continued to obsess over my mistakes in the competition, despite Mom's reassurances.   And as soon as we got home, I walked to my bedroom, pulled my local competition medal off the wall, and stuffed it into a shoebox under my bed.

My complete rejection of failure and an undying competitive spirit had taken me from Boon to Harvard (I was the first person from my high school to go there), then to a Ph.D. and an M.D., and finally propelled me to one of the best internal medicine residencies and rheumatology fellowships in the country at UCSF.   But the process was also both emotionally and physically tiring, and near the end of my training at UCSF, I decided I needed to wind the whole thing down.   So, I refused an offer from the university to join the faculty there.   To accept the faculty position meant that I would be taking another spin on the roulette wheel of achievement, for in the academic setting there are a clearly-sequenced series of steps, starting with assistant adjunct professor and ending with tenured professor, that mark professional advancement. And that journey would require a tremendous amount of work, something I just wasn't up for anymore. Plus, I wanted to make money and the faculty position offered to me was only seventy-two thousand dollars per year. I had student loans totaling over one-hundred thousand dollars, a new baby on the way, and I lived in one of the most expensive areas of the country. Furthermore, I never had had money; neither growing up nor in the fourteen years I spent after graduating from college going from graduate school to medical school to residency to fellowship. Now, at thirty-six, I was ready for a real job with real pay.

And that's when little Cade County Hospital came to my rescue, offering to pay me three times more than UCSF. I also liked the fact I'd have dual responsibilities at Cade, particularly since I had no interest in practicing just rheumatology. There were simply too many chronic pain patients, such as those with fibromyalgia, which could be emotionally draining. Hospitalist medicine, on the other hand, involved the care of inpatients, and so it was necessarily a more intense and exciting experience. In that role, I would be literally saving lives, which also minimized the chance that I'd become bored, something that did tend to happen very easily with me.

At Cade, I would join a group of seven physicians, each of whom practiced a different specialty. They were all devoted, likable people who functioned effectively as a team, something I appreciated, given my background in sports. Members of the group treated each other like family, and every year they vacationed together over Labor Day Weekend. And since the group had been in existence for thirty years, there was stability as well.

When I signed the contract in May of 2002, I effectively pulled the ripcord on academia, something I had never envisioned happening. But I felt the decision was a healthy one. No longer would I have to worry about accumulating degrees or symbols of recognition. And I was convinced my love of patient care would transcend any boredom I might experience from being away from the stimulating university setting. Instead, I could just settle down, establish my little corner in the medical universe, and live with the contentment that I was practicing something I had taken more than a decade to learn.

Two years later, it was clear that I wasn't the settling type. I was restless and plum out of challenges. I needed something to make me feel alive again.

So, I called Lance.

"Just wanted to check in to see where your thinking was regarding my involvement in Follicle Research," I said.

"Thanks for your call, Max. I still haven't decided. I've been pretty busy with lab work."

"I completely understand, Lance, but I want you to know that my Ph.D. in pharmacology would be an excellent complement to yours in biochemistry."

"You make a good point," he replied. "What are your feelings regarding DMSO?"

"I've looked into it, and I think I'd be comfortable with prescribing the drug. I'd still like to do a little more due diligence, though."

Of course," he replied, now sounded excited. "Tell you what. Why don't we start with a non-disclosure agreement? I'll fax it to you later today."

I hung up the phone feeling good about something for the first time in a while.

The faxed non-disclosure agreement (NDA) arrived later that day. I reviewed the document for less than five minutes before signing and faxing it back to Lance. Within an hour, I received a call from him.

"Hello, Max. Lance Starling here." I could feel his energy flowing through the phone. "Thank you for the NDA. Just wanted to talk to you a bit about our product. Is this a good time?"

I had a scheduled meeting in five minutes, but I replied, "Sure."

"Great. The hair peptide is a hormonally-based therapy. It's a relatively short sequence, but its uniqueness lies in its folding characteristics."

Peptides are found everywhere in nature, including the human body, where they perform various functions. For example, peptides are in fingernails, ligaments, tendons, bone, muscle, and hair. Peptides can also be hormones, naturally-occurring chemicals that have wide-ranging effects on the human body. Testosterone, which improves muscle strength, deepens the voice, causes hair growth and stimulates sex drive, is one well-known example.

"Is it similar to an endogenously-occurring hormone?" I asked.

"Yes."

"Which one?"

"I'm not comfortable sharing that with you right now."

"I understand. Can you tell me its target receptor?"

In order for a peptide to produce its effect, it needs to attach to a structure called a receptor, which is found on cell walls. If the peptide is the key, the receptor is the lock. But in order for the key to fit into the lock, it must be cut into a very specific pattern. Similarly, the peptide must have a certain conformation in order to be effective.

"The peptide attaches to a receptor found in a specific region of the hair follicle," Lance continued. "Utilizing computer modeling, I have been able to produce a structurally-modified version of a naturally-occurring peptide that interacts very strongly with this receptor."

His voice was deep and reassuring, and his diction was so perfect it seemed like I was listening to an audio book. My meeting could wait for another day. He went on to describe his research in even greater scientific detail, which I found enthralling. It was clear to me that Lance had an exquisite understanding of the science he was investigating. And I assumed that his results had been impressive, since he had retained the services of a prestigious Boston law firm to assist in patenting the product. But when I asked one too many questions about the peptide's behavior in the human body, Lance transitioned into a discussion of hair growth physiology, clearly concerned I might figure out the identity of the peptide.

"Even though the scalp is bald, there are still hair follicles present," he said. "This is critical to understand. Since they are still present, they simply need to be turned on again. They need to be brought out of hibernation. My drug does just that."

Lance hesitated, to allow me to assimilate his words. By this point, I was convinced he was absolutely brilliant, but I was still concerned about possible legal and ethical issues regarding DMSO. Although I doubted there would be any problems, I reminded Lance that I wanted to consider this a bit more before committing to essentially handing over the privileges of my medical license.

"Of course, of course, I completely understand," he reassured me. "In the meantime, let me ship you some product so that you can try it yourself."

"That would be great," I replied, not even trying to disguise my excitement.

This would be my chance to see whether the treatment was legitimate.

Conversation complete, I returned to my care of patients, but it was hard to concentrate because Follicle Research remained on my mind, and I was relieved when the end of the day finally arrived. I went to my office and tried calling Alice to tell her I'd be home late, as I needed to look for an apartment, but she didn't answer. Since she always carried her cellphone, I knew she simply didn't want to talk, so I left a message. Then I spent several hours searching online until I found an apartment I liked, calling the landlord to set up an appointment for the next day. Afterwards, instead of going home, I surfed the internet for another hour or so, hoping to avoid contact with Alice if I got home late enough.

When I finally walked into our apartment later that evening, Alice was asleep on the couch, a book resting on her lap. I hadn't seen her face so relaxed in a long time. I switched off the light and stood in the dark next to her, feeling particularly melancholic and reflective. I covered her with a blanket and went to the bedroom to get undressed, stopping on the way to check on Jessica, finding her asleep. I didn't feel tired, so instead of going to bed, I grabbed a warm jacket and my grandpa's old woolen plaid hunt cap and went out into the late San Francisco night.

As I walked down 24th Street in Noe Valley, I began thinking about the beginning of my relationship with Alice, when we'd spent every free moment together. I'd hurry out of the hospital so just I'd have an extra ten minutes to spend with her. When I walked down the street holding her hand, I could feel her pulse, strong and steady against me. An indescribable feeling of connection and oneness, bordering on erotic, would carry me along. Three years later, it was hard for me to comprehend how such a state of connectedness with another person could be so thoroughly lost.

Unable to come to an explanation, I adjusted my cap and looked at my watch. I had been walking for close to an hour and my mind was as exhausted as my body, so I decided to head home. Just to the west, fog partially illuminated by the city lights was hung up on Twin Peaks. San Francisco was quiet now. Inside the apartment, I peeked into the family room and found Alice still asleep on the couch. I went to the other end of the apartment, undressed and climbed into bed, falling asleep almost immediately.

# CHAPTER FIVE

Three days after my last couples session with my wife, I left work early to view the potential new apartment located less than a mile away from our old one, where Alice and Jessica would remain.   Nearly identical to the apartment I shared with my dissolving family, it felt like fourteen hundred square feet of a transitional object.

"A big person's teddy bear," I thought to myself as I signed the lease on the spot.

I left the apartment and sat in my car, reflecting.   I remembered a card Alice had given me for our first Valentine's Day.   In addition to being a doctor, Alice was a talented artist, and she had constructed the card entirely from scratch.   On the front, she wrote:

Both a wild thought, mutually caught
The moon is calling us
In a whisper, it says it's true
A house of hope exists for me and you.

Inside, she created an outline of a couple lying down in embrace, using strings, beads and glue.   Around the contours of the bodies, she wrote a poem:

The moon is calling us.
And I hear myself say,
I would like to be next to you,
If you want me to.
I would like to get next to you,
If you want me to.
Holding,
Skin to skin.

Tears started to form as I reflected on the beauty of her words, but I quickly brushed then away.   I had now been sitting in my car in the driveway of my new apartment for over thirty minutes and decided it was time to go home. When I arrived, Alice was still at work, and I decided to use the free time to call Mom.   After telling her about my new place, I sensed something was wrong, and asked her what it was.

"I wanted to tell you earlier," she said, "but I didn't want to worry you too much.   I know you are having a hard time."

I took off my tie and sat down, realizing from the tone of her voice what was up.

"Don't tell me it's the cancer," I said.

"I'm sorry," she said quietly.

My whole body went numb.

Mom had been diagnosed with non-Hodgkin's lymphoma a decade earlier at the age of forty-eight.   I had received the biopsy results from Dad on my twenty-fourth birthday, on a day I was in the lab doing research.

"She has that stuff," was all he'd managed. I nearly dropped the phone. Mom always seemed indestructible to me. She never got sick, never even seemed tired, and was always on the go. She was the one radiating energy from the moment she awoke. And now she could die? It seemed too unreal to fathom.

The doctor told that her lymphoma was slow-growing, which was both good and bad news. The good news was the average life span after diagnosis was seven years, a long time in the world of cancer. The bad news was that since it was slow-growing, it wasn't curable; it could only be put into remission, but eventually the cancer would come back. And since Mom's cancer wasn't growing quickly, there was no benefit in early treatment. We would simply wait until her lymph nodes and bone marrow filled up with malignant cells, and then she would undergo chemotherapy.

Initially, she went to her doctor's appointments on a regular basis. After a while, however, she couldn't see the point of it so she stopped going. She was feeling great, enjoying life, and couldn't be bothered with the hassle. Before we knew it, seven years had passed since her diagnosis. Lymphoma became a distant memory and we rarely discussed it.

That changed when I returned home that Christmas during my final year of medical school. Even as I spotted her from a distance in the airport, I noticed the lymph node swelling on both sides of her neck. I tried to act casual, but she could tell from my eyes that I knew.

Later, while I was wrestling luggage into the trunk, she turned to me and said, "I guess it's time for me to go back to the doctor."

I felt a lump form in my throat and went to hug her, but she sensed my sadness and quickly pulled away.

"Your nephew and niece can't wait to see you," she said, touching my cheek with the back of her hand. I nodded, cleared my throat, and walked to the passenger side.

"We're calling the doctor tomorrow," I said across the top of the car as we both opened our door.

Her oncologist, a lovely woman who cared for Mom like a family member, ordered a series of blood tests. The next day, Dad and I accompanied Mom to the appointment where we received the grim news: Mom's cancer had progressed significantly. She would need to undergo chemotherapy. Dad looked like he might topple headfirst onto the floor.

Chemo started two days later. She didn't get sick with that cycle of chemo, nor with any of the other ones she received over the next four months. Other than losing her hair, chemo represented a mere blip in Mom's life, and she continued playing in her golf league through the entire course of treatment. Because she wore a wig and never complained, most people didn't even know she was undergoing treatment.

Then, for the next six years, the cancer was again in remission and we never discussed it. Until now.

"Max? Are you there?" Mom repeated, bringing me back to the present.

I cleared my throat and stood up from the couch. "Sorry, Mom. What did you say?"

"I went through more chemo about three months ago, but it didn't work."

"You never told me."

"It was a difficult time for you."

I couldn't believe how selfless Mom was. I wondered how much more difficult my marital problems had made her chemo treatments. "What do they want to do now?" I asked her.

"A bone marrow transplant."

My stomach churned, and I tried not to sound too alarmed. "Well, that sucks. Did the doctor give you any idea of a prognosis?"

"She said there was a fifty percent chance I'd be cured," Mom said.

A coin toss. My mom had become a number. I felt sick.

"Did she talk about the risks of a bone marrow transplant?"

"Ohhhh, just a little," she said in an oddly high-pitched, singsong voice. "Only that there was a twenty percent chance of dying from the procedure itself."

All that came out of me was, "But you're not a typical patient."

Mom laughed. "That's exactly what I told her."

If anyone could handle a bone marrow transplant, it was Mom. Also, I knew Dad would be there to support her, as he had done with her first go-round with chemo. At that time, he had made her protein shakes when her appetite was poor, helped with housework, and provided emotional support. I had been so proud of him.

"I know you'll be fine, Mom," I managed.

"I have no other choice," she quickly replied.

After I hung up, I stood looking out the window. The rays of the setting sun sent sparkles of orange-yellow light glancing across the houses lining Noe Street. The blue sky, progressively darkening, was blurred by the tears that were forming. I had recently lost a wife and a family life, and now I had learned I might also lose my mother. To top it off, I wasn't happy with my job. I felt like my world was collapsing upon itself.

# CHAPTER SIX

I was born on the shores of Lake Erie in Euclid, Ohio when Mom was twenty-two and Dad was one year older. We lived in Cleveland for three years before moving to California where my father sought greater opportunity (he had been working in a steel mill), warmer weather, and escape from an overbearing father. It was a courageous act for a young man who carried little more than hope and the thousand-dollar loan in fresh hundreds given him by my grandparents.

On arriving, we stayed with distant relatives while Dad distributed a resume listing his job experience as manager of Al's Burger Shop. Al was my grandfather, a carpenter for the city of Cleveland who had never owned a burger shop. Evidently, Dad felt that such white lies were justified by circumstance, and I never asked Mom about her thoughts regarding this. I do remember Dad relaying the story proudly, as though the strategy was a testament to ingenuity, rather than a bald-faced lie.

Eventually, Dad, a scratch golfer who grew up playing the game at the course behind his house off Lake Shore

Boulevard in Euclid, got a job as a golf professional at a local country club. This seemed to work for him until the day he quit in protest at his boss's refusal to sponsor him for a pro tour qualifying event at a course in northern California, short-circuiting his dream of becoming a professional golfer. His impulsiveness was ill-timed, as our family had few financial resources, but that was Dad, and later, that would become me.

Jobless again, and without a back-up plan, Dad found employment as a cook at the nearby Howard Johnson's. Those were lean years for the family as he slowly worked his way up to a management position. When I was five, he was transferred to Tempe, Arizona, where he became manager of the restaurant there, but our family continued to struggle financially. I can still remember the night Dad had to work late and Mom didn't have enough money to buy food for dinner, so she served my brother Danny and me potato sticks and water. Many years later, she told me it was one of the lowest points of her life.

Dad drove our only car to work, so if Mom needed groceries, she would walk the two-mile roundtrip to the supermarket with my brother in the stroller and me walking next to her. On the way home, I had to alternate between carrying my brother and pushing the stroller, now filled with food. Later, Mom took a part-time job at that same supermarket as a check-out girl, which eased our financial situation somewhat. Although more talented in many ways than Dad, Mom saw her responsibilities through the prism of family, and so she had no real career ambitions. She took the job because she had to, establishing a life-long pattern of irrepressible spirit and determination.

At five foot six, with a slender, athletic figure, Mom was a pretty brunette, with her best physical attributes being her blue eyes and her well-rounded backside, features that I inherited and was reminded about over the years. She was the oldest of four children, and was often put in the position of caretaker for her three brothers. It had to be that way, she said, because Grandpa and Grandma owned a bar and were gone most nights. Mom cooked dinner and made sure the brothers bathed, brushed their teeth and got into bed on time. Even later, when I was an adult, Mom was the glue that held the siblings together. This strong sense of family caused Mom to grieve when Danny and I grew apart as we got older.

She had given birth to me and my brother in her early twenties, whisked away to California far from the siblings who meant so much to her. She later told me she cried every night for two weeks, but after that she determined never to feel sorry for herself again. It wasn't Mom's style to wallow in self-pity. Perpetually smiling, bouncing with endless energy, Mom explored the world with a child-like eagerness.

She was a kind person, willing to spend hours with anyone who needed to talk, and because of her natural empathy and her sharp mind and judgment, women in the neighborhood frequent sought her ear. She also had a talent with numbers, and I remember being amazed by how rapidly she could calculate the exact sale price on discounted clothes. But it was her indefatigable optimism that was Mom's greatest gift, and it got her through four bouts of cancer later in life.

Although it was clear she loved us dearly, she had no tolerance for misbehavior, a fact that was reinforced by a squeeze on the upper arm that immediately elicited pain. From the look on her face, I always knew when it was coming, and I learned to brace for the discomfort, before finally realizing all I had to do to avoid it was behave.

Mom believed in fulfilling commitments, so I almost never missed a day of school or a sports practice, despite constantly going from one to the other. And integrity was essential. One day in third grade, I stole a magnet from the classroom. Feeling guilty, I told her about it when I got home that night. Obviously upset, she told me to take it back to school the next day and apologize to everyone, not only the teacher but also the students.

"And don't expect me to help you. You've gotten yourself into this, now you deal with the consequences."

The following day, I was barely able to stand while delivering my mea culpa to the class. Shaken, I returned to my desk, and as I sat down, I caught a glimpse of Mom hiding in the hallway. She'd come to make sure I was okay.

Because of Dad's long work hours at Howard Johnson's, we didn't spend a lot of time with him during the early years in California and Arizona. But that didn't stop him from trying. Sometimes, when he'd return home late at night, he would wake up Danny and me so he could spend a couple of minutes talking with us. He loved to hug the two of us at the same time, while proclaiming, "my two sons," or "my two boys." In the darkness of the Tempe night, my brother and I would smile at each other, happy to be so loved.

I can remember when I was seven and Dad borrowed a friend's Volkswagen Westfalia Camper to take us on a fishing trip. On the second night, Dad built a big fire on the shore of a lake, and we roasted marshmallows while he fished.   As the night wore on, the sounds of the wilderness grew louder, including the howls of coyotes that seemed very close.   It was frightening for little boys, and we clung to Dad, who remained calm and reassured us.   I can still remember looking up at the brilliance of the starry Arizona sky, my head tucked into the crook of Dad's warm elbow.

Dad was tall, dark and handsome, president of his high school class, and a good athlete with excellent hand-eye coordination.   And he passed some of his skills on to me. He showed me the proper techniques for football, basketball and baseball and built contraptions to help me practice.   He taught me the proper "triple threat stance" important to all sports, even before it was called "the triple threat stance."   He taught me how to cast a fishing pole and to use a rubber worm to catch largemouth bass in the small farm ponds that we fished.

"You have to tease them with it, make the worm look alive and then when they hit it, let them run for a little before setting the hook," he advised.

He showed us how to safely handle and shoot a shotgun so that we could go hunting with him.   He snuck out of work early so he could spend time with Danny and me, even giving up golf, the sport he loved so dearly, to maximize his time with his sons.   He protected and stood up for me, like when my Pee Wee football coach yelled at me excessively.   And Dad taught me that when greeting someone, I should give a firm handshake, look the person in the eye, and speak in a clear voice.

Dad also encouraged me to work hard and never give up.   Possessed with a fighting spirit, he liked to say, "I don't have problems, I have opportunities." Although I appreciated the sentiment, and knew Dad was not one to back down from a challenge, I also knew he didn't actually believe the first part of that phrase. In fact, he thought he had plenty of problems, so much so that he looked at life suspiciously, as though the universe held a perpetual full house to his pair of twos.

It was this pessimism, along with his underlying anger problem, that gave Dad a dark side. My first experience with it was on a family vacation to the White Mountains in Arizona when I was six. On that trip, we stayed in the middle of the forest in a log cabin, complete with a wood burning stove, four uncomfortable cots, and an unfinished wood floor. Each morning, we awoke to the smell of fried eggs and bacon prepared by Mom. During the day, we went fishing with Dad, and then at night, we roasted marshmallows under the stars. For three days, it was a little boy's dream vacation.

On the fourth day of the vacation, Dad suggested Mom take us on a picnic while he fished. Per his plan, we dropped him off at spot where the mountain stream slowed and collected into a deep hole. We then drove a mile or so down the road to a picnic area. After parking, we played in the woods for a while, waded in the frigid stream, and then sat on the banks warming up in the sun. Afterwards, we made our way to a picnic table where Mom had set out lunch. We had just started eating when I heard Mom suddenly exclaim, "Oh, no!"

Alarmed, I asked her, "What's wrong?"

"Your Dad," she replied, nodding her head in the direction of the road.

I turned to see Dad stomping towards us, veins bulging in his head, the fishing rod clutched tightly in his right hand. He was still a hundred yards away but was already shouting.

"I told you one o'clock! Where the hell were you? I just had to walk the whole way!"

Mom sat speechless for a moment. Then she scrambled to intercept him, hands up, trying to placate him, but his anger blasted right through her efforts.

"You guys are sitting here eating lunch while I'm waiting for you. Get in the car!" he ordered us.

We started cleaning up our picnic, but Dad was already in the driver's seat.

"Get in the car!" he repeated as he stuck his head out the window. Danny and I scrambled to finish the job.

"Leave it," Mom said quietly. Dropping everything, we hurried to the car. As I was about to get in, Dad looked back and saw that I was still holding my soda.

"Don't bring that in the car!" he ordered. My hands started to shake. There was no trash can nearby. What should I do?

"Just put it on the ground!" Dad bellowed.

I set the can down, clambered into the car, and had barely shut the door when Dad peeled out of the parking lot, still yelling about the soda. I sat silently, unable to comprehend how such an idyllic moment had gone so sour.

"Now come on, Doug," Mom said, trying to defuse the situation, but that only caused Dad to re-direct his ire towards her. This went on for a few more minutes before Mom yelled, "That's about enough! All of this over a misunderstanding?"

Eventually, Dad settled down, but the damage was done, as an awkward nervousness spoiled the remaining two days of vacation.

When I was eight, Dad was transferred to a Howard Johnson's in southwestern Ohio, where he was promoted to manager. We settled into a modest three-bedroom house in the small town of Boon, a place that was almost entirely white and lower middle class. I entered school halfway through second grade and had no difficulty gaining new pals, perhaps because I had the strongest leg in kickball and an Incredible Hulk metal lunch box.

Later, in fifth grade, when I was a member of the Boy Scouts, the Pinewood Derby was held at our school. This was an event where Scouts, with the help of parents, built their own cars from wood and then raced them. Each of us was given a kit containing a block of pine, plastic wheels, metal axles and four nails. The finished car had to use all nine pieces, could not exceed a certain weight or length, and had to fit on the track. Seemed simple enough.

I brought the kit home, dumped it on the kitchen counter with the rest of my stuff and started rummaging through the cupboards for snacks.

"What's that?" Dad asked.

"Something for a Scouts contest," I said.

He walked over to the counter, picked up the block of wood, and asked, "What kind of contest?"

As I explained, Dad's eyes grew bright with excitement, particularly when I told him we could design the car however we wanted. Dad loved working with wood, having learned the skill from his carpenter father.

Grandpa took driftwood from Lake Erie and turned it into road signs, saving the city money in the process. Dad was equally resourceful, and he had built multiple pieces of wood furniture for our house, including the cabinet in my room that held my stereo eight-track player and music collection.    Dad's best and most impressive work, however, had been the large living room extension he had constructed off the kitchen, a task he had completed almost entirely on his own, although I felt I played a major part as his second in command.    My role consisted primarily of ferrying tools, nails and screws to Dad, and I performed my duties with great pride, convinced that I was doing something important for my family.

"How long do you have before the race?" he asked.

"Two weeks."

"Maybe we should start," he said, pulling out a piece of paper.    He then began sketching rough models of various car designs.    Within an hour, we had decided on a prototype that resembled a door stop, postulating that the low sloping front would decrease wind resistance.    To create it, Dad used a table saw to cut the block into the desired shape.    As he did so, I stood next to him smiling, wood dust settling on my plastic goggles, admiring his strong forearms and the steadiness of his hands.    I couldn't imagine anything much cooler than building that car with my dad.

Afterwards, Dad showed me how to sand the wood smooth and round the edges.    Finished with the basic design, we weighed our fledgling car and found it was two ounces below the maximum-accepted weight.    A heavier car was a faster car, so Dad drilled a hole in the bottom

50

and filled it with melted soldering metal.   Task completed, we then debated paint colors, eventually concluding that candy apple red with a gold racing stripe would be really flashy.   Dad let me do most of the painting, although he took care of the racing stripe, as it required a bit more precision.   The only remaining step was to put on the axles and wheels.   The former looked too wide for the car, so Dad narrowed them, which I agreed did improve the aesthetics.

Unfortunately, it also meant the car would no longer fit the track.

"I'm sorry, but this car has been modified against Derby rules," the Derby official proclaimed as he inspected my car.   I'll have to disqualify it."

Dad moved in quickly.

"How 'bout if we fix it right?" he asked.

The man frowned and shook his head.   But then he looked at my dour face and its sudden absence of color, and said, "If you can do it within thirty minutes, I'll consider it."

In a flash, we were back at my house, and Dad was working rapidly to fix my car.   Dad was great at things like this, like most of the other neighborhood fathers. Everyone in our town was blue collar, it seemed, with a strong sense of community.

When Dad was finished, my car was regulation, but it wasn't very fast, and I didn't win a single race.   It made me wish Mom was there; she would have made me feel better by saying something positive like, "It doesn't matter, your car looked the best."   She was the perfect counter-balance to Dad, whose modus operandi was to complain and criticize.   But Dad didn't complain this time.     Instead, he apologized repeatedly, accepting full responsibility for my misfortune.     I felt a little bad for him because I hated when Dad was unhappy; I even hated worrying about the possibility of him being unhappy, because I had seen what Dad's unhappiness could lead to.

Dad's worst anger outburst occurred one summer day while his mother was visiting.     At the time, Mom and Grandma were in the kitchen preparing dinner, and Dad was standing to the side, reading the paper.     Danny and I were seated at the kitchen table playing "Sorry."     I don't remember why the argument started, but within minutes there was shouting between Mom and Dad. And then, before anyone realized what was happening, Dad picked up a knife sitting on the counter, backed Mom into the counter, and held the knife to her throat.

"I'll do it!     I'll do it!" he yelled, as Grandma tried to pull him off.

Mom leaned backwards over the counter to create some distance, shouting, "Go ahead!" with pure hatred in her eyes.

Danny was hysterical, screaming, "Daddy, don't!"

I sat still, unable to move or speak, trying to make sense of the unspeakable.

The tension lasted for a minute or so before Grandma was able to talk him down, gently taking the knife from him in the process.

"I'm outta here," he said, stomping down the hallway towards the front door.     Along the way, I heard him shout, "I can't take it anymore," followed by a loud noise, which I later discovered was caused by him punching a hole in the closet door.

Once he was gone, the house was deathly quiet, save the sound of Mom's weeping coming from her bedroom. Dad didn't return until the next day, and when he did, he removed the damaged door, reversed the hinges, and put it back in place. But the hole remained, and each time I opened the door to retrieve my coat, it reminded me of the darkness in the house.

Fortunately, despite his destructive temper and unhappiness, Dad never touched us or Mom. And although his temper sometimes made it hard to see, we recognized his inherent goodness. But even when he wasn't overtly angry, Dad was often irritable. "Crabby," was the euphemism Mom used. It created an atmosphere of constant unease. We became experts at reading his facial expressions and body language so that we could reduce the chances of a big blow-up. But we couldn't be perfect, and so inevitably the anger would come. Dad could get mad if I closed the door too loudly or made the smallest verbal faux pas. Even to this day, I'll look for Dad's expression when certain potentially inflammatory topics are brought up, that familiar tightness in the pit of my stomach.

Dad's varying moods confused me. I loved him so much and knew that he loved me dearly, but he could be so unpredictably mean. I resented his arbitrary authority, so much so that over time I came to resent any authority I viewed as unfair. This carried over to sports, where I clashed with coaches who were overly strict. My junior varsity basketball coach was one such person, screaming at me for the smallest mistakes on the court and stirring up such strong emotions in me that I had to focus intently on not punching him in the face, even if he was the pastor of our local church.

Dad always had trouble handling stress, one source of which was money. The restaurant business was not particularly lucrative and Dad never made more than thirty thousand dollars a year, which was less than the salary earned by the workers at the large factory nearby. And as the manager of the local Howard Johnson's, he had to deal with the daily personnel problems inherent to the restaurant industry. But instead of leaving his frustrations at the job, Dad brought them home and took them out on his family.

Later, I would learn Dad had been fighting demons generated from years of emotional abuse at the hands of a harsh father who rarely allowed Dad to enjoy life as a child or adolescent. He had to be home earlier than everyone else, was often saddled with difficult chores, and bore the brunt of his father's displeasure with whatever bothered him at the moment. I knew Dad tried to transcend his own difficult experience and that he had a good heart, but he could never shed his past. He tried outrunning it by dragging us to California and Arizona, but it always caught up with him, and in turn, us.

As Dad's favorite son, I felt particularly responsible for his happiness. This feeling was something I never shared with anyone, and I doubt Mom ever realized I felt that way, but I can remember when I was ten and first became aware of the guilt. Dad had decided to take Danny and me to watch a ballgame. I really did not want to go, but I didn't have the heart to tell Dad because I thought he would be disappointed and then angry. So, I almost went. But at the last minute I backed out. Dad was surprised but not angry, and yet I cried with guilt after he left, confusing Mom.

If dealing with Dad's anger wasn't difficult enough, we also had to endure frequent fights between our parents. Sometimes they would go a week or two without speaking to each other. I hated the silent dinners, the only sounds made by silverware against plates. I learned to eat quickly and with my head down, thinking of school or my friends to pass the uncomfortable time. To this day, I still eat rapidly.

Although I didn't feel responsible for their fighting, I internalized it nonetheless. I worried about it, thought about it (even when I was at school), prayed that it wouldn't happen, and then when it invariably did, I would feel sad and anxious.

I remember one night when I was eight and Mom and Dad got in a huge blow-up just as I was getting ready for bed. Mom retreated to the bedroom while Dad took up his usual post in front of the TV, shouting at her until she slammed the door shut. I waited for a couple of minutes, and then tip-toed down the hallway to my parents' bedroom door. There, I sat on the floor with knees pulled tight against my chest, my bright orange Cincinnati Bengals pajama bottoms too short for my rapidly growing legs. Then I pressed my ear against the door and listened to my Mom cry. When the sniffles finally stopped, I quietly opened the door and slipped inside. Mom was lying on the bed, covering her face, her hair in disarray. As I entered, she quickly sat up, wiped her tears, and smiled faintly.

"It's okay, Max.   I'm fine," she reassured me.

I toed the shag carpet, trying not to cry.   Mom came over and hugged me.   I could feel her body trembling as she rubbed my back.

"Mommy, do you love Daddy?" I asked her.   Her hands stopped and her body grew rigid.

And then she said, "Sometimes."

Mom did the best she could under difficult circumstances, I suppose.   She was essentially a buffer between my father and us, and in being one, received the brunt of his emotional angst.   She sacrificed her own personal happiness for the sake of what she thought best for us, feeling that a dysfunctional family together was better than one apart.   It was when I was an adult and going through my divorce that she explained it, in part, by telling me that she always thought people gave up too easily on marriage.   That relationships were hard.

I often heard her trying to placate Dad, giving him little pep talks, using her favorite expression: "Things always work out."   But at what cost?   She didn't succeed in shielding us from Dad's emotional abuse and so in that way she failed us.   She could have left him and taken us along.   She could have at least given him an ultimatum. But she didn't, and so his behavior continued, unabated.

In her defense, she truly believed she was doing the right thing.   She thought her undying optimism could overwhelm Dad's negativity, and to a certain degree, it did.   But it wasn't enough, and our dysfunctional family dynamics affected my brother and me.   Danny reacted to the turmoil by acting out.   Not excessively, as he was generally a well-behaved boy, but he would get defiant sometimes with Mom and Dad over silly things, like when they told him to clean his room. I dealt with the stress much differently by seeking refuge within. In the process, I discovered an inner strength that I could rely on to provide solace regardless of the chaos at home. I didn't need anyone else. I learned I could take care of my own emotional needs.

# CHAPTER SEVEN

One week after Alice and I decided to separate, my cousin's husband helped me move out while Alice kept Jessica away. The process took longer than anticipated, however, and Alice returned with Jessica just as I was finishing. On my last trip out, Jessica, now one year old, stood at the top of the stairs, watching as I picked up a lamp to carry downstairs. "I'll see you soon," I said, hugging her tightly.

"Daddy go?" she asked, looking puzzled. I kissed her on the cheek and scrambled down the stairs before I confused her further by starting to cry.

Later that night, I sat alone at an old kitchen table left by the landlord. Partially unpacked boxes and and crumpled newspapers surrounded me. It was so deathly quiet that I could hear the slow in and out of my breath, which became shallow and quick whenever I thought of Jessica. Away from her, I felt so alone. The family I had long wished for had suddenly evaporated; despite my beautiful, innocent child, I couldn't keep us together.

When I climbed into bed just before midnight, I didn't feel the least bit tired, despite my lack of sleep over the previous week.    I fluffed my pillow and tried to find a comfortable position in bed.    Outside, I could hear the commotion caused by the late-night clean-up of the closing Chinese restaurant behind my apartment.    I pulled the pillow out from under me and put it on top of my head.    It quieted the sounds but not the racing thoughts.    I began to think once again about Alice.

I felt I could never do enough to fully please her, and so I lived in a state of constant striving, discomfort and guilt. This caused me to feel bad about myself and when the source of that feeling was someone I loved deeply, the result was devastating. She seemed so inflexible and unfair with her insistence on a rigid code of conduct. But I was not a person to be contained, and so I rebelled, which caused her to push for even greater control.    She needed to feel safe, and according to her, the best demonstration of that would be consistency on my part. However, it seemed I just couldn't meet her standard, and, quite honestly, I probably lacked the maturity to do so.    It seemed I couldn't sustain the effort required in a relationship, and that contributed heavily to Alice's perpetual uneasiness about us.    It certainly didn't help that I could take her for granted at times.

Several weeks after signing the non-disclosure agreement, I received a notice in my work mailbox that a package was waiting for me in shipping. I nearly sprinted down the two flights of stairs to the ground floor, signed off on the small box, and went directly back to my office, where I ripped open the package. Inside were several six-ounce vials of a brownish liquid with a strong chemical odor. Included was a device that looked like a miniature version of a lawn roller, studded with tiny spikes, called a derma-roller. The device was to be rolled back and forth across the bald scalp, leaving barely-noticeable, non-bleeding holes which theoretically allowed better penetration of the medication.

Using a calibrated medicine dropper, I applied about an ounce of the hair peptide to the bald portion of my scalp and used my fingers to spread the liquid evenly. Then I moved the derma roller back and forth across my scalp to drive the medication into the deeper skin layer. After several minutes of gardening my own head, I was nearing my pain threshold rapidly and so I stopped, put away the equipment and washed my hands.

Then I began walking back to the medical ward. As I did, I noticed a pleasant tingling feeling.

"Ah, the sweet sensation of chemistry at work," I purred to myself.

I smiled at patients and staff passing me in the hall, reveling in my good fortune. Hair would soon be sprouting from my barren head.

The corridor was long, however, and by the time I reached its end, my smile had disappeared. The tingling sensation had intensified to the point that I began to feel like a live power line had been downed on my scalp. Several minutes later, my head seemed to spontaneously combust, causing me to run to the nearest bathroom to extinguish the flames that must certainly be shooting out of my head. But when I looked into the mirror, there were no flames, not even any redness.

Tears of pain wet my cheeks, but I sucked it up and stayed with the discomfort. I didn't dare wash off the caustic shit—oh no! —because I was going to grow some hair, goddamnit! Eventually, however, the burning became intolerable, and so I turned the faucet on and cupped my hands under the running water. Just then, the pain started to fade, almost imperceptibly at first but then more rapidly. Within minutes it was completely gone, leaving me with a refreshing scalp tingle. I wiped away the tears, cleared my throat and emerged from the bathroom feeling energized to see patients.

For the next month, I went through the same routine, twice a day, every day. Apply hair peptide, roll a spiked barrel over my head, and suffer through ten minutes of a scalp conflagration. I was setting a new standard for commitment, even for me. And then one day near the end of the month, I began noticing tiny new hairs. Little wispy things at first, that later grew bigger and were followed by others. I felt a surge of newfound enthusiasm for life. Maybe I could recapture some of my youth after all, even if everything else in my life seemed broken.

While my hair was growing, I continued to struggle with my separation from Alice. And because we needed to communicate regularly regarding Jessica, healing seemed to progress slowly. I slogged through those early days as best I could, pinning hopes of happiness on Jessica and Follicle Research. If I focused my efforts there, everything would be okay, I told myself.

In the meantime, Alice and I had begun seeing a divorce psychologist to help us determine how to best handle Jessica through the separation. The psychologist was an older woman located in the Marina District of San Francisco, and I hated going to see her. I was angry with Alice for insisting on this and I thought the sessions were the worst sort of parental intellectualization of childcare. Some sessions were truly ridiculous, like the one where we discussed whether it was best to drop off Jessica at the front door, the bottom of the stairs, or the top of the stairs. I just tried to focus on what was best for Jessica and together Alice and I came to an agreement that we would share custody equally within six months.

But for now, I still had Jessica only twice a week. Fortunately, Alice understood how much it pained me to be away from my daughter and so she graciously offered me the opportunity to join them for dinner on any night. Despite the poisonous atmosphere of divorce, I could count on Alice's character to make her do the right thing, which brought me more solace than I might have imagined. Her goodness in the face of turmoil helped anchor me, and I didn't hesitate to take her up on the offer, making my way to her house three or four nights per week, where the three of us would sit around the table like a pseudo-family, creating some of the most awkward moments of my life.

"How's work going?" she would ask, fiddling with Jessica's bib.

"Fine. How about with you?" I would ask, jabbing at my broccoli.

"Fine."

"Have you been working out?"

"Yes."

"That's good."

Sometimes I would look up to see Alice staring at me, cheek resting against a closed fist, tears in her eyes. I would smile at her, and she would return the smile. We were still in love; that had never changed. We just couldn't find a way to be together and avoid the terribly destructive arguments that we both loathed. So, we exchanged our marriage for a new kind of partnership, galvanized by our love for our child.

New hairs seemed to be popping up all the time. I could barely contain my excitement over my imminently thick locks. At the end of two months, I snapped a photograph of my scalp and compared it to one I had taken before starting treatment. There was clear evidence of hair growth. At the current rate, I estimated I would have a full head of hair within twelve months.

During this time of rapid hair growth, Lance and I continued to communicate daily, sometimes for an hour or more, talking about a variety of topics both professional and personal. We were keenly interested in figuring out a way to make the hair peptide even more effective. Like two science enthusiasts, we discussed everything that might be of relevance, things with complicated names like dihydrotestosterone, steroid biosynthesis, parathyroid hormone, dermal papilla cell, soluble molecules of the dermis, bone morphogenic proteins, TGF beta, Wnts and sonic hedgehog. We spoke about lithium, "AGE-breakers", intra-follicular peptide delivery, the pilosebaceous unit and the B2 region of the hair follicle.

I loved every moment, finding the conversations fascinating and challenging. I was consistently impressed by Lance's mind, particularly his ability to synthesize and present complicated scientific information. I found his intellect seductive, and I looked forward to every conversation, almost waiting by the telephone like a love-struck teenager. I was so wowed by him that there were many times when I doubted I could match his level of talent. So, I devoured every bit of scientific information I could find regarding anything about hair, including its growth and loss, structure, life cycle and function, spending many late evening hours in this pursuit. Besides increasing my knowledge base, those nights filled the sizable void created by the absence of Alice and Jessica, and distracted me from Mom's poor health and my increasingly unsatisfying job.

I felt I was developing a good sense of Lance through those innumerable phone conversations. I knew he had grown up in Louisiana, the product of a schoolteacher and a physicist. His mother, however, was an alcoholic and his father, a philanderer who spent most nights away. Lance was alone much of the time, and because those important emotional attachments with his parents never fully formed, he had a problem with intimacy. Instead of people, his relationships were mostly with science and math, and so much of his adolescence was spent engaged in various scientific pursuits, such as designing his own experiments.

Being from a small town in Louisiana, he did a lot of hunting and fishing, but he tended to do it alone. His social isolation was deepened by constant bullying by neighborhood boys who took advantage of his physical slightness. Later, at the age of sixteen, he began lifting weights to add some bulk to his skinny frame, but bulking up failed to erase the insecurity born out of his previous physical shortcomings. Eventually, Lance would graduate from Vanderbilt with a degree in biochemistry. Fascinated by the human body, he had gone on to become a chiropractor. At some point, however, he had given up his career to pursue scientific research, and that is when he had come across the hair peptide.

His obsession with the peptide had taken a toll on his marriage, and when I initially met Lance, he told me he had just gone through a divorce, made more difficult because they had a daughter. This shared experience drew me still closer to Lance, so that I considered him not only a business partner, but a friend as well, even before I met him in person. As it would turn out, however, that meeting would not take place until a little over a year after I first contacted him.

Early on in my relationship with Lance, it occurred to me that I should perform a thorough background check, particularly since I had become so heavily invested in Follicle Research, both in terms of my time and the use of my medical license for the DMSO. I tried searching various data bases for scientific publications authored by Lance, but I was unable to find any. This seemed odd, as nearly every graduating Ph.D. student has published his work somewhere. But, figuring it might be a sensitive topic, I never broached it with Lance. After all, I didn't want to hurt my chances with Follicle Research, and I wasn't about to insult the man who was giving me the opportunity of a lifetime. By then, I had probably talked with Lance over one hundred hours by phone, covering topics both professional and personal, and felt I could trust him. A complete background check would be an unnecessary waste of time.

One of my earliest contributions to the company was to develop an overall business strategy, consisting of an internet-based approach. Specifically, I proposed setting up a website which would allow me to perform online medical consultations with patients interested in purchasing the product. Patients could then purchase the peptide directly from this site, and the medication could be shipped to customers from compounding pharmacies that we'd contract with to produce it. Centralization of the process would reduce the costs of an already expensive treatment. Over time, as demand inevitably grew, I would oversee hiring other physicians to assist with the online consultations.

I also pushed Lance on the need to perform a clinical study, which I would design, to formally evaluate the safety and effectiveness of the drug. This data would lend scientific credibility to our product. Since we were not seeking FDA approval (and did not need it because the peptide was a topical preparation, known by some as a "cosmeceutical"), the study did not require a placebo group, the usual standard of FDA-approved clinical trials. Strictly speaking, the designation of "cosmeceutical" meant the peptide was not a drug, as defined by the FDA, and thus not subject to the usual rigorous regulatory requirements of pharmaceuticals. This was not unusual, as there were several cosmeceuticals already on the market that had taken this approach. This important legal distinction would save a significant amount of research time and money.

Lance was enthusiastic about my ideas, particularly the online selling of the peptide. But in terms of the clinical study, he was more subdued, telling me, "That's definitely something we'll want to do at some point." Regardless, he must have been impressed with my contributions because, two months into our relationship, he invited me to join Follicle Research as a partner. He could not pay me, as the company had no revenue, but he guaranteed an ownership stake, the exact amount of which we would discuss later. I didn't hesitate to accept his offer. It seemed like the chance I had been waiting for my entire life, and I immediately ramped up my participation.

My first project was to find a new penetration enhancer for the hair peptide. The DMSO just wasn't going to work. Most people would not set fire to their scalp every day even to have hair, and I wasn't completely convinced that using my medical license to prescribe the chemical was sensible. So, we started an exhaustive search for possible solutions. Eventually, we came up with a cocktail of three difference substances that seemed to work in studies we performed in the lab.

Confident now in our formulation, Lance agreed we needed to synthesize enough peptide for a clinical study. He decided the production process should take place at a university laboratory in Charlotte, North Carolina. He had a friend who worked in the lab, a technician named Oliver, who agreed to work for us making the peptide after hours for low pay. It was a time-consuming task, but he never seemed to mind, and he never asked what the peptide was for. He was perfect for our purposes.

As I continued to ramp up my involvement with Follicle Research, Mom had finished the extensive preparation for her bone marrow transplant. Dad had accompanied her on all the visits and he did it without asking or expecting credit.

The doctors told Mom the average length of stay in the hospital after transplant was twenty-five days.

"Yeah, right," she said as she relayed the information to me. "There's no way I'm staying that long."

On the first day, the doctors gave her a massive dose of chemotherapy in an attempt to kill every single cancer cell in her body. The cost of such a high dose was that it obliterated her bone marrow as well, in addition to causing her hair to fall out and creating terribly painful ulcers in her mouth and esophagus that made swallowing even a small amount of liquid nutrition difficult. Despite that, she rarely asked for pain medication. "Tylenol is fine," she told the disbelieving nurses.

Five days after the doctors dumped the poisons into her body, she was given an infusion of her own bone marrow cells that had been collected a month earlier. Then, it was simply a matter of waiting for the cells to migrate to her empty bone marrow space, set up shop and start creating a new marrow. This could take up to three weeks, if it happened at all. But before that happened, Mom was particularly vulnerable, as she had no effectively functioning immune system. As such, she could quickly die if she developed an infection.

Generally, the process of undergoing a bone marrow transplant completely wipes out the patient's energy, and the simplest of tasks, such as walking to the bathroom, become onerous. But that didn't happen with Mom. She stayed in bed only to sleep at night. Otherwise, she was either sitting in a chair or walking the hallways. Irritated doctors trying to round on her often had to hunt her down.   She refused to accept the sick role, even spurning the hospital-issued gown.   By the fifteenth day, her new marrow started churning out white blood cells, indicating a successful transplant.   Two days later, she was done with the hospital, so she packed her bag and waited impatiently for the doctor.

"I don't think so," was her response when he suggested a few more days of hospitalization.

I had inherited Mom's fighting spirit, and in combination with my competitive drive, it took beyond the confines of a small southwestern Ohio town to the Ivy League.

But Mom didn't necessarily help me in that particular pursuit.   In fact, when I asked her about the Ivy League (my high school football coach had sent games films to several of the prestigious schools), she couldn't name any other than Harvard and Yale.

"Why do you want to know?" she asked.

"Because Coach thought maybe I could play football there."

Mom gave me a "you're so cute" smile.

"That would be wonderful, but those schools are very difficult to get into.  Have you thought about applying to Ohio State or Case Western?"

It sounded like the Ivies were beyond my reach. And so, I forgot about them until several weeks later when I received recruiting letters from the football programs at Harvard, Princeton, and Yale.  The Princeton coach said he would be traveling in Ohio the next week and wanted to meet me.  I was thrilled.  Coach arranged a meeting in the football offices at the high school.  He invited a classmate named Mark, who was another outstanding student-athlete, to join us.

The Princeton coach met with us for thirty minutes, telling us about both the football team and the university. He showed pictures of the beautiful campus, including the big football stadium, and talked about the difficulty of getting admitted to the school. Once there, we would be challenged as both students and athletes, he told us, adding that not many people could handle the rigors of playing an intercollegiate sport while carrying a full course load. The meeting was intimidating, but also exciting. By the end of his presentation, I was completely intrigued by the idea of going and wanted to at least give it a try.

But Mark thought differently. "It seems too hard," he said, after the coach left. "It's too far away."

I couldn't imagine how he could pass up such an opportunity. Although we were close friends, the disconnect could not have been greater.

"Well, I'm going for it," I replied, unaware that I was embarking on an eighteen-year quest that would take me on a decidedly divergent path. I would think about that day many times over the years, particularly after the arrest.

Meanwhile, my school's guidance counselor was suggesting I apply for a cooperative program offered by a university in Detroit, consisting of alternating six-month periods of taking classes and working for General Motors. I believe the school counselor felt she was suggesting a real opportunity, as we lived in a small town where only fifteen percent of the two hundred and forty graduating students attended college. And for those who did go away, most returned to Boon afterwards. I figured just maybe I could aim a little higher.    In fact, I always knew I would leave; I needed to have new experiences and challenges not afforded by Boon.  I had wrung everything I could out of the place, and it was time to move on.  I would not be just another Boon graduate.

As it turned out, football was my ticket.    I was invited on paid football recruiting trips to Harvard, Princeton and Yale.    When my baseball coach heard about this, he pulled me aside one day at school.

"I think you're too skinny to play college football, Max.  Maybe you should think about baseball."

It was true that although I was six foot two, I only weighed one hundred and sixty pounds.    But I knew I could train and get bigger.    Furthermore, I was certain I had the athletic talent to play.    Instead of dissuading me, his doubt simply strengthened my resolve.

"Thanks, Coach," was all I could manage.

My first trip was to Harvard, and I needed to inform my teachers I would not be in school that Friday.  My history teacher was Mr. Ellison, who was also the track coach.  When I told him I was going to visit Harvard, he laughed at me.

"Yeah, right.  I'll need documentation."

The next day I brought the travel itinerary, which was packaged in a professional-appearing folder with "Harvard University" printed on the front.  I dropped it on his desk when I walked into class.  He was busy reading something, and when he saw it, he picked the folder up and spent several minutes looking through it.  When he finished, he placed the document back on his desk.  Later, while we were in the midst of a school assignment, he slid the folder onto my desk while walking past, never speaking a word about the subject again. I got a similar brush-off from others, and so I made of point of keeping my college selection process low-key.   I had hoped that people would share my enthusiasm for my remarkable opportunity, particularly since only one student had attended an Ivy League school in our high school's one-hundred-year existence.   Instead, people seemed uncomfortable discussing it.

My recruiting trip to Harvard took place over St. Patrick's Day weekend in 1984.   Mom accompanied me to the terminal, and I waved at her as I walked down the jet way.   The moment I lost sight of her, I was suddenly overcome with a feeling of being very alone, but by the time I reached the plane, I had a huge smile on my face.

"Welcome aboard," the flight attendant said as I boarded.   "How are you?"

"Excited," I answered as I strode onto the plane for my first flight without my parents.

Not surprisingly, it was an overcast day in Boston as we made our approach into Logan Airport.   When we broke through the clouds, the brownstones, the irregular streets, and the harbor came into view.   I pressed my face tightly against the window as I tried to take it all in.

A coach was waiting for me when we landed, and he drove me straight to the campus, where I was introduced to my freshman host.   I then attended a class in Sanders Theater inside Memorial Hall, a famous old building built in honor of those who died in the first World War.   The theater seemed mammoth, with endless rows of seats that went straight up.   I sat there in that historic place with real live Harvard undergrads and felt swallowed up by the hallowed surroundings. Before the class ended, I knew I had to attend Harvard.

Another highlight of the trip was my meeting with Joe Restic, the long-time head football coach and a living football legend. Tall and soft-spoken, he was a grandfatherly type who nonetheless shook my hand with ferocity as he welcomed me into his office. As I sat down, I noticed a large window afforded a fantastic view of Harvard Stadium, one of the most historic sports venues in the country. Coach Restic spent several minutes describing the college football experience, but I barely listened. Instead, I imagined myself in a Harvard uniform, playing in the glorious stadium just outside.

Near the end of the interview, he put his elbows on the desk, clasped his hands in front of him, and leaned forward. Then, in a slow, deliberate voice, he asked me, "Tell me why you want to come to Harvard."

Without hesitation, I pointed out the window and said slowly and surely, "Because I want to play in that stadium."

He blinked and pulled his head back a little, surprised by the confidence of my response, which made me think for a moment, "Oh shit, maybe that was a little too brash." But a smile soon relaxed his wrinkled face and my anxious energy, and, with that new connection, he stood up to see me off.

"We'd love to have you, Max," he said, shaking my hand with the same tenacity he showed in our introduction.

I smiled as I made eye contact with him. Then I floated out of his office. Twenty-five years later, it still doesn't seem real that someone at Harvard would actually want me.    That kind of stuff just doesn't happen to people from Boon.

After the recruiting trip, Harvard arranged for an interview with a graduate from the class of 1959 at his home in an affluent suburb of Cincinnati.  I dressed in my nicest clothes--a pair of dress pants, shirt and sweater, and my beloved penny loafers.  Thinking it might help, I wore my only pair of argyle socks.  Mom drove me to the man's house, and I was silent in nervousness the entire trip.  As I walked to the front door, I looked back to see her pulling out of the driveway.    She waved as I knocked on the door.

Soon, a middle-aged man welcomed me into the nicest home I had ever been in.  We sat in overstuffed leather chairs in his study and talked for the next forty-five minutes.

"Can you tell me some of your favorite books you've read?" he asked.

I squirmed in the chair and cleared my throat.    My mind raced for possibilities, but I had trouble coming up with an answer.    The simple truth was that I rarely read any books.    I didn't have time.    I played three sports in high school and was in various school plays.    After practice for both, I wouldn't get home until nine, at which time I would eat dinner and then do homework.    Very few people in my high school read books anyway.

"I liked *Raid on Entebbe*," I replied, remembering a book about Israeli commandos I had read the previous summer.

"Why's that?" he asked.

"Lots of action.    And those guys were really brave."

74

He looked at me blankly and waited.    Behind him, his bookshelves were spilling books.    I doubted *Raid on Entebbe* was there.

"Anything else you liked about the book?    Narrative flow?    Structure?    Character development?"

*What's he talking about?*

"The dictator Amen…Amin maybe…seemed pretty ruthless.    So did the PLO."

"I see.    Okay…"

My feet were soaking the argyle socks.    I started to cross my legs because it seemed more sophisticated, but found it uncomfortable so I stopped.

"Why do you want to go to Harvard?"

I immediately relaxed.    I had an answer to this question.

"Because Harvard graduates are doing things, and I want to do things."

In my mind, I couldn't be any clearer.

The man smiled slightly.

"You know?" I asked.

He nodded.

*Was he agreeing or just laughing at me?    Did I sound stupid? Ah man, he definitely knows I'm a fucking hick now.    He'll probably start asking me if I go cow tipping.*

"What are your favorite classes?"

"I like math and science, mostly."

"Why's that?"

"I guess I've always liked numbers.    And I've always had good science teachers, like my chemistry teacher, Mr. Hensley.    He's amazing, and he goes to all our basketball games."

"What would you like to do after college?"

"You mean job-wise?"

He nodded.

"Something where I use math and science, I guess. Maybe electrical engineering?"

The man looked at his watch. "Well, I think our time is up."

I wanted to jump up and run out, but the driveway was empty. Since the interview had ended early, Mom wasn't back yet.

Sensing my panic, the man gave me a benevolent look and said, "It's okay, you can wait here."

"That's alright, I'll just stand outside," I said, reaching for the door handle.

"It's snowing," he replied, putting his hand on my outstretched arm. "Come on, let me show you some of my books."

I followed him over to the bookshelves. He stood with his back to the books and swept his arm across an entire shelf, which I found funny because it reminded me of the "Price is Right" models showing off a new car!

"This is my collection of Greek mythology. Have you read any of these?"

I didn't know what Greek mythology was. We had studied *The Canterbury Tales* in our literature class, but I thought that was more English than Greek.

"You know, *The Iliad*. *The Odyssey?*"

"I think we're saving that for the spring semester," I said.

I looked outside and saw Mom pulling up in our Ford Mustang. I nodded towards the direction of the window.

"Ah yes, I see. Well, then, Max, it was a pleasure. Good luck to you, young man," he said shaking my hand.

I nearly sprinted to the car. As soon as I sat down, Mom asked, "How was it?"

"Just drive," I said through clenched teeth, staring straight ahead.

When we were out of sight, I relayed the events to Mom. She started laughing.

"Mom, it's not funny," I protested. "I want to go to Harvard."

She stopped laughing. "Don't worry, honey. You will," she said with certainty.

In the end, I was admitted to Harvard, Princeton and Yale. Although my grades were fantastic and my board scores good, it was my football skills that ultimately were the determining factor. I knew that and was okay with it. I just needed the opportunity. Once I got that, I knew I would take care of the rest.

I opened my last letter of acceptance while sitting in Mom's car outside the Pizza Hut, waiting for her to pick up dinner. I held the letter to the car window as she came out of the restaurant. Puzzled, she walked towards me with her head cocked slightly to the side. When she got close enough, she stopped, and I watched her eyes dart back and forth across the paper. When she finished, she stood there smiling momentarily before succumbing to the inevitable tears. Her boy was going to Harvard.

I felt so good in the moment, not only for my accomplishment but also because I knew it would knock Dad out of his depression for a while. But I also knew it would make things more difficult for Danny, as my shadow that he was already living in would grow even longer. We never talked about it, of course, but then again, we rarely talked about anything of substance.

I told a few classmates at my high school about my acceptance to Harvard. The reaction was always muted. Some people rolled their eyes. Others gave me a strained "Congratulations." After a while, I stopped telling people, and even when I would return home from college for various breaks, I was careful not to talk about Harvard or wear any clothing bearing its name.

# CHAPTER EIGHT

Five months after our separation, Alice dropped off Jessica for a weekend stay at my place. As I took my sleeping daughter into my arms, I noticed Alice staring at me.

"Can we talk for a little?" she asked hesitantly.

"Sure. Come on in."

We walked into the front room of my apartment and sat down. Jessica was still sleeping, and I lay her down on the couch next to me.

"Looks the same as my place," Alice said, looking around. It suddenly occurred to me she had never been in my apartment before.

"Yeah. Made the move a little easier, I guess."

She nodded, a sad look on her face. "I wanted to tell you something I think you should know," she said, her voice trembling. "I've started seeing someone."

"Oh, no," I said reflexively. I felt like cold water had been dumped on me.

"It's Jerry."

I knew Jerry. Alice had dated him throughout most of college. I knew he still loved her, as he had made numerous attempts over the years to get back together with her. It was never clear to me why she hadn't done so, but I had speculated privately that after our separation she might. Still, the news took me by surprise.

"It's so soon," I complained. "How could you move on so quickly?"

"We've been spending some time together recently, and I think I want to give the relationship a chance."

"But how do you know we can't still work it out?" I asked, sounding as desperate as I felt. Alice looked at me sympathetically, which made me feel even more pathetic.

"Our relationship is over," Alice said firmly. "It's better if we think of ourselves as parenting partners."

Her words stung, even though I knew they were true. I just hadn't accepted that reality and refused to do so now.

"Will you at least consider it?" I pleaded.

"No, Max. I'm sorry," she replied, getting up to leave.

"Please?" I was embarrassed even as I asked.

"Bye, Max," she said gently, before walking out of the apartment. I sat there for another half hour or so until Jessica woke up. In that time, the finality of the break-up resonated through me, and I realized I needed to move on.

But it wouldn't be easy. For me, the emotional wound was still wide open, and I struggled with the unfairness of her pain being eased by a new person. Then one evening while we were having dinner, Jessica mentioned that Jerry had read her a bedtime story. This crushed me, especially since Alice had suggested, and I had agreed, that we would not introduce Jessica to a potential romantic partner until at least six months of the relationship had passed. And even then, the other parent would be notified first.

"It's different with Jerry. He's a family friend," she rationalized when I brought this up to her.

"But you're dating him, and we had an agreement."

"I didn't think it would be a big deal," she said, with less conviction.

I knew that had the situation been reversed, there would have been hell to pay. "How could you let him read her a story in bed? Do you know what that does to a dad? Do you have any concept of how painful that is?"

"It was just a couple of minutes, and Jessica asked him to."

"This is such a violation, Alice."

While I steamed about it over the next several days, Jerry unexpectedly called me. I was driving at the time and pulled over to take his call.

"I want to apologize if I offended you, Max. It was not my intention."

"It just isn't right. Do you understand that?"

"I really do. It won't happen again."

"Alice should know this is wrong," I pushed.

"I don't want to minimize it in any way, but I just read to Jessica for a short while after she asked me to."

"That's not the point. Alice and I had an agreement."

"I understand, and I just wanted to say, sorry."

Although I appreciated the call, the whole episode still bothered me. *I* was Jessica's father; not Jerry. It didn't matter that he was a great guy.

My self-pity lasted until a friend, tired of my whining, told me, "Max, your daughter can't have too many people that love her. Get over it."

Although it hurt to see Alice move on with someone else and to know that another man was spending time with Jessica, I realized I had no choice but to accept it. My daughter deserved nothing less. And as time wore on, I realized that I could not have hand-picked a better person to be around my daughter than Jerry.

My wife might have been sleeping with someone else, but at least I was growing hair. And soon I would be rich. That would show her.

While Oliver toiled away making FR-1, Lance and I, via frequent phone conversations (we still hadn't met in person), began examining ways to set up our own laboratory. In addition to space and equipment, we needed a cheap source of amino acids. I called multiple suppliers around the country trying to get the best price. Still, the powdery substance was prohibitively expensive. Frustrated, I called Lance.

"I've gotten pharmaceuticals pretty cheap from China before," he said.

"What pharmaceuticals?" I asked, a bit alarmed.

"Oh, just something I was working on before," he replied, before quickly adding, "Let me contact a few of those Chinese companies and see what they can do."

Within several weeks, we had purchased a supply of amino acids from China for far less than the cost of US manufacturers. We tested all samples for purity and were quite satisfied with the results, so we signed a contract with the company. It would not be the last time I turned to China for a bargain on chemicals.

Although we no longer had money to pay him, we persuaded Oliver to produce FR-1 in our new lab by dangling a 0.5% ownership stake in Follicle Research, which he accepted. Although he was efficient, the construction of the peptide was time-intensive. Each step required a waiting period, and there were often errors. Upon completion, the resulting mixture would be run through a special process called high performance liquid chromatography which would purify the mixture so that only the desired peptide would be left. The final step would include the addition of the special penetration enhancers we concocted.

However, to proceed effectively, we needed money. I felt we should look to venture capital funding. But Lance wanted no part of that; he was not about to give up a significant ownership stake in a company that he had started and which had a potential blockbuster treatment. He had already conservatively valued the company at one hundred million dollars.

"Huh?" I had blurted when he told me.

"Yeah, like eight zeros."

"How do you come to that number?" I asked.

"There are fifty million men and thirty million women balding in America, right? If we capture just five percent of that market, we would have a total of four million customers."

"That seems like a fair number," I said.

"Now, if we earned a profit of twenty-five dollars per patient per month of treatment, that would be a total profit of one hundred million dollars."

"One hundred million dollars every year," I said. "Wow."

"Max, that's one hundred million dollars *per month*," Lance corrected.

"Holy shit."

"And those numbers are for the US only. It could be five times that with worldwide sales."

I was speechless.

"So, the valuation of one hundred million is actually a conservative one," Lance said.

The possibilities made my head spin, and I became obsessed with making Follicle Research a success. But to get there, we needed funding. We started by considering angel investments, which would allow us to retain majority ownership. For reasons I would discover later, Lance had an extensive network in professional sports, and he began contacting those sources. In the process, he came across a personal physician for professional athletes, movie stars and wealthy businessmen who offered to put us in touch with one of his clients, a man named Sam Sirotka. Sam lived in Dallas and knew the owner of a Texas professional sports franchise quite well. His family had made their fortune during the US oil boom in the fifties. He had parlayed that success into a number of well-placed real estate investments that exponentially grew the family fortune. And, importantly, he was bald.

We arranged for a meeting in Dallas in early December, a little over a year since I had become involved with Follicle Research. It would be the first time I met Lance in person. He was my Steve Austin, the bionic man, upgraded to one-hundred million dollars.

As I waited for the Dallas meeting, my personal life was improving. Alice and I had already filed for divorce, and those proceedings were completely non-contentious.

The pain of the ten-month-old separation was fading, and I had started to get used to the idea of another father figure in Jessica's life. Most importantly, I now had fifty percent custody of Jessica, per the agreement worked out with the child psychologist. Now three, Jessica had started preschool at Eureka Learning Center in Noe Valley. At home, she loved to hang out with Daddy. When we weren't dancing to the Wiggles, we colored together or played board games like Chutes and Ladders or Zingo. Sometimes, we walked the three blocks to Mitchell's Ice Cream in the Mission District, where Jessica always ordered her favorite flavor: cinnamon apple butter. I loved to watch her big eyes glow with excitement as she furiously licked away. "Daadddyy," she would protest in mid-scoop, her ice cream-rimmed smile in full display. But I couldn't stop myself, and I often found myself staring at my daughter, unable to believe my good fortune.

Jessica was still below the fiftieth percentile in weight and height, but she was nonetheless healthy and already showing evidence of the athletic ability she inherited from her parents. She was a marvel of balance and agility compared to her peers on the playground and a daredevil as well, with one of her favorite activities being head-first dives down the big slide at Douglas Playground, which caused more than a few disapproving looks from New Age San Francisco parents.

I spent every moment I could with her, and I rarely hired a babysitter. Sometimes, this caused me to miss out on social events, but every time I compared the value of the event against time spent with Jessica, my daughter always won out. And so, it was that when my best friend

Greg came into town and I had Jessica, we would spend our evenings at home.

I had met Greg freshman year at Harvard in a dorm room in Mathews Hall over a game of caps, a drinking game whereby opponents sit approximately eight feet from each other and attempt to toss bottle caps in the other player's beer-filled cup.

He was one of the largest people I had met, standing six-foot-four and weighing two hundred and fifty pounds. Already balding and with hulking shoulders that were perpetually arched forward, he cut an intimidating presence made even more so by his big, booming voice. But his spirit was gentle.

"Hi," he said as he greeted me. "Wanna play?"

"Sure."

We introduced ourselves as I sat down for my first game of caps. The game achieved its desired effect and by the end of the evening, I was rather drunk, finding myself stumbling with Greg to the Tasty, a tiny one-room diner and lunch counter in Harvard Square, for the first of what would be many late-night Huskie burgers over the next four years. As we sat at the narrow counter made of yellow linoleum and had our grub, Greg told me a little about his background.

He had attended Nobles and Greenough School for high school and then completed a post-graduate year at Choate Rosemary Hall, a highly selective and prestigious private boarding school located in Connecticut. Whereas fifteen percent of my high school class had attended college, fifteen percent of his Choate class had been admitted to Harvard. His mother worked in commercial banking for Bank of Boston, rapidly rising to

Senior Vice President and thus becoming the highest positioned woman at the bank, while his father was a successful residential real estate development in Denver. They each made more in one year than Dad could make in ten. Greg had grown up mostly in Wellesley, Massachusetts, in a home that was worth many more times than ours.

Regardless of the educational and economic differences, we would become best friends, and I was thrilled he was in San Francisco.

Now a successful investment banker like his mother and living in Denver, Greg arranged his business trips in such a way that we saw each other regularly throughout the year. One of those trips occurred a week before the Dallas meeting. After dinner, we settled onto the couch, while Jessica gathered her dolls on the floor to play nearby. I had talked with Greg only sparingly about Follicle Research and now he wanted to know more.

"How'd you meet this guy?' he asked me, taking a sip of beer.

"Would you believe online?"

Greg's eyes narrowed and he frowned. Then he shook his head. Conservative, careful, and reasonable, he was now also concerned. "How do you know he's legitimate?"

I shifted uncomfortably on the couch. Jessica was taking the clothes off all her dolls. I watched her, mostly to buy time to collect my thoughts. It was a good question, of course, particularly since I hadn't done any formal due diligence about Lance's background.

"Because I've talked science with him over and over," I said. "With my background in pharmacology, I could spot a bullshitter. This guy knows his stuff."

That seemed to reassure Greg, and his face relaxed and he nodded slightly. "If you say so, I guess. But I wouldn't commit myself too much."

"Don't worry, I'm not"

"So, what's your role in all of this?" he asked.

"Basically, I'm a partner in the company."

"So, you getting paid?"

"No, but I have equity."

Greg shook his head and said, "Now hold on a second. That's a big risk. If it doesn't work out, you'll have done all this work for nothing."

"It's worth the risk. I believe it's going to succeed."

Greg pushed on, turning his body towards me. "But how will you fit this in? You have a full-time job and Jessica half-time."

"I'll work on the nights and weekends I don't have her," I said confidently. "Don't worry."

As I said this, Jessica handed Greg a half-dressed GI Jane doll. The doll looked tiny in Greg's huge mitts.

"Very good, Jessica," he said to her. "Do you want me to help you?"

She nodded and so he lowered his giant frame onto the floor next to her. She jumped into his lap and watched as he started putting on GI Jane's fatigues. Just as he finished, he turned to me and said, "Just make sure everything is legit."

"Come on, now," I said, waving my hand at him. "You have nothing to worry about."

Meanwhile, I was still struggling with my work at the hospital, made worse by interactions with patients like Leena, a drug addict who had tragically contracted HIV from being raped. In almost inexorable fashion, her life began to unwind after she was told of the infection. She started smoking methamphetamine and refused to take medications. Her disease advanced to AIDS, and then one day, she woke up with a terrible headache. She started vomiting, so a friend brought her to the ER, where I was called to admit her to the hospital.

Leena was sweating profusely when I walked in on the activity surrounding her in the ER. The bright fluorescent lights made her face look particularly pale. She was agitated and confused, arguing with the nurses trying to place IV's in her arms. Her long brown hair was soaking wet and her nonsensical words tumbled across rotten teeth, a typical consequence of long-term meth use. Her face was gaunt and her body thin, which was not surprising given the appetite-suppressing effects of the drug. Most concerning, her neck was as rigid as a board. It was clear that Leena had meningitis, a serious infection of the membranes that cover the brain and spine. The spinal tap confirmed the diagnosis, and she was started on multiple antibiotics and admitted to the ICU.

Leena was not expected to survive. She had a poor immune system due to her advanced AIDS and the infection, pneumococcus, was a dangerous one. When informed of the prognosis, her mother simply shook her head, as if to say, "I expected this". Leena remained in the ICU for 11 days, but to everyone's surprise and relief, she eventually recovered and was transferred to the medical floor.

It was there that I had numerous opportunities to interact with Leena, but I found my attempts to really connect with her were difficult and largely unsuccessful. The violence and shame of the rape had inflicted a deep psychological wound and the methamphetamine had destroyed her soul, leaving a vacuous shell of a woman. And I think it was my inability to connect emotionally with this woman that left me with the unsettling feeling of wanting, even needing, to feel real empathy for her, but whatever empathy I experienced was mostly intellectual. I *thought* empathy, but barely felt it. I did genuinely hope, however, that the gravity of her medical illness combined with ongoing outpatient psychotherapy and sobriety would provide the impetus for change.

There were lots of hugs and thank you's and promises the day Leena was discharged from the hospital. But she failed to attend any of the three appointments I scheduled for her during the two weeks after she left the hospital. She also didn't pick up any of her medications, and when I tried to call her cell phone, it was disconnected. A subsequent conversation with her mother confirmed my worst fear: Leena had resumed her meth use.

My interaction with Leena came just when my feeling of disconnection with my patients was progressively worsening to the point where I felt I was in full occupational crisis. Not only had I lost my intellectual satisfaction in the job, I was now losing empathy for my patients. But how could that have happened? I went into medicine because I was once a patient. And my road to becoming a doctor had been filled with so many fortuitous occurrences that I should have been nothing but thrilled to have such an honor.

That journey, which had started in a hospital bed at Beth Israel, was immediately complicated by a major obstacle: I had never taken pre-meds or the MCAT, the standardized examination required of all students applying for medical school. To even try to take the MCAT would be useless, as it tested knowledge gained from pre-med coursework. The only solution was to finish graduate school, attend a two-year pre-med program, and then take the test. All of that would take another three to four years, which was much too long for someone with my general level of impatience. I needed to come up with an alternative path.

As I considered various strategies, I realized I had already taken many of the first-year medical school courses as part of my doctorate program (I was in graduate school at the time). If I could figure out a way to complete the first-year curriculum, I could apply for entrance into the second year, a strategy that could work, but only if the admissions office would waive the pre-med and MCAT requirements. And the school that did that would have to be in Boston, since my college girlfriend, Laurie, with whom I was still in a serious relationship, worked at a law firm in the city. It was an ambitious plan that had a small likelihood of success, but something deep in my gut told me it was the right path.

I went to see the Director of Admissions for the Boston University School of Medicine to discuss the issue, but she told me I couldn't get into medical school without the usual admission requirements and that the only way a student could be admitted to the second year is if someone dropped out of school. Apparently, the number of positions in each class of every medical school was fixed and could not be increased.

"But maybe there could be an exception due to special circumstances," I suggested.

"I doubt it," she replied.

I wasn't dissuaded, however, and moved forward with my plan, taking the remainder of the first-year medical school courses—some of them only with permission from the course manager—and completing my doctorate program requirements. Then, I submitted an admission application. Two weeks before the start of the school year, a student dropped out of the incoming second-year class and I was given his position, much to the surprise of my new classmates who had quietly given my plan little chance of success. I think even my parents were taken aback, and I can remember their brief silence after I gave them the news over the phone. On a personal level, I felt very grateful and blessed that I had been given the chance by the Admissions Office, and I was committed to making the most of it.

I did well enough to be elected to Alpha Omega Alpha, the medical school honor society, and to be named the best student in Internal Medicine, the field that I decided ultimately to pursue. Mom, Dad and Grandma flew out for graduation. Wearing my black robe with three green stripes on each arm while standing among my fellow graduates, I felt nearly overwhelmed as we recited the Hippocratic Oath, which ended with:

*So long as I maintain this Oath faithfully and without corruption, may it be granted to me to partake of life fully and the practice of my art, gaining the respect of all men for all time. However, should I transgress this Oath and violate it, may the opposite be my fate.*

I could never imagine, as I so earnestly repeated those words, that ten years later, in a federal courtroom three thousand miles away, a judge would angrily read those same words to me, as my very freedom hanged in the balance.

But for now, as we filed out of the auditorium, I felt a sense of incredible privilege and responsibility granted to me by society. My hands shook as I tucked the diploma under my arm. And then I saw Mom to my left, sitting about five seats in. She had a look on her face I'd never seen before, one that transcended pride, love and joy. A look of complete satisfaction. It was so striking that I felt compelled to go to her, despite the strict instructions we had been given not to break the line.

She met me halfway.

"We did it, Mom." I whispered. "We really did it."

I had never felt so thoroughly humbled. It was hard to conceive that the small-town boy from Ohio was now a doctor. It was an outcome that I would never have imagined growing up in Boon. I might as well have said I was going to be President of the United States.

She hugged me for a few moments, pulled back, and then grabbed my cheeks with both hands, her face nearly touching mine. And smiled. Her mascara had run, and I wiped it away as I smiled back at her. I handed her my diploma and she held it tight against her chest, leaning forward slightly, as though she were trying to wrap her body around it. As I returned to the procession, I glanced back and thought how beautiful she looked in her brand-new dress.

Finished with medical school, I was thrilled when my first call night of residency arrived. I grabbed a pair of the baby blue scrubs with the large, circular UCSF seal on the front and put them on. On my waist, I wore a fanny pack that contained the essentials--the UCSF Housestaff Handbook, the Sanford Guide to Antimicrobial Therapy, Tom Evans's ECG Crib Sheets and a pen light. The only thing missing was my stethoscope, and once I hung it around my neck, I was ready for battle.

It wasn't until four in the morning that the hospital quieted down. Taking advantage of the opportunity the lull provided, I made a break for the call room for some shut-eye, but because I was so excited about my first night on duty, I couldn't sleep. Instead, I got out my pen light and started reading the Handbook. At five, I'd had enough, so I walked the hallways for a time until I came across a set of windows that faced west. As I moved toward them, I was struck by the spectacular sight of the first light shining on the Pacific Ocean. I stood in awe as the ocean became progressively bluer and the distant hills of Marin took shape.

Suddenly, my beeper went off, causing me to jump. The ICU needed me, and as soon as I entered the unit through a large set of automated steel doors, I was immediately intercepted by a nurse who redirected me into the nurses' station.

"The fifty-six-year-old patient in bed three was brought in two days ago after suffering a cardiac arrest at home," she said. "She's basically brain-dead, and her husband wishes to talk to a doctor."

I noticed some staff nearby who were smiling and laughing as they engaged in conversation. In my newness, I could never imagine reaching a point where patient care became just a job. Didn't they know people were dying around them? Shouldn't there be more respect? I turned back to the nurse.

"What's he want to talk about?"

"He wouldn't say."

I glanced around the corner and saw the man sitting bedside with his face in his hands. Wide-eyed, I looked back at the nurse. She frowned and lifted her hands, as if to say, "Are you going or not?" I really did not want to, but I was the doctor now and didn't have the luxury of refusing, so I walked slowly into the room and introduced myself. The man lifted his head from his hands and helplessly looked at me.

"Thank you for coming, doctor," he said. "Can we talk?"

Hesitating for a moment, I nodded. Then I guided him to a nearby empty room. He dropped into a chair and stared for a long minute or two.

"I think my wife is dead," he said without looking at me. "And I could've saved her."

"Can you tell me what happened?"

He shook his head and muttered something unintelligible. He cried quietly for a bit, and I moved close and put my hand on his shoulder. He cleared his throat and started talking to the floor.

"You know, Mary was only twenty-four when I met her," he said.

The change in direction caught me off guard, and all I said in return was, "Uh, huh," as I settled back into my chair.

"She was a flight attendant. Attractive, perky, full of energy. A friend set us up."

"What'd you do on your first date?" I asked, gaining my bearings.

He looked up at me and smiled slightly.

"Can you believe we went bowling? Hell, it was 1963. We all bowled," he said with a chuckle.

"Sounds fun."

"Yeah, it was," he said, staring into space, thinking. "Wanna know something crazy?"

I nodded.

"So, we're there bowling and every time she gets up, I'm checking out her body. I'm doing this with every frame, and then I start getting this feeling of familiarity. Deja vu or something. Suddenly, in the eighth, it hits me. I had met her a year before in the supermarket."

"What triggered your memory?"

"Her butt. I remembered her butt," he said, causing me to laugh.

"Did she remember yours?" I joked.

He smiled. "No, but she remembered me. She said, "Oh, yeah! I thought you looked familiar, too!""

"Serendipity, I guess."

He nodded. "We got married six months later and bought a house. Those were some good years."

"How many children did you have?"

His smile faded, and he looked down again. "That never worked out."

"Oh, I'm sorry," I said, feeling foolish.

"It's okay," he said kindly. "She changed after that. Seemed like her nerves started getting the best of her."

"Did she see a doctor?"

"No. She started drinking instead. Created some embarrassing situations. I did my best to help her, but she couldn't seem to give it up. And I loved her too much to give up on her. So, I hung in there."

And so it went for the couple as the years started piling up. Eventually, both retired, but in her extra time Mary began drinking more. One night during dinner at home, Mary decided to finish off the bottle of wine. A short while later, as Bob was at the kitchen sink washing dishes and Mary was still at the table finishing the last bit of her steak, he heard a strange muffled sound.

"I look and she's frantically grabbing her neck and her veins are bulging on her forehead. It took me a moment before I realized the steak had gotten stuck in her throat."

By the time Bob covered the ten feet separating him from his wife, Mary had fallen to the floor, gasping for air and turning blue. Within seconds, she was unconscious. And then suddenly she stopped breathing, her body limp and lifeless.

"One moment you're washing dishes and the next moment your wife is dying in front of you," he said.

Bob responded immediately by trying to pull the piece of meat out of her mouth, but he could not find it. So, he quickly sat her up, knelt behind her and repeatedly performed the Heimlich maneuver to no avail. He called 911 and returned to Mary to perform CPR.

"Nothing I did worked," he said.

"I think you made absolutely heroic and textbook attempts to save her life," I said, trying to reassure him. He dismissed my comment with a wave.

"She was limp, lifeless, but I kept trying and trying to revive her. It seemed like the paramedics would never come. Our entire life together flashed through my brain."

Eventually, the paramedics did arrive and were able to place an IV and a breathing tube in her. But thirty minutes had passed. Too long for the fragile brain to be deprived of oxygen. The medics took her to our hospital where she was found by both the emergency room and admitting physicians to have no meaningful neurological functioning. The grim prognosis was relayed to Bob, and Mary was admitted to the ICU. No one wanted to give up that quickly.

"But now I know she's dead," Bob said, his face twisted into a combination of anguish, disbelief and emptiness. He looked and acted like his soul had been vacated.

I tried to find something to say, but all that came out was, "I'm so sorry."

By this time, it was seven in the morning, and I could see other medical residents arriving for morning rounds.

"Would you mind staying here with me until her doctor arrives?" he asked. "By the way, my name is Bob."

I quickly touched the back of his hand. "Of course," I replied and introduced myself.

Within minutes, the third-year resident who had admitted Mary to the hospital came into the room with a neurologist. After a brief discussion, he asked both Bob and me to accompany him into Mary's room. I watched as the neurologist went through the almost robot-like motions of the physical examination. When he was finished, we stepped outside, and the neurologist turned to Bob.

"I find no evidence of any higher-level brain functioning. She's displaying only primitive reflexes on exam. This finding, combined with the amount of time her brain was without oxygen, tells me her chance of any recovery of brain function is essentially nil."

Bob's shoulders shook as he cried for a few moments. When he stopped, he seemed to be thinking.

"Let's stop this madness," he said.

"I'm sorry?" the neurologist replied.

"I want her taken off life support," he said, before starting to cry again. I put my hand on his back and noticed he was trembling again. "I can't believe I'm killing my wife," he said.

"You're not killing your wife," the neurologist said. "You're simply allowing her to pass naturally."

"It's all my fault she choked. I'm her husband. I should've protected her."

"It's not your fault," I said quickly, feeling the full weight of his misguided guilt.

After several minutes of discussion, we all returned to Mary's room. The resident asked the respiratory therapist to disconnect Mary from the ventilator. Bob sat in a chair next to her bed, holding her hand and fiddling with her wedding ring.

The respirator let out a long sigh as it shut down. This startled Bob and caused him to begin crying again. By now, the resident had left the room, and I was alone with Bob and the rhythmic beeps of the cardiac monitor. My medical degree, the tools in my fanny pack and the stethoscope around my neck, were useless now. Bob needed only my humanity.

As her breathing became shallower and the color drained from her face, the beeps from the monitor slowed to the cadence of a tolling clock.    The nurse came in and mercifully turned everything off.

When she did, I noticed Bob had become stoic, even determined, and I admired his fortitude in that painful moment.

As I watched the early morning sun filter into Mary's room that day, my thoughts turned to a long ride I had taken from New York back home to Boston three years earlier, after I had coughed up chunks of blood on the green grass of Central Park, leaving my youth behind and starting my journey to this place.    The blood was from my lungs and was caused by Wegener's Granulomatosis, a disease diagnosed by doctors at Beth Israel Hospital in Boston.    It was in that hospital that I was started on the medications that would eventually take away my fertility, but that would also save my life.    And it was from that hospital bed that I first realized I wanted to be a doctor.

Now a doctor fresh out of medical school, my experience of Mary's death at Bob's side validated just how much I wanted to help people, and sometimes that help consisted simply of being present, of caring.    Even in the midst of tragedy, I felt a certain sense of gratitude that I had been guided through a remarkable set of circumstances to that moment in my life.

Seven years later at Cade County, I still wanted to help people, but it seemed I had lost my zeal for my job.    I needed something new, something to get me excited again.    Something that provided a goal that I could work towards.    I decided that goal would be Follicle Research. It would stimulate me, challenge me, and bring me recognition and fortune.    Maybe it could even make me immortal.    And then people would really know the boy from Boon had accomplished something.

# CHAPTER NINE

Although the wait seemed interminable, the day of the Dallas meeting finally arrived. By now, I was very anxious to meet Lance, as the only image I had come from a picture of his bald scalp and a brief self-description. "Pretty muscular and pretty hairy," he had told me. "And since my hair hasn't grown back all the way, I'm wearing a wig."

Lance arranged for us to stay at a hotel downtown. I picked him out as soon as I walked into the lobby. He was crossing in front of me, headed for the elevators, carrying a large duffel bag on his right shoulder. He was a burly man, a little less than six feet tall, very thick in the shoulders, with a short, muscular neck and large head. Tight jeans hugged his bulging thighs, and he walked with his free arm extended from his body, as though it were counterbalancing the weight on the other side. Light tan boots kicked out to the side as he walked, suggesting he had just dismounted from the horse he rode in on. I thought if I squinted hard enough, I might see the faint vapor trail of anabolic steroids curling off him.

"Lance!" I shouted across the lobby, causing him to stop abruptly and turn around. We made eye contact, and then he smiled and began walking towards me. He was an average-looking man with thick eyebrows and a wide nose, his generous forehead being his most distinguishing feature. But his long, brown wig was parted down the middle, making him a poster child of the eighties feathered look.

*This is the genius I've talking science with for the past year?*

As I went to hug him, he thrust his arm forward to shake my hand, resulting in an awkward semi-punch to my abdomen. I pulled back, and we both laughed, shaking hands as we did.

"Great to finally meet you, Lance," I said.

"Likewise," he said, fidgeting with his luggage.

I cleared my throat. He reached for my bag. And then we spoke simultaneously.

"Can I help you with that?" he asked.

"Let me go check in," I said.

We laughed uncomfortably. He pulled back his hand, put it into his pocket, and brought out a cell phone. "While you're checking in, I've got some calls to make," he said. As he dialed a number, he added, "By the way, I put us in the same room. That way we can talk about Follicle Research."

I nodded my head and moved towards reception.

*The same room?*

By the time I got upstairs, Lance had already unpacked and was lying on the bed, finishing a phone conversation.

"I'll have three months' worth shipped out in the next couple of days," he said, before hanging up.

"I didn't realize we had any FR-1," I said, as I set down my bag.

"I was talking about something else. A little side business I have," he said, getting up for the bathroom.

"What side business?"

He sized me up briefly.

"Well, you know I have a number of contacts in the sports world."

I nodded. Lance had told me he had founded a vitamin supplement company whose products purportedly helped athletic performance. He had sold the company five years earlier but had maintained connections with professional athletes.

"Through that network, I have been working with a physician to supply hGH for pros."

"hGH?"

"Human growth hormone. It's a performance-enhancing drug used by athletes. It's pretty popular."

"Isn't that illegal?" I asked, not very familiar with the drug that later would become notorious because of the famous athletes who would be busted for using it.

"I work with a physician who prescribes the drug."

"Interesting. Where do you get it?"

"China."

"Are you sure it's safe?"

"Of course."

I didn't ask another question. The truth was that I didn't want to know any more. I was already involved in an incredible opportunity, and didn't want to screw it up. What Lance did in his free time was his business.

The meeting Lance and I had scheduled with Sam Sirotka was to be brief and informational only. He had a full schedule that day and was not interested in having any substantial business discussions. Nonetheless, we viewed the meeting as a very important opportunity for us and, given our dwindling cash, we were becoming desperate. We considered a formal presentation, but thought that might seem too much like a sales pitch.

We arranged to meet in the lobby of the Fairmont Hotel at ten-thirty in the morning. Lance made sure we were there thirty minutes early. Right on time, a tall and physically fit man in his late sixties strolled over to us and introduced himself as Sam. He had a pleasant Southern drawl and a nonchalance about his demeanor. Absent was an air of privilege, which I figured was the result of good parenting. He seemed sincerely happy to meet us.

"Let's go have breakfast," he suggested, as he maneuvered behind us, placed a hand on each of our shoulders, and gently guided us across the lobby to the restaurant, where we were promptly seated. Sam grimaced slightly as he glided into his chair.

"Two-hour yoga session today," he explained.

Lance and I nodded.

"I'm just getting fruit and coffee," he said, refusing the waitress's menu offering. "I hope you boys don't mind, but I have another meeting scheduled in an hour."

"No problem, Sam, we're happy to have the opportunity to meet you," Lance reassured him.

"I hear you boys maybe got something big."

My pulse quickened. Lance didn't hesitate.

"Sam, we believe we've found a cure for baldness. Not just for the bald spot on top of the head, but also for balding areas in the front where the hairline used to be. Our product works like a hair switch. It turns the hair follicle back on, causing it to produce normal, mature hair again. And it's a safe product that you apply directly to the scalp."

Sam nodding his head impassively. The waitress had arrived with coffee. We watched in silence as she went around the table, filling our cups. As she did, I thought about my conversations with Lance about how we needed to do animal studies to make certain the drug was safe. For financial reasons, we had never gotten around to doing them. Instead, we simply assumed the drug was safe. I suddenly realized what a tremendous leap of faith that was.

Lance then began summarizing our research efforts to date. Sam maintained eye contact with Lance the entire time. After a while, he interrupted.

"What about patent issues?"

"We feel we have a strong patent position," Lance replied.

"How do you know that?"

"Think of our patent like this knife," I said, placing my butter knife down straight in front of me. Lance raised one eyebrow at me. Sam tilted his head slightly and squinted.

"This knife can move from here to here," I said as I rotated the knife back and forth forty-five degrees in each direction. "The area covered by this knife encompasses all the combinations of our peptide that are effective. Any configuration outside of that area does not work. Our patent covers all the effective combinations."

Sam scratched his head and stared off into space. Lance scratched his chin, staring at my knife. It seemed logical to me. Just when the silence started to feel really uncomfortable, Sam spoke.

"I think I understand. How will you produce this product?"

"We currently have a lab in Charlotte."

"How much does it cost to make it?"

"We're working on production costs," Lance replied.

"I'm sure you are, but my question was, how much is it?"

Lance repositioned himself in the chair and coughed. It always came down to money, but we had prepared for the meeting by analyzing different production methods. Just then, the waitress arrived to take our order.

"Eggs benedict," I said, without opening the menu.

I waited until the waitress wrote down our orders, collected our menus and left the area before speaking.

"We have produced the molecule with excellent purity in our private lab," I started. "We have done this by making several different modifications in our production methods. However, we have found that even large-scale synthesis using our methodology is quite expensive."

"How expensive?" Sam pushed.

"To build a synthetic production facility, it would cost anywhere from two to six million dollars and take one to two years. The cost to produce one month of treatment for one patient would be one thousand dollars."

Sam grimaced.

"However, if we contracted with an existing facility in China, we could start producing the peptide within six months. That would lower the cost to four hundred dollars for one month of treatment."

I looked at Lance, and on cue, he continued the conversation.

"We have also examined something called recombinant technology. This is a scientific method whereby an animal, microbe or plant is genetically modified to produce a peptide. Huge vats of special bacteria could be used to pump out peptide twenty-four hours per day. This could bring the cost down to less than one hundred dollars per month."

"That's better, but it's still too expensive, fellas."

"We agree. That's why we think tobacco is the answer."

"Tobacco?"

"We can use genetically-modified tobacco plants to produce our molecule. It is the perfect production choice for multiple reasons. First, the US Department of Agriculture views the tobacco plant as a "non-food, non-feed" plant, exempting it from the usual regulatory requirements of the FDA. Second, the tobacco plant is perennial and, once planted, it yields three crops per year for six to seven years before replanting is needed. Third, there are thousands of unused acres of tobacco land in the Southeastern United States. Fourth, the USDA has limited the use of land planted for tobacco used for smoking, but freely offers permits for the planting of tobacco for other uses, such as medicinal. Fifth, the plant could be genetically modified in such a way that other tobacco plants would not be affected. Sixth, we think the US tobacco industry will back the project, as it would place tobacco in a more favorable light."

"Fascinating stuff, boys. Go on."

"It will cost about a million dollars to modify six to ten tobacco plants. Those plants will yield enough seeds to plant hundreds of acres of modified tobacco. We estimate it would take six to twelve months before seeds would be ready to plant."

"Who is gonna tend the land?" asked Sam.

"That part is easy. The infrastructure is already in place. The land and the farmers are there. In fact, there is plenty of under-utilized land so the farmers would welcome the business. Plus, there is a facility in North Carolina that can process the tobacco leaves into pure peptide."

"So how much would it cost, using tobacco?"

Lance leaned back in the chair, a fat cat after the big kill.

"Once in place, the cost to produce one month of treatment would be twenty-five dollars."

Sam leaned forward, placed both elbows on the table, and rested his chin on his clasped hands. He slowly scanned Lance's face and then looked at me. He pulled his arms off the table and played with his left cuff link. Then he took a sip of water and cleared his throat.

"Does this stuff really work?" he asked earnestly.

"We'll let you be the judge," Lance said, nodding at me.

I pulled a set of pictures out of my shirt pocket and placed them in front of Sam.

"These are before and after pictures of two patients who received treatment for five months," I explained.

Sam picked up each picture, holding the Before picture in his left hand and the After picture in his right, and studied them for several minutes, eyes darting back and forth between each pair.

I watched for a minute before telling him, "The second set of pictures are of my scalp."

Surprised, he quickly looked up at me. Then he held up my "before" picture and compared it to my scalp. Moments later, he began to smile, relaxing a bit as he did. Then he set the picture down, gripped the edge of the table with both hands, and leaned formed.

"I'm in," he announced.

We had scheduled a second meeting in Dallas to take place later that day. To gain working capital for our hair peptide development, we had generated another business idea around a procedure called mesotherapy. This technique was first used in France twenty years earlier and involved a series of injections of a specialized drug cocktail into body areas with excess fat, such as love handles, back of the arms and under the chin. Tiny needles were used to give a series of closely-spaced injections, which in turn would cause the breakdown and elimination of fat from those areas of the body.

I had researched mesotherapy extensively, studying the physiology of fat cells in highly technical detail, particularly the pharmacologic manipulation of fat metabolism. Most of this information was gleaned by reviewing basic science research studies in animals that used highly sophisticated measuring devices. By extrapolating the results of these studies to human beings, we were able to formulate a cocktail consisting of four substances. Eventually, we had developed an idea of building a business around our formulation, utilizing a business-in-a-box strategy that would incorporate a franchising model. To support this, we would develop a standardized training program and would supply all equipment and product. We named the business Forever Lithe.

For the Dallas trip, we had arranged a meeting with a prominent plastic surgeon, Dr. Nicholas Cooper, and his business partner, Frank Lawry, to discuss Forever Lithe. I had emailed Frank several days before the trip in an effort to expedite the process, as we were desperate for money.

Frank's response was simple: "All possibilities will be discussed."

That was good enough for us. We arrived at Dr. Cooper's office with only a couple of minutes to spare, our breakfast meeting having lasted nearly three hours.

We were greeted in the waiting room by the office manager who escorted us through a beautiful, modern clinic to the doctor's private office where Frank and Dr. Cooper were waiting for us. After introductions, we began discussing the philosophy of mesotherapy, but the doctor was already familiar with it, and wanted more specific information about our proprietary cocktail. We told him our treatment was several times more potent than others on the market.

"Do you have evidence it works?"

"There is plenty of evidence that mesotherapy, in general, works," I said. We think our formula is more effective. To test this hypothesis, I have written a full clinical protocol. We were hoping you'd be interested in performing the study here. You could probably publish the results."

I handed him the ten-page clinical study I had written the week before the trip. He spent about five minutes flipping through the pages, stopping to read certain sections more carefully.

"We have a state-of-the-art photography studio where we can do before and after pictures," he offered, putting down the document.

"That's essential for the study," I replied.

We then spent the next fifteen minutes talking about the study logistics.

"I'm very interested," the doctor concluded.

"We would need to know the costs of the study," Frank interjected. "And since we're conducting the study, we would need special consideration when it came to discussing the business end."

"Of course," Lance reassured him.

"Well, this is definitely something we'd be interested in," Frank said.

We spent another fifteen minutes discussing financial arrangements before Dr. Cooper informed us that he had to get back to his patients.

"Of course," I replied, standing up.

"Hey, you guys want some Botox injections before you go?" he asked us.

I wasn't sure whether I should be grateful or offended.

"Why not?" Lance answered.

I nodded in agreement.

Forty-five minutes later, we walked out of the clinic, crow's feet fading by the minute.

We had a celebratory dinner that night at a pricey seafood restaurant downtown. We were giddy from the events of the day. We ordered an expensive bottle of champagne and toasted ourselves. Everything was finally coming together.

Lance seemed particularly sentimental as he filled my glass.

"Max, I'm really happy you're here. I've never worked so well with a partner. I love our conversations, how we think and talk about science. It's helped development so much."

I thought he might cry. His arms bulged out of his polo shirt. His wig remained perfectly coiffed.

"I think we can do some big things together," he continued. "I want you to have a greater part of the business. I'd like to offer you fifteen percent ownership in the company."

Flabbergasted, I put down my fork and looked at him.

"I'm honored, Lance," I said.

"I want you to always be a part of Follicle Research."

"I would love that," I said, beaming.  Then, I lifted the glass of champagne in salutation, and drained it.

That night, I could barely sleep because of my excitement.  "Small town boy makes it big," the headlines would read.  I couldn't believe I had become involved in such an amazing opportunity.  Awash in self-congratulations, I began reminiscing about when I first became seriously interested in a career in science.

It had begun senior year of college when I took a psychopharmacology course.  At the time, I was a psychology major and fairly happy with it, but I was still looking for something a bit more scientific. Psychopharmacology—the study of the effects of drugs on the brain--felt like a perfect merging of the two fields.  I decided to meet with the professor to discuss career opportunities.

"A master's degree might be a good idea, Max," she said with a smile, catching me off guard.

"Actually, I was considering a Ph.D."

She frowned slightly and looked off in the distance, as though she were preparing to say something uncomfortable.

"I'm not quite sure a Ph.D. is for you," she said squarely.

My chin dropped as I stared at her, speechless. Those were the type of things I expected to hear back at Boon, not at Harvard. She squirmed uncomfortably in her chair and then said in a soft, almost apologetic, voice, "Why don't you consider doing a year of research before making a decision?"

*She doesn't think I can handle a Ph.D. Maybe she doesn't think I'm smart enough.*

I wanted to tell her to go fuck herself, but I liked her and she hadn't handed out grades yet, so I simply said, "Thanks. I'll look into it." Then I left without asking for the reason why she felt that way. Perhaps I simply didn't want to hear it, whatever it was.

On the twenty minute walk back to my dorm room, I thought how far I'd come since freshman year. I remembered my favorite class that year: Expository Writing. It was taught by a timid graduate student who wore a ridiculous bow tie and the same khaki sport coat to every class. He arranged the seats in a circle each time, thinking that it would foster a more collaborative experience. It didn't. Regardless, I loved the course, even if my small town-ness was occasionally on full

114

display, like the time I wrote a paper describing an old cemetery in Harvard Square and the "rod" iron fence surrounding it.

"Wrought!" my professor wrote in big capital letters on the first page.

One of the more embarrassing moments occurred when we were discussing Jane Austen's *Pride and Prejudice*. The conversation centered around the importance of environment and parenting style on character and morality development.

"I think Mrs. Bennet is mostly responsible for Lydia's poor moral judgment," one of the students argued. "Just look how she conducted herself in public. And her social climbing was unabashedly opportunistic."

I was itching to jump in. "That daggone Mr. Bennet isn't the best role model either," I offered.

Time seemed to stop as everyone stared at me. Then it occurred to me.

*I just said daggone. In Expos class.*

So frequent was its use back in Boon, I hadn't ever given it a second thought. Now surrounded by valedictorians and perfect SAT scores, I felt like the hick I most certainly was.

Other similar episodes—like the time I read a flier about a social event and asked my roommate what hors d'oeuvres were—sometimes plagued me.

"Looks like cheese and crackers and sandwiches cut into small pieces, if you ask me," I said sourly, when we arrived at the event.

But now, four years later, I was ready to take my education to another level. By the time I arrived back at North House after the meeting with my professor, I was certain I would get a Ph.D. But it was too late to apply for the coming fall, and so I did take the professor's advice after all, and through a convoluted series of contacts, I found an opening as a research assistant at the Alcohol and Drug Abuse Research Center (ADARC) at McLean Hospital, a psychiatric hospital affiliated with Harvard Medical School. Over the next year, I conducted research examining the effects of alcohol on the human brain, using MRI scans.

At the end of that year, I applied for graduate school, deciding eventually to enroll in a behavioral neuroscience doctorate program at Boston University School of Medicine. I would be working in the laboratory of Conan Kornetsky, an early pioneer in the study of how various street drugs affected the brain. Once there, I bounced around the lab trying to find my niche before Conan, who had become my mentor, mentioned to me he was considering bringing a new technology to the lab that allowed for the study of brain metabolism in exquisite detail. He wanted to know if I'd be interested in being the graduate student using the technology, and I immediately agreed. The research was labor-intensive, so I was given a research assistant to help me. With another pair of hands, my research progressed very rapidly compared to that of my fellow graduate students.

After the first year of graduate school, I decided to switch my field of study to pharmacology, as I considered it to be more rigorous. I went to the department chair with my CV and transcripts and informed her of my intentions. As she sat reviewing them, I saw a look of confusion on her face.

"I don't see any documentation that you've taken organic chemistry, let alone biology or physics."

"That's true, but I have taken several other science classes and have done well."

"But a course like biochemistry, which is required work for a doctorate degree in pharmacology, would be very difficult without organic chemistry."

"Perhaps, but I think I can memorize the formulas, even if I don't fully understand their meaning."

"And your advisor supports this?"

"Absolutely."

"Well, I'll need to speak with him."

In the meantime, I told Mom about my intentions.

"If that's what you want to do, you should go for it," she said.

"I think it will be a lot harder than the program I'm in now," I told her.

"You've been able to handle every other thing in life you've set your mind to. I don't think this will be any different."

That was all I needed to hear from her. Eventually, after some persistence on my part, the prerequisite requirements of the pharmacology program were waived for me, primarily because of my performance in graduate school to that point and because various people in positions of influence apparently liked me. Although it was an unusual situation, I always knew that it would work out, and when it did, I was very grateful. Three years later, I graduated with a Ph.D. in pharmacology. I was officially a scientist.

# CHAPTER TEN

The Dallas trip created significant momentum that Lance and I were eager to capitalize on. Within several days after our return, Lance arranged for a meeting to take place the first week of January in Las Vegas with the oil man, Sam Sirotka. This time, his close friend and business associate, Larry Josephs, would be present, along with Dr. George Findley, the man who had first introduced us to Sam. They scheduled a Saturday arrival aboard Sam's private jet and would leave the following day. Their sole purpose for coming was to hear more about our hair peptide and to discuss a potential business partnership. In typical efficient Lance fashion, he also arranged for a meeting about Forever Lithe to take place the night before.

We expected the weekend to bring significant financial compensation and increased product exposure, as the two businessmen, in addition to their own wealth, had an extensive network of similarly wealthy contacts. Larry and his wife had started a small medical supply company fifteen years earlier and had built it into a national business with over one thousand employees. Then, several years previously, they sold the business for two hundred million dollars. Although only fifty-one, Larry was now retired and generally didn't want to be bothered, but apparently could be coaxed into the right business opportunity from time to time.

We decided to prepare a Power Point presentation for the men. Since the hair peptide was Lance's creation, I thought he should make the actual delivery. He refused, however, stating that his anxiety would be too overwhelming, which would create a bad impression. I was thrilled to do it for him. The preparation was easy and took only a few days, due to all the discussions we'd had over the previous year.

As we worked on the presentation, it reaffirmed our belief that we were sitting on a veritable gold mine. The potential market size was astronomical; the effectiveness superb. Consequently, we needed a setting that would match the grandeur of our science. We chose the Bellagio.

I arrived in Las Vegas on Friday afternoon and waited for Lance in the beautiful lobby of the hotel, spending the time marveling at the many glass-blown art pieces there. Thirty minutes later, I saw Lance hurrying in the front doors. I greeted him with a handshake, mindful that hugs, based on my Dallas experience, were off-limits for him. He was particularly nervous, continually wringing his hands and taking short, quick steps from side to side, like he was trying to stamp out an entire ant colony with his two feet. His forehead was moist. He immediately wanted to go over our itinerary in detail.

"Lance, relax. We have another day before meeting them. Let's just get ourselves situated and then go have some fun."

My words seemed to calm him somewhat, and after checking in, we proceeded to a lovely room with two queen beds. Upon arrival, I took off my shoes, jumped into bed and turned on a college basketball game. Lance, on the other hand, fastidiously unpacked his clothes, refolded them, and placed them in drawers. He then hung several shirts and pairs of slacks on hangers. Finished with his housekeeping, he went into the bathroom to speak on the phone. I was able to make out several different conversations from his muffled voice behind the door. Per usual, I had no idea whom he was speaking with.

As scheduled, our meeting with Frank, the Dallas businessman with whom we had discussed Forever Lithe, and his wife would take place on Friday night at Aqua Knox, a seafood restaurant in the Venetian. Lance was dressed and ready to go an hour early, and he spent the next twenty minutes impatiently pacing the room, exhorting me to hurry up. He had his usual tight-fitting short-sleeved shirt on, a powder blue one, with a pair of khaki's and brown shoes. Even his best attempts at fashion were awkward. I wasn't sure if it was because he was a redneck from Arkansas or a closet nerd who spent too much time in the lab.

Dinner that evening was dedicated to exquisite food, stimulating conversation and an endless stream of alcohol. We spent only a brief amount of time discussing Forever Lithe, as we had already covered all the relevant details previously. Lance, who didn't drink much, laughed frequently and engaged fully in the conversation. This was his wheelhouse, a relaxed setting where he could demonstrate his vast fund of knowledge about a seemingly endless number of topics. He had a unique ability to make even the most difficult concepts understandable and interesting. Given that, it was not surprising he dominated the conversation. Intermittently, I would glance around the table and find the others transfixed by him. The king was holding court.

The long dinner ended at eleven. Lance was exhausted because his anxiety about the trip had prevented him from getting adequate sleep the week before.

"I'm hitting the sack," he said wearily.

"Ok, I'm gonna check out the casino," I replied.

He gave me a disapproving look, but I wasn't about to lose an opportunity to shoot dice. By 11:30, I had established myself at a rowdy craps table at the Bellagio. The minimum bet was $50, but I didn't care. I was about to be rich from the hair peptide. And I loved the drama, because with drama usually came a dilemma, and that dilemma created a challenge which I could then conquer, causing me to feel fully alive and validated as a person. The mundane was for much less interesting people.

For three hours and through many drinks at that craps table, I felt really alive. But eventually I spent most of my money and nearly all my energy, so I returned to the room and slipped into bed. Lance was snoring loudly. Clearly, the Ambien I had prescribed for him had worked.

Drums were playing in my head when Lance woke me at around ten in the morning. Fully dressed, he stood over my bed, insisting I get up so that we could review our presentation scheduled for that night.

"Later, Lance. I need to sleep. Can you grab me some ibuprofen?"

He handed me two and a glass of water and after washing them down, I turned away from him, pulled the covers over my head and slept for another two hours. When I awoke, I met him for lunch, where I was subjected to an intense review of all aspects of the hair peptide.  It was a complete waste of time from an informational standpoint, as I already knew the details intimately.  But it seemed to soothe Lance, and so I suffered through it.

When we returned to our room, I lay down for more sleep while Lance began making his mystery phone calls. He shook me awake several hours later.  His face was intense and much too close to mine.  I was already sick of his constant, excessive urgency.

"Time to get ready," he said firmly.

By 4:45, we were both dressed in nice shirts and slacks. Lance was in all black.

"Looking good," I said to him as he emerged from the bathroom.

He smiled briefly before popping a pill into his mouth.

"What was that?"

"Valium," he answered.

This was not the time to tease him and so I gave him my best sympathetic smile and patted him on the back as he walked by. "We'll be fine," I told him.  As we prepared to leave, it occurred to me that a year had transpired since I first became involved in Follicle

Research. It had been a whirlwind of events that was about to reach a climax.

Soon, we were knocking at the door of one of the Tower Suites on the twenty-fifth floor. An impeccably dressed middle-aged man in a navy pinstriped suit answered. Lance greeted Dr. Findley first and then introduced me as "Dr. Max Kepler."

"Max is fine," I said as I shook his hand.

"My pleasure," he replied.

He then invited us into a large, elegant suite with dark brown wood furniture. There was an elliptically-shaped table overflowing with hors d'oeuvres. I still found the term for appetizers funny but tried not to smirk. Next to the table were large windows that allowed a spectacular view of the lake and fountains below, and Las Vegas beyond. On the other side was a comfortable-appearing, tan couch.

Dr. Findley had black hair, slicked back and receding, with just a hint of gray, which was much more prominent in his closely-cut beard. His nose was refined in shape and his eyes, brown. Although he was a handsome man, what I found much most appealing was his demeanor. He had an air of calmness and goodness to him.

We engaged in small talk until I started to get restless and glanced at my watch. Dr. Findley saw this and quickly reassured me the other two would be there soon. Embarrassed by my social gaffe, I acknowledged his remark with a smile and nod of my head. Within minutes, there was a knock at the door. Dr. Findley got up to answer it and Lance and I exchanged here-we-go looks as we sat passively at the table, trying to feign casualness.

Dr. Findley greeted the two men at the door, and as they entered, we, in turn, stood to greet them. Sam was the first through the door, looking fit, as before, and behind him was Larry, a short, slightly overweight man with a friendly smile and a big, booming voice. After exchanging pleasantries, we settled into seats around the table, Lance and I on one side and Sam and Larry directly across from us. Dr. Findley sat on a nearby couch.

"How did you guys do in the casino last night?" Larry asked as I opened the laptop.

"The craps table was uncharitable," I said.

"Dice were not nice?" Larry asked, before throwing up his hands and bursting into a fit of laughter.

The rest of us laughed at his hullabaloo.

I swung the laptop around to face the men. This allowed me to make eye contact with them as I spoke. I had long ago memorized the presentation. Sam and Larry were smiling and quietly talking to each other as I set up.

"Thank you for coming, gentlemen," I started. "Follicle Research believes they have found a cure for baldness."

The smiles faded from the faces of Sam and Larry.

"There are fifty million men and thirty million women in the United States who suffer from baldness. This, of course, represents a tremendous market opportunity."

Both men sat upright in their chairs as I started describing the life cycle of a human hair, complete with pictures and diagrams accompanied by descriptions in layman terms. I also discussed why and how a hair follicle stops producing hair. The scientific discussion was out of their comfort zone and so they asked me a few questions, some of which Lance answered quite eloquently. Once satisfied that their questions had been answered, I moved on to a description of our product and how it worked.

I then showed a series of Before and After photographs of patients who had been treated with the peptide. The visuals caused both men to nod repeatedly in approval.

Next, I turned to the product financials. I started by reviewing the price of the product per month for each patient, with our projected revenues, based on assumptions of product market penetration. When I showed them the final numbers, the two men blinked, as though they didn't trust what their eyes were telling them. I paused, partly for effect, and asked them if they had any questions before I proceeded. They both shook their head no.

I ended the presentation with a summary slide, concluding that, "This is the first peptide-based treatment that has been shown to not only slow down hair loss, but also cause new hair growth, quickly and safely, without the need for a prolonged FDA-approval process. This treatment will revolutionize the treatment of hair loss," I emphasized. Then I sat back in my chair and waited. I couldn't help but smile.

Dr. Findley was the first to speak.

"Gentlemen, we've heard an impressive presentation tonight. Lance and Max have something here...something that has the potential to bring dynastic wealth."

His words lingered in the air, causing everyone to pause momentarily as the words washed over them.

Sam and Larry tried their best to suppress their excitement. Turning towards each other, they shared a silent smile. A minute passed before Sam finally spoke, looking at Larry as he proceeded.

"Well, it sure is a compelling story. Thank you for the presentation. I think Larry and I need to talk more and then let's arrange to meet for brunch tomorrow to talk business."

Larry nodded his head in approval. His clatter had been quieted.

Lance and I were disappointed we would have to wait another day.

It was 6:30 and people were hungry.

"How about we all go to dinner," suggested Dr. Findley. "There is an excellent steak house downstairs."

When we arrived, the maître d' told us there was a three-hour wait, but Sam palmed a lump of cash into his right hand and within ten minutes, we were being led to a table. Over the next several hours, we ate beef and drank expensive red wine on Sam's tab while the Texans regaled us with stories of hunting expeditions in Alaska, big sporting events they had attended and various famous people they knew.

Later that evening, I could barely sleep as I contemplated the "dynastic wealth" about to come my way. My life would be transformed, and that would bring meaning and satisfaction. I had transcended all the recent unfortunate events in my life—divorce, job dissatisfaction, Mom's poor health, and even my own mortality—to reach new heights.

# CHAPTER ELEVEN

Within a week of returning home we signed an agreement with Sam and Larry in which they pledged to provide us with seventy-five thousand dollars, payable in three equal installments over the subsequent six months, to help fund our research. In return, we granted them a perpetual two percent royalty on worldwide sales of all products that utilized our patent. We also committed to providing the men with a sufficient supply of product to test effectiveness on five people for six months. And the product had to ready within three months.

The last installment was to be paid after the clinical testing phase, and we could then enter into good faith negotiations for both additional funding and further product development, with the idea of an eventual 50/50 percent partnership ownership.

We were a little disappointed in the total amount of money given, but Sam and Larry wouldn't budge on the figure.

"You only have evidence it works in two people," Larry explained. "Plus, I think anyone trying to start a new business should be a little hungry. I think it's healthier and leads to greater productivity."

Agreement in place and money in the coffers, I was eager to spend the next several months churning out FR-1 for both our Vegas agreement and for use in our own clinical trials. Future fund-raising would be much easier if we had convincing data. But we were having technical problems with our outdated lab equipment, which was draining our financial resources, even with the seventy-five thousand dollar Las Vegas investment. We needed more money, and Forever Lithe seemed like a potential good source.

I decided to take the lead on Forever Lithe, primarily to show my gratitude to Lance for offering me the partnership, although I knew it would be difficult to find the time, what with my full-time job, shared custody of my daughter, and Follicle Research. In retrospect, it was an impossible challenge, but I convinced myself I could handle it, just as I had managed all the other challenges in my life.

After our Dallas meetings, Frank Lawry had called several of Lance's acquaintances to ask about him. It sounded like simple due diligence, but Lance didn't like it one bit. In fact, he called Frank and told him the deal was off, which seemed like an overreaction to me. I tried pressing Lance about why it caused him so much discomfort, but he refused to discuss the issue, mentioning only that "I don't like people snooping around in my life." I gave up on the discussion because I was afraid of upsetting Lance further. It would be much later before I discovered the real reason for his reaction.

Since the plastic surgeon in Dallas was out along with Frank, I suggested opening mesotherapy clinics in the Bay Area, where I could both generate revenue and perform a clinical study demonstrating effectiveness of our formula. Once that was completed, we could start selling our cocktail as part of the business-in-the-box strategy. Then I could pull out of the clinic altogether. I estimated it would take about one year to reach that point.

First, I contracted with a graphic design company to develop a logo, stationery and business cards for Forever Lithe. I hired a website designer, spending about twenty-five thousand dollars in the process. I found office space in a medical building in San Francisco and signed a subletting contract with the owner, who was a chiropractor. I opened another office in Oakland, on the second floor of a building that housed a Korean beauty shop. Then I fine-tuned the protocol for the clinical study I had written previously. Lance contributed almost nothing to this process, and, in fact, I never even bothered to send him the business cards I had made for him.

Several months after starting Forever Lithe, I realized our business-in-a box concept could be used only in California, as it was illegal to ship the mesotherapy cocktail across state lines. I discovered this only after reviewing federal regulations regarding compounded pharmaceuticals, and I was quite upset with myself for my lack of due diligence. But by this time, I was all set for business and had already spent thirty thousand dollars in the process. I wasn't about to admit defeat. Instead, I modified the plan to include franchising clinics only within California, which would still provide plenty of revenue.

I hired a nurse to assist me with the procedure, intending for her he eventually take over for me. Since I was working at the hospital during the day, I scheduled patients during evening and weekend hours, during those times I didn't have Jessica. Our first patient was scheduled in our San Francisco office on a Wednesday evening. It took me almost ninety frustrating minutes to fight rush hour traffic on the drive from Cade County to my downtown office location. The patient was a thirty-five-year-old schoolteacher who never seemed to be able to get rid of the fat on the back of her arms.

I discussed the procedure at length, and gave my opinion as to whether her treatment expectations were reasonable (they were). I emphasized that mesotherapy was not a treatment for obesity, and I would only treat patients who had attempted to lose fat though diet and exercise. The patient was required to read and sign a detailed informed consent, which she did.

I began by slathering an anesthetic gel over the backs of her arms, waiting fifteen minutes for the full effect. Then I cleaned the area thoroughly and placed clean sheets around the treatment site. After mixing the four ingredients that comprised the mesotherapy cocktail, I filled ten syringes and made injections approximately one inch apart into the back of each arm. The patient received a total of fifty injections, with each one feeling like a bee sting.

"Thank God, it's over," she said with a sigh as she got off the examining table. "I don't know how I'll go through another four sessions, though."

I then reminded the patient that she would be swollen and sore for the next week.

A similar scene played out with each patient, and I started to realize that, although some patients were achieving excellent results, it was a lot to go through so many patients simply refused to start or dropped out of treatment. The volume wasn't nearly what I had anticipated, and after six months of lackluster business, I began to consider stopping the procedure.

It was then that I had a particularly uncomfortable interaction with a patient. He was a thirty-year-old man who had lost over one hundred pounds several years previously. He still had some love handles that he simply couldn't get rid of and so he came to me, inquiring whether mesotherapy might help him. After evaluating him, I thought he was a good candidate for treatment. I did have some reservations, however, about his ability to tolerate the procedure, given his history of anxiety. Consequently, I spent a longer amount of time going over the procedure and side effects with him. With some trepidation, I commenced treatment and his first two sessions went without much difficulty. By the third session, he was thrilled, as he was already seeing some positive results. He decided he wanted to try a higher dose to shorten the overall treatment duration.

"I can do that, and it will lead to a more rapid effect. But you have to understand that a higher dose will cause more swelling and discomfort, and those symptoms will last longer," I warned him.

"I can take it," he told me.

Several days after the higher dose treatment, he called me in a panic, worried that his pronounced swelling would be permanent. I reassured him otherwise, telling him he just needed to be patient. My reassurance did not have the desired effect, however, and he called me repeatedly over the next ten days, sometimes several times a day. His anxiety rendered him unable to work some days, and he required extra visits to his psychiatrist and adjustments of his medications, for which he blamed me. Eventually, the swelling went down and he acknowledged that he had ended up with a good cosmetic result, but he never returned for another session. I made no attempt to convince him otherwise. Unfortunately, it would not be the last time I heard from him.

Meanwhile, Lance had starting tinkering with a new formulation of the hair peptide that he thought would be more potent. I thought this was a bad idea, as we still hadn't produced the peptide supply required by our Vegas contract. In my mind, instead of trying new things, our efforts needed to be focused on churning out product that we knew worked and that we had to deliver. Although we could theoretically make a stronger peptide, it was unknown whether it would translate into improved hair growth.

Lance was adamant, however, and convinced Sam we should delay delivery of product so that a new, better version could be produced. To Sam's lay person mind, this sounded great, and so we went back to the receptor binding studies and computer modeling to create a more potent peptide. After six weeks of work, we had developed a version that was ten times more powerful, at least in the lab, and by that time, I, too, had bought into the idea.

After months of tinkering, our manual synthesizer was now working consistently, and so Oliver began cranking out FR-2, as we dubbed it. Within two months, we were able to ship out enough of the drug to supply five people for six months, thus meeting the terms of our Vegas contract. I received my supply several weeks after that and immediately began applying it, expecting fantastic results within months. Then, I figured, the funding would truly roll in.

And the good news kept coming. Through a convoluted series of contacts, the CEO of a major US hair product company became interested in FR-2. I immediately prepared a tear sheet for his review and several days later, we discussed our product via a conference call. He wanted proof of efficacy, and we offered to send him photographic evidence, but he was not interested. Instead, he wanted his company to conduct its own clinical trial, and we agreed to supply enough peptide for a small six-month trial.

We failed to tell him we had no available FR-2 and no cash to produce it; nor did we even have evidence the new peptide worked. I pointed this out to Lance after the call was over, but he was convinced the peptide was effective and that he could get money for production costs. Since he had no job, I wasn't sure from where. I assumed it was leftover capital from the vitamin company he had sold five years earlier. Or maybe his hGH business was doing really well. Whatever the source, I didn't care, as long as we kept Follicle Research going.

A month of self-treatment with FR-2 passed by and I was surprised that I hadn't noticed any new hair growth. I brushed aside my concern, convinced the hair would eventually manifest. But then at two months, there was still nothing, which prompted me to take a picture of my scalp and compare it to a pre-treatment photograph. I nearly panicked when I realized that not only was there no new hair growth, it appeared I had less hair! Was it possible FR-2 was causing hair loss? Sensing a disaster, I called Lance. He sighed heavily when I gave him the news.

"Have you heard from Sam?" I asked.

"He emailed me this morning and said no one is seeing hair growth."

"Holy shit! What the hell are we going to do?" I shouted.

"I'm not sure. Oliver analyzed the peptide again and it's ninety-five percent pure, so it wasn't a mistake in synthesis."

"Then it must be the peptide itself," I said.

"Maybe it would work better if we added things like epidermal growth factor, vascular endothelial growth factor, basic fibroblast growth factor, maybe some others. I could send them out and have people mix it in with their peptide."

"You might as well add magic pixie dust. You know the science. Those things won't help."

"I don't have any other solution."

"I do. We need to go back to what works and scrap the FR-2," I said.

"But we've already made FR-2, and we're in the process of making more for the hair product company study."

"Well, that sucks, but the shit doesn't work and we have people depending on us. We have to go back to FR-1."

"How are we going to explain this to Sam?"

I could hear the fear in his voice.

"We're going to tell him the increased potency we saw in the lab is not translating into hair growth. That's science for you, Lance. We both know that. Just because we see something in the lab, that doesn't mean it's gonna work in human beings. At least we still have FR-1, and we know that works."

"Give me some time to wrap my head around this. I'll get back to you in the next day or so."

"Make it quick" I said, ending the phone call.

When I got home that night, I tossed my supply of FR-2 into the trash.

After two days, I hadn't heard from Lance. He didn't return my messages or emails. Just as I started to worry about him, he called me, and I could hear the excitement in his voice.

"I've thought about it more. I'm convinced if we add the growth factors, FR-2 will work."

"Have you lost your mind? That doesn't make scientific sense."

"I've already sent off the factors to Sam," he interjected.

"You know this will only weaken our credibility more when it doesn't work, don't you?"

"I think it's gonna work."

He had never been so irrational, and so I simply hung up on him. His anxiety had overwhelmed him and in his desperation, he had ditched sound scientific reasoning for nothing other than conjecture. Inevitably, it would be a disastrous strategy, if allowed to continue. We still had a chance to salvage our relationship with Sam, but instead of admitting a problem and trying to rectify it, Lance had compounded it. Critical time was being wasted giving people an ineffective treatment that had the potential to destroy our reputation.

"This has to stop," I said to Lance when I called the next day. "We need to go back to FR-1 right now."

There were several sighs, followed by silence. I waited patiently for him to speak.

"They'll think we don't know what we're doing," he said meekly.

My mind raced with possible solutions. I decided we didn't need to tell them the complete truth. They were lay people and probably wouldn't understand it anyway. Our science was rigorous; the drug just didn't work.

"How about this?" I suggested. "We'll send a letter telling everyone there was a production mistake. That will buy time to make FR-1 again. They'll never even know we switched back to the old formula."

"Can you write the letter?" Lance asked, renewed enthusiasm in his voice.

Within two days, I had composed a letter explaining away the ineffectiveness of FR-2 in the first paragraph:

We have just identified a problem with one of the amino acids in the hair growth formula. We generally receive the amino acids from a single supplier, but several months ago they ran out of a certain amino acid. To avoid a production delay, we ordered from another supplier. The initial batches of the amino acid from the new supplier were of high quality but our routine quality control analysis revealed a problem with subsequent supplies. Consequently, the hair growth product that was made utilizing this faulty amino acid has greatly decreased potency.

Desperate to salvage our company, I was willing to manipulate the truth. In my mind, it was a relatively benign maneuver that served a higher purpose and thus was justifiable. Plus, we could still depend on the effectiveness of our initial peptide.

The letter was sent out two days' shy of our one year anniversary of the Las Vegas meeting. We had wasted a year of progress with a combination of production delays and an ineffective version of our peptide. Our credibility had taken a serious hit, and Sam stopped taking our calls, even after receiving our letter of explanation.

We needed to start over again, making FR-1 and looking for money.

# CHAPTER TWELVE

Around the time disaster was striking Follicle Research, I received an email from a Chinese doctor named George who had seen my Forever Lithe website and was interested in starting a mesotherapy practice in his hometown of Shenzhen. He had recently established a clinic where the doctors performed various cosmetic procedures, such as Botox and Restylane, a facial filler used for deeper wrinkles. They wanted to add more services and decided that mesotherapy would be most appropriate. After several weeks of email discussions regarding its theory and practice, George invited me to China to teach his doctors the procedure. He agreed to pay all expenses and provide a stipend. I thought the trip was an excellent idea because I could both travel and get my mind off Follicle Research and my divorce.

In advance of the trip, I prepared an introductory talk on the procedure, and packed a large Styrofoam container with all the ingredients for the mesotherapy cocktail. George picked me up at the airport and took me directly to the clinic for the presentation. When we arrived, I discovered they had erected a ten-foot-high poster of me next to the main entrance. In one of the best examples of photo editing, they had taken a picture I had provided from my brother's wedding and altered it to show me wearing a white doctor's coat and a black stethoscope around my neck. I was holding a clipboard and on my head, was a thick mop of hair, which seemed odd since people were about to see I had much less hair. I chuckled to myself as we walked past the poster and into the building.

George escorted me to a conference room where I was surprised to find over one hundred people waiting. Several local television camera crews were there to cover the arrival of the American doctor. Unfortunately, my luggage had not made it on the plane, and so I showed up at the reception in T-shirt, shorts, and flip flops. The attendees gave me puzzled looks as I walked in, but once I explained the attire and started the presentation, everything seemed to flow smoothly. Afterwards, there were many questions, photographs and interviews, and then an incredible spread of food was brought out. After about an hour of eating and drinking, I was completely exhausted. Sensing this, George escorted me out of the party and across the street to a modern hotel. I checked into a beautiful room with a computer, internet access and a wet bar. I collapsed onto the bed and as I faded away, I heard George remind me not to drink the water.

Loud knocking woke me several hours later, and I opened the door to find George standing there with my luggage. He told me to get dressed for dinner and soon afterwards we took a cab to a restaurant/theater showing a series of live vaudeville-like performances. It was a happy, family-type atmosphere, and we spent the next hour or so eating and watching the entertainment. At the conclusion of dinner, I was guided behind the stage and down a long hallway lined on both sides with a series of doors. We entered one of them halfway down the corridor and found a group of George's friends sitting on couches, taking turns singing karaoke and drinking shots of beer.

We sat down and immediately someone poured us two shots of beer each. A short man with big ears was doing a poor rendition of a Celine Dion song. Within minutes, the door swung open and an older woman wearing elaborate clothing and excessive make-up led a group of scantily-clad, beautiful, young women into the room. I realized what was happening just seconds before George waved his hand in the direction of the women and said, "take your pick." I had been told this was one way the Chinese entertained their business guests.

I deferred with a smile and then tossed back the next shot of beer. Every fifteen minutes or so, a fresh collection of women would parade into the room until every man had a companion. After two hours of this, George picked out a woman for me. She snuggled up next to me and smiled. Her English was limited to "hi" and my Chinese to "nie hou." We spent the rest of the night playing some Chinese dice game that did not require any verbal communication. She had expectations for a more personal interaction, and thus was surprised when I stood to leave without her, but, by that point, I was struggling to speak even my native language. I took one final shot of beer before stumbling out of the establishment arm in arm with George, who slipped my "date" some money as we left.

I awoke the next morning in the same clothes, shoes still on, my head pounding. I stumbled into the bathroom and poured myself a glass of water. It was halfway down before I realized what I was doing. I considered forcing myself to vomit, but my head was hurting too badly so I wandered back to bed. It was only half a glass anyway.

Six hours later, I was forcefully expelling fluid from both ends of my body, seemingly without pause. I couldn't believe that much liquid could come out of me. By the next day, I was so weak I had trouble getting out of bed. A nurse from George's clinic came to the room, inserted an IV and started hydrating me. Just as I was feeling sure that I would be unable to see the ten consultations scheduled that day, I heard a knock at the door. Wearing underwear and a tank top, I shuffled to the door with the IV stuck in my right arm, carrying the bag of fluid in my left hand. When the door swung open, I found George standing there with five wide-eyed patients. Reluctantly, I invited them in and for the next several hours, I provided mesotherapy consultations from the hotel bed, stopping only for intermittent scrambles to the bathroom.

Two days later, I was feeling much better, and I spent the remainder of the week teaching the clinic doctors how to mix the mesotherapy cocktail and administer it. Near the end of my stay, George offered to take me on a tour of the pharmaceutical-manufacturing factory where he had part ownership. It was a beautiful, modern facility with state-of-the-art scientific equipment and rigorous cleanliness standards. George proudly pointed out the laboratory conformed to Good Manufacturing Practice (GMP) standards and was approved by the China SFDA, which was the equivalent of the U.S. FDA. The factory manufactured botulinum toxin, otherwise known as Botox, and human growth hormone (hGH).

Later, at lunch, George inquired why I wasn't using Botox in my Forever Lithe practice.

"I never really thought about it."

"We could set up an arrangement where I would supply you with Botox."

I laughed and shook my head.

"Thanks, George. That's kind of you, but it's probably not a good idea."

"Why?"

"I doubt the FDA allows it. And I don't want to get into any trouble."

"I understand, Dr. Max," he said, before returning to his lunch.

We never talked about the issue again during my trip, but I thought about it quite frequently. Having just come from his beautiful factory, I had no doubt the drug was safe. And I was sure I could get a good price.

After I returned from China, I began shutting down the mesotherapy practice, despite relative success with the procedure. It just wasn't a viable solution for me, as the volume was inadequate and the procedure was mind-numbingly boring. But I still had not paid back the debt incurred when I started the business, let alone generated any money for Follicle Research. I decided I urgently needed to find another service to offer at the clinic. Botox injections seemed like logical choices, especially after watching the procedure in George's clinic and seeing the high level of patient satisfaction. It looked like an easy, fun way to make money.

I enrolled in injection training courses and received certifications upon completion. Next, I placed advertisements in the *San Francisco Chronicle* for "Introductory Offers on Botox" for patients who wanted to "Look Younger!" I then contacted Allergan, the pharmaceutical company that manufactured Botox. Each vial cost five hundred and eighty-five dollars and, based on what I planned on charging patients, I could generate a net profit of four hundred dollars per hour.

Those were good numbers, but I wondered if I could do better. I decided to ask George for a list of his prices, just for comparison purposes. I don't remember actually thinking I would buy from him. At least that's what I used to tell myself much later when I looked back and tried to justify my actions.

The best time to contact him was morning, his time. That was late evening in California, and so one night I found myself sitting at the computer, Yahoo Messenger opened, waiting for him. I began reading a research paper on hair growth while I waited, and then, about thirty minutes later, I heard the familiar beep indicating George was available. After exchanging pleasantries, I asked about botulinum toxin.

George: Our American doctors are very happy with the results. I told you before, we have good product.
Max: I remember.
George: Perhaps you want to try some?
Max: I don't think so.

George:  You can order just a little, for sample.

Max:  I guess I could do that.

George:  I can offer $110 per vial if you buy 10 vials, but I'll charge $50 for shipment.

Max:  It's $485 per vial here.

George:  Too expensive for same drug.  You see my factory.

Max:  Yes, I did, and it's a very nice factory.

George:  For orders over 20 vials, I can offer free shipment.

Max:  How about only 10 for now?  When can you ship?

George:  I make a shipment upon arrival of payment. If I ship on Monday, you'll get it on Wednesday.

Max:  Great.  How would you like payment?

George:  Wire transfer to my bank account.

Max:  So should I use Western Union?

George:  Please.  This is very simple.  But be sure not to write wrong name.  Do not miss any words of the name, otherwise I could not take the money.

Max:  Can you stay online 5 minutes while I complete the transaction?

George:  I'll wait for you.

Max:  The maximum that I can wire online with Western Union is $999.

George:  So you have to make two transfers.  The total amount is $1150.

Max:  I'll have to send the rest tomorrow.  Can you let me know when the first transfer worked out?  I'll email the confirmation for the second transfer tomorrow.

George:  I'll go to Western Union now.

My first illegal act took 37 minutes and 40 seconds to complete, requiring only a few keyboard strokes and mouse clicks.   Of course, in my mind I was just ordering some drug to use on myself and some friends.  It wasn't like I was going to be injecting patients.   I could order the FDA-approved stuff from Allergan later.

I received the package of botulinum toxin in five days.  As George promised, it was packed in dry ice and still cold. After picking it up from Cade Hospital shipping and receiving, I kept it in a refrigerator in my office for the rest of the day.   When I opened the package that night at home, I found ten small unmarked glass vials containing powder.  I removed one, placed it in a padded envelope, and sent it Fed Ex the next day to our Charlotte lab for testing.

Oliver used high performance liquid chromatography to determine that the powdered substance was indeed pure botulinum toxin.  Next, he performed several tests for sterility, which showed the drug to be uncontaminated.  Satisfied the drug was both the real thing and clean, I decided I could start injecting it.

The first person I used it on was myself.  It was an arduous process.  I tried my best to steady my hand as I placed four injections around the outside of each eye where the crow's feet formed, but each injection hurt and my eyes began to water.  I went very slowly, using the bathroom mirror to guide me, and by the end, I had four bleeding holes around each eye, sweaty palms and a sick stomach.  I needed ten minutes on the couch to recover. The misery was worth it, however, for within days the wrinkles disappeared, and there were no side effects.

Next, I offered to inject several Cade County staff members for free, which allowed me more opportunity to practice technique. Everyone was uniformly happy with the results, and so I felt no need to reveal the drug's origin. Not only was it irrelevant, but it could unnecessarily worry them. To my way of thinking, I was doing something I was good at: figuring out a way around the system.

By this time, patients had started to respond to the advertisements, which meant I needed Botox quickly. I still had six vials remaining of the Chinese version, and with Allergan's drug costing over four times more, it seemed senseless not to use it. I already knew it was safe and effective, even though it was not FDA-approved. But who cared about the FDA? It was filled with a bunch of poorly paid and under-qualified government employees, and there was no doubt I was smarter and better-trained. I could make my own decisions and didn't have to follow their arbitrary rules. Anyway, everyone knew it was a politically charged, autocratic bureaucracy in the pockets of the large pharmaceutical companies who were only interested in preserving their profits. Who could blame me for being resourceful enough to maneuver around them to find a safe, cheaper alternative?

I didn't think of it as illegal to import the botulinum toxin. Rather, I thought it was more of a regulatory thing. If I ever got caught, I figured I would probably receive a cease-and-desist letter, or the equivalent, from the FDA. But that wasn't going to happen because no one besides George and me would know about it. And I would make nearly four hundred dollars more of pure profit per vial, money I desperately needed to keep my dream alive in Follicle Research.

I injected my first patient one week later. She was a forty-five-year-old mother of two. She wore a bright yellow sweater and had her hair pulled into a ponytail so that I could see her wrinkles more clearly. She carried a designer handbag and wore expensive jewelry. She had never received Botox before and was literally bouncing in the chair in anticipation.

"My husband doesn't know I'm here," she confided in me. "He'd probably kill me."

"He'll be happy when he sees the results," I said.

"I'm using my milk money," she said, winking. "With the great deal you're offering, he'll never notice."

After having her sign the informed consent, I went into another room to mix the botulinum toxin so that she wouldn't see the unmarked vial. Afterwards, I performed the injections in less than ten minutes, and when I finished, she hugged me excitedly and promised to call me a week later with her results. I received her call during my Tuesday afternoon clinic at Cade County. I stepped into an empty room for privacy.

"I can't believe how much younger I look," she gushed.

"And your husband" I asked.

"He said I looked well-rested and then asked if I was using a new facial cream. He has no idea." She giggled as she said it.

The conversation reaffirmed I had made the right decision.

The patients started rolling in, and the results were uniformly fantastic. Everything about my use of botulinum toxin was done standard of care, including the informed consent process, the technique itself, the chart documentation, etc. The only thing marginal was the source of the drug, but I reasoned that my due diligence had dispensed with that potential problem. After a while, the source of the botulinum toxin simply stopped registering in my conscious thought. In fact, I eventually brought the vials into the examining room with me, and let the patients watch as I drew up the drug into a syringe.

I never told anyone about the origin of the drug. Multiple patients asked me if I was using "real Botox" and I always answered, "Yes." I wasn't lying, after all; it was real botulinum toxin. Botox was just a name. We use generic drugs all the time in medicine, and this was no different. Of course, I couldn't attest to the safety of the drug on an ongoing basis. I only knew the first batch was safe, since we had tested it. After that, I never tested the drug again. There was no need, I had George, and he was a doctor and, by now, a trusted ally. Plus, I had seen his beautiful factory. My rationalizations had become increasingly elaborate. Without them, I would not have been able to engage in such conduct. But for now, the full flame-out was gaining momentum.

Soon I would be funneling my profits into Follicle Research, and we could move even closer to our dream of creating the first truly effective treatment for hair loss. To me, that eventuality, as gargantuan and life-changing as I could ever imagine, justified my means. Plus, growing up, I learned from Dad that skirting rules was sometimes acceptable, as long as it didn't hurt anyone, proof of this being the false resume that helped Dad land a job when we first moved to California. There were other examples too, with one of the most memorable being Dad's old Zing Ping putter that he had bought when he was in his twenties. It was a legal putter, but Dad had modified it by melting lead onto the back of the putter face. The heavier weight stabilized the club through the stroke, thus improving consistency. This led to better golf scores, which was great, except for one thing: it was illegal to modify the club in such a way. Did it hurt anyone? Not really. Dad wasn't a professional golfer, so he wasn't taking prize money away from other golfers. But he often bet on the golf course, so he won money from other players with his illegal club. This never seemed to bother him. He even called it "the illegal," as though that was a badge of honor.

My grandfather was similarly crafty. As a carpenter for the city of Cleveland, he had access to an almost unlimited supply of tools. And he used that access to "collect" tools for his own personal use. In fact, Grandpa had a comprehensive collection at home, probably worth several thousand dollars, that he accrued over the years. Many of those tools were passed down to my father, who used them regularly during my childhood. The source of the tools was never a secret; apparently, it was well-accepted that employees of the city of Cleveland "collected" these things.

I had done a similar thing during graduate school—"collecting" my own set of tools-tape dispenser, pens, calculator, paper, folders, etc.—from the lab where I was working. A fellow graduate student saw me take one of these items and raised a fuss about it.

"Don't worry about it," I told him. "What's the big deal?"

The items had been paid for through research grants, most of which came from the government, and since there was no real victim involved, in my mind it seemed reasonable to simply take such things. Plus, I was a poor graduate student who had little discretionary income.

Remarkable as it sounds, especially since office supplies are not the same as drugs injected into patients, the importation of Botox registered in my morally-shrinking brain as similarly reasonable, particularly since I was convinced the drug was legitimate and that there would be no victims. That assumption was flawed, of course, by the fact that I could never actually guarantee the safety of a drug coming from a Chinese factory. For all I knew, the Chinese government was using me to import biologic weapons. Instead of using sound reasoning, I simply assumed the drug would always be safe, thus preventing my mind from ever fully stopping at the ethical speed bump.

I did tell Mom about my importation of Botox when I was back home, and she did not like it.

"Now, Max, are you sure that's legal?" she asked.

"It's fine, Mom. Plus, no one is going to know anyway."

"That's not the point. It better be legal. You could get in a lot of trouble."

"It's really no different than some of the things Dad and Grandpa have done."

"It's a lot different. Plus, you're my son and a doctor. I expect more out of you."

I walked away without a word, but it would not be the last I heard from her about the subject; in fact, she mentioned it every couple of weeks or so. And the more

I convinced myself that the importation of the drug was just a regulatory thing, the more this irritated me. After a while, I simply stopped listening to her.

After only four months, I had already treated about fifty patients with botulinum toxin. But every so often, even when Mom wasn't hounding me, I would revisit the ethic quandary, usually when I was placing another order with George.

Max: I do worry about legal issues, though. If I ever have a bad event (even if it's not due to your drug), I'll be in trouble.

George: We do have a few side effects, but same as Allergan Botox, and very easy to treat.

Max: I'm not really worried about the side effects but the trouble I could get into for importing a drug from China.

George: I know. American FDA is very strict. But FDA will not know.

Max: They could know if someone brings a lawsuit against me. They ask for records of drug purchases. So, I'll use mostly your drug and occasionally the one from Allergan.

George: Yes, probably a good idea to have Allergan product too.

The conversation convinced me I needed to order a supply of real Botox, but I decided to wait until after I had fully recouped my initial investment in Forever Lithe. Once I reached that point, I would only use the real stuff. But I never made the transition; the money was just too easy. I would continue to use the illegal drug to a calamitous end.

I never told anyone other than my parents and Lance about the source of my botulinum toxin, not even the psychiatrist I had started seeing when Alice and I had separated. I now realize that my failure to disclose this information to him, despite multiple opportunities to do so, was clear evidence that I knew that what I was doing was wrong. But I never considered this in any real way during that time. I also knew that had I still been with Alice, there was no way I could have continued in my illegal behavior. She would have been far too vigilant.

But I wasn't with Alice. Not in the least. In fact, Alice had gotten married in a quick ceremony at City Hall while I was in China. Furthermore, she was three months pregnant. Her separation from me was now complete, and she had started a new family.

But I was in a new relationship, too, even if it was just a business arrangement. And although we weren't family and didn't have children together, Lance and I were going to do some amazing things.

# CHAPTER THIRTEEN

As I began making more money with Forever Lithe, I considered transforming the clinic into a wellness center. My thoughts were shaped in part by my experience of taking care of patients with chronic diseases in my rheumatology practice and my feeling that a more holistic approach to these patients, particularly those with chronic pain, would lead to a better quality of life. But this approach was not encouraged by western medicine or the existing U.S. heath insurance structure, and so instead I was forced to use various narcotics for pain that I felt could be managed more effectively by utilizing non-medical (and non-insurance-covered) modalities such as water therapy, yoga, acupuncture, and various vitamin supplements, to name a few. I felt that if we could use such approaches to not only treat disease but to improve the general quality of life, patients might have fewer future medical problems. And if we were thorough in this regard, it might even be possible to extend the human life span.

Meanwhile, anti-aging clinics were opening all over the country. Lance and I had frequent conversations about the topic of anti-aging, discussing at length various treatments that might minimize or even reverse the aging process. Lance explained his theory of aging one day in a phone conversation.

"I'd say in its most fundamental form, aging is the cumulative damage to cells that make up the tissues and organs of our body. Over time, this damage leads to declining function. You realize the maximum life span for humans is about one hundred years, whereas it's only four years in a mouse!"

"That's 'cause there's genetic differences between the two species," I pointed out.

"Yes, and so if there are genetic differences, there must be differences in the aging mechanisms."

"The efficiency of DNA repair is probably better in humans," I hypothesized.

"Don't forget about the types and quantities of antioxidant enzymes."

"And no doubt there are different rates of free radical production."

Free radicals are oxygen molecules produced in response to various stressors in the environment, such as excessive sunlight, bad food and certain chemicals. The production of free radicals is known to play a role in heart disease, cancer, osteoporosis, and Alzheimer's disease. Given this, it follows that preventing free radicals to form and oxidize will mitigate the aging and disease process. Therefore, various antioxidant supplements, such as Vitamin C, Vitamin E, Q10, lipoic acid, carnosine, glutathione, and N-acetylcysteine, might extend human life, or at least improve its quality.

The fundamental problem, however, is that a person can never take a high enough dose of antioxidants to produce the desired effect. Either not enough is absorbed by the body or high amounts in the stomach cause nausea, vomiting and/or diarrhea. A method of bypassing this problem is to give the supplements intravenously. Lance believed so strongly in antioxidants that he had been self-injecting vitamin C and glutathione three times a week for the past three years. In that time, he had never had so much as a cold. Furthermore, he had also been working with the hGH physician in Seattle to administer antioxidants for the treatment of various conditions such as hepatitis and cancer.

Eventually, I had plans to introduce some of these therapies, among others, into my Forever Lithe clinic as part of its evolution into a center of wellness. However, this strategy of promoting wellness vis-a-vis various supplements was not well-accepted in the medical community, mostly because there was no proof these therapies actually worked. But proof would be hard to come by, primarily because no one would be willing to pay for the large clinical trials necessary. Companies will only pay for expensive trials when they hold a proprietary interest in the compound being studied. But with substances like vitamin C that anyone could manufacture, there would be no incentive to pay.

On a grander scale than my Forever Lithe clinic, Lance and I had long discussions about Follicle Research developing new therapies for wellness and anti-aging. Our long-term goal was to turn Follicle Research into a company with multiple product lines addressing these unmet needs, the research to be funded by the zillions we were going to make with the hair peptide. We intended to turn Follicle Research into a pharmaceutical powerhouse at the forefront of new and exciting treatments that might not only enhance quality of life, but extend it as well.

One anti-aging approach that we were particularly interested in was hormone replacement therapy using testosterone and human growth hormone, otherwise known as hGH. There was already some published research on the use of hGH for this, and anti-aging clinics were employing the therapy all over the country. And although I had been uncomfortable when I had earlier learned Lance was supplying hGH to professional athletes, I had since spent a lot of time investigating ways in which the hormone could be used in a medically responsible manner.

The rationale for the use of hGH was simple: the levels of hGH peak when men are in their twenties and then decline throughout the remainder of life. The greatest decline occurs from age twenty-five to forty-five, and by age eighty-five, the levels are a third of their previous peak strength. Research suggests this drop might be responsible for some of the physical changes that occur to the human body over time. If so, it would follow that restoring hGH levels to their youthful levels might reverse some of the age-related physical changes in the human body.

I spent the next several weeks reading every possible study about hGH. In my research, I came across the first clinical trial of hGH replacement in elderly men, which was published in the preeminent medical journal, the *New England Journal of Medicine*, in 1990. The investigators compared the effects of six months' of hGH injections on twelve men, ages 61 to 81, to an age-matched control group. Drug injections caused an average gain of 8.8% in lean body mass and an average loss of 14% in fat (without diet or exercise), improved skin texture and tone, and increased bone density. In a summary of their results, the researchers wrote: "The effects of six months of human growth hormone on lean body mass and adipose-tissue mass were equivalent in magnitude to the changes incurred during ten to twenty years of aging."

Other clinical studies have confirmed that low-dose GH treatment for adults with GH deficiency not only increases muscle mass and decreases fat, but also improves quality of life. It also has a favorable effect on "bad cholesterol" and other health parameters. These benefits occur without significant side effects.

But these studies were done in patients with low hGH levels to begin with. No one has ever studied the use of hGH in "normal men" over the course of a lifetime. Given the length of time needed to assess the effect, these studies would be very difficult to perform, and so any support for the anti-aging theory of hGH supplementation comes from inference and anecdotal reports from anti-aging clinics. After reviewing the literature, I felt the evidence supported the use of low dose hGH for anti-aging, without significant risk of side effects, and so I decided to try it on myself. I asked Lance to send me some.

I spent lots of time researching the best dose to use. I discovered that the youthful pituitary gland secretes approximately 1-1.5 units of hGH per day. I figured up to 2 units per day would be safe, and so that's the dose I began injecting each night before bed. After ten weeks of therapy, I experienced many benefits, including more energy, improved sleep, a younger appearance, quicker recovery from workouts, improved muscle tone, and improved mental well-being.

Because I had played sports my entire life, I was well aware of the benefits of physical training, and I believed I was getting as much out of my daily injections as I would from a moderate weight training program, without any side effects. Even for a scientific skeptic like me, I found the drug impressive. It was like a workout in a syringe.

I decided I needed to test the drug on others, and the most logical choice was my father. At that point, Dad was sixty-five years old and experiencing some of the usual effects of aging. He would be a good candidate for hormone therapy, and after several conversations, I was able to convince him to try the drug, which he self-injected. He was thrilled with the results, particularly on the golf course, where he found he hit the ball further and recovered more quickly, with less aching in his knees and back. The difference was so obvious that his golfing buddies asked him for his secret.

"A new exercise program and diet," he usually told them.

"Well, it sure as hell is working," was the normal response.

Seeing the beneficial effects in Dad, my brother decided to give it a try. He also was pleased with the results.

With all three Kepler men happy with their hGH experience, and after more exhaustive research regarding the drug, I decided to start incorporating hGH into my Forever Lithe practice. I asked my website designer to create a page devoted entirely to hGH, where I summarized the benefits of hGH and offered treatment to qualified patients. I didn't worry about safety issues, as I had done my homework regarding the risks and benefits of hGH and would only be prescribing the drug at low doses. Unlike Lance, I was not interested in performance enhancing high doses used by pro athletes.

I researched prices for hGH and found the average cost was about fifteen dollars per unit. I opened Yahoo Messenger late one night to discuss hGH with George.

George: We are selling.

Max: I'm aware, George. Is it safe?

George: Good Manufacturing Practice (GMP) certified.

Max: What kind of price could you give me?

George: I could do $2.50/unit.

Max: How many units are in a vial?

George: 15.

Max: I'll buy 50 vials.

George: Please use Western Union again. Ship to same address?

Max: Yes, please.

George: I mark it as "tissue culture media in vitro use, not for use on humans, plant tissue only". I hope there will not be problem in the Custom.

Max: I'll be selling it to patients and they obviously would like professional-appearing vials. Could you send some labels as well?

George:   We need to print some.
Max:  Make sure the labels don't say China on them.

I was thrilled.   Even if I sold hGH at fifty percent off
the average U.S. price, I would still make a great profit.
I was truly on my way to turning Forever Lithe into an
aesthetic and anti-aging clinic that would generate large
revenues.   Then I would finally be able to provide the
money needed to accelerate development of the hair
peptide for Follicle Research.

Meanwhile, Lance told me he was continuing to supply
professional athletes with the drug.   This bothered me,
not only because high doses of it could be unsafe, but also
because it was illegal.   Plus, the issue of performance-
enhancement drugs in professional sports had become a
hot media topic.   The BALCO (Bay Area Lab
Cooperative) scandal had erupted several years earlier
when agents of the Internal Revenue Service, Food and
Drug Administration, and the San Mateo Narcotics Task
Force conducted a house search at the BALCO facilities
in Burlingame, California.   In the search, containers with
labels for various steroids and hGH were found, along
with lists of BALCO customers, including major league
baseball players, track and field athletes, and an Olympic
boxer and cyclist.

The US Government, in response to the BALCO
scandal and the increasing use of hGH as a performance-
enhancing drug, was beginning to crack down on anti-
aging clinics that were using hGH.   Additionally, US
Customs had stepped up their attempts to stem the flow of
the drug into the country.   After several seizures of drugs

intended for other doctors he was doing business with, George was getting nervous.

George: But I'm afraid of Custom. What if it is stopped in the Custom?
Max: Why are you afraid of Customs?
George: If they stop it.
Max: Well, what can they do?
George: It's difficult to say.
Max: There's nothing we can do about it right now; we'll just deal with it if it happens. Have faith, my friend.
George: I hope it's okay.
Max: If not, I'm going to have to make trips to China just to get supplies.

I still didn't think I could get in much trouble. The importation of hGH, like botulinum toxin, was just a regulatory issue, and I was using the hormone in a medically-responsible manner. I was so certain that everything was fine that I became indignant when several of my shipments were held up in Customs, prompting me to call and inquire about them. Each time I called, I was shuffled around to several different people, each saying they had no idea about the packages, which I later learned was a stall tactic by ICE (Immigration and Customs Enforcement). At the time, however, I couldn't believe the incompetence of the Government.

Undaunted, I was determined to get hGH into the country and so I suggested having it sent to my parents' house in Ohio. George was still nervous, however, fearing that if Customs held it up he'd have to pay for the lost drug, but I assured him I'd cover the cost if that

happened.    In the end, however, I never did have the
drug shipped to Ohio; I didn't want to get my parents
involved.

A few days later, I was making rounds at the hospital
when I received a forwarded call on my cell phone from
my Forever Lithe 800 number.    I had purchased the 800
number to add legitimacy to the business, but I didn't
have enough volume to justify an answering service.
Thus, all the calls were forwarded, and when I received
such a call, I usually answered in an altered voice to give
the illusion I had a receptionist.    It felt ridiculous, but it
seemed like something I should do.

"One minute," I said when the caller asked to speak
with the doctor.

I sheepishly made my way out of the patient's room
and to the end of the hallway.    The linen cart had been
left there, and I moved behind it for greater privacy.

"Dr. Kepler here," I said.    "How can I help you?"

"My name is Jill Monroe, and I came across your
company on the internet recently and had a few questions
about mesotherapy," she said, before adding, "You have a
very impressive website, by the way."

I then spent several minutes answering her questions
before she suddenly changed the subject.

"Are you an anti-aging specialist as well?" she asked.

Since I was more interested in this than in
mesotherapy, I quickly answered, "My practice is slowly
evolving in that direction."

Just then one of the custodians came to retrieve the
linen cart, giving me a quick smile as he did.    I turned
my back and faced the window as he wheeled it away.

Across the expansive San Francisco bay shimmering under the midday sun, I could see the golden-brown Oakland Hills. I had always loved this view, ever since I first came to Cade County, and I had started relying on it to bring me calm during chaotic days.

"The reason I ask is one of my sorority sisters who now lives in Baltimore, she was injecting something like HHG or something. I can't remember."

"Ah, yeah..." I said, stalling for time as I made my way to the stairwell for improved privacy. Finding no one there, I continued. "Do you mean hGH? Human growth hormone?"

"Yeah, that's it," she said excitedly. "Do you know what that is?"

I could hear someone from below climbing the stairs.

"Of course, but that's an entirely different treatment," I said.

"Is that the same thing professional athletes use?"

I could see that the person coming towards was a colleague. I nodded at her as she went by, and she gave me a puzzled look. I waited until she had passed through the door before continuing.

"Yes, athletes do use it but at much higher doses. I would never, under my care, allow a patient to use that much."

Jill's tone seemed to increase in intensity as she said, "This was something my girlfriend was using and she said it made her lose weight."

"It definitely does. But I wouldn't use hGH just for fat loss. There's a lot of other beneficial effects, which I've listed on my website."

"I know that she really likes it."

I was starting to get nervous having this discussion while at work so I told her, "If you're interested in hGH, we'd need to meet in person so that I could get a sense of what your expectations are for the treatment. I would have to establish a trust relationship with you because all patients have to be very safe with the drug and willing to be very compliant in terms of following up. That's something I feel strongly about."

"That makes sense. Another thing, I'm kind of scared of needles. If you're doing the injection, that would be better."

"It's a simple injection. You can do it. It's like an insulin shot. It's a very, very small needle you give yourself once a day. I'll teach you how to do it."

"When can I start?"

I wasn't comfortable with how pushy she was being so I suggested, "How about if we meet first so that I can better understand your goals. I prefer a more holistic approach instead of just using the drug to lose weight."

"Maybe it could help me with my workouts."

"You'll notice a significant improvement in your muscle tone and definition. You'll feel more energized. It's not a high; it's not a drug like that and it's not an anabolic steroid. Basically, you want to replace declining hormone levels."

"So, it's kind of like estrogen pills for older woman."

"That's a good analogy. I would say it's a supplementation, not an augmentation. If you use it the proper way, it's very healthy and beneficial. Let's talk about it more when you come in."

We then scheduled an appointment for one week later, and I returned to my morning rounds.

The following week, Jill arrived at my Oakland office on time but had, according to what the owner later told me, supposedly gotten lost and gone into the Korean beauty shop downstairs before her appointment, wandering around the salon as though she were looking for something.

"Doctor upstairs," the irritated owner had told her after she found Jill talking with one of the massage therapists. According to her, Jill did not seem flustered or embarrassed by her mistake and had simply nodded before heading upstairs. I greeted the pretty, thirty-six-year-old brunette wearing slacks and a tight tan blouse. She tucked her long hair behind her ear as she introduced herself, looking directly at me with friendly blue eyes as she did.

Once seated in my office, she glanced quickly around the room. I reached into a manila folder and pulled out an informational sheet, which I handed to her.

"After you've taken some time to read this, I'll answer any questions you might have," I said.

She nodded and started reading. As she did, I finished cleaning up a few empty syringes and soiled gauze from the previous Botox patient. Several times, I noticed Jill looking around. Figuring she was nervous, I said, "We'll take all the time you need to make sure you're comfortable."

She smiled warmly and returned to the information sheet. After a few minutes, she said she was finished but had some questions.

"No problem," I reassured her as I grabbed more paperwork from a nearby file cabinet and handed it to her.  "But first, please complete this comprehensive medical questionnaire."

"Wow, is this really necessary?" she asked sweetly.

"It is," I said.  "I need a good understanding of your medical history in order to be safe using hGH."

"I understand," she said, and then started filling out the forms.  A short while later, she nonchalantly asked, "So do you have offices all over?"

"Just two," I said, turning to look at her.  She gave a quick nod.  I turned back to the counter and pulled a vial of hGH out of the padlocked refrigerator.  I then locked the refrigerator and added, "A San Francisco office and this one."

"Which is bigger?"

I opened the drawer containing the insulin syringes and took one out.  "The San Francisco office has five rooms."

Nervous small talk, I figured, but it continued.  "You must see a lot of patients," she said.

"A fair number," I replied, then answered several more questions, including where I grew up, where I went to medical school, and where I lived now.  I interpreted her questions as an attempt to get to know me better, and I remained patient with her inquiries.  Nonetheless, there was something unusual about her behavior that I couldn't quite place.  Maybe it was that her questions, although probing, did not feel like those of an anxious patient. Rather, her inquiries seemed to be more of the fact-finding nature.  For someone who had never used hGH, she seemed too knowledgeable, and I considered the possibility that she was trying to use hGH as a performance enhancement drug, perhaps for body sculpting or something similar.  I just wasn't convinced she was truly interested in only the anti-aging properties of the drug.

"I don't really have any medical conditions other than migraine headaches," she said, handing over the stack. She looked past me at the vial and syringe sitting on the counter and appeared to be trying to read the label.

"Next, I'd like for you to read and sign this informed consent," I said, handing it to her.

"Can you just go over it with me?"

"Sure," I said, as I sat down. I started reading it aloud and soon after she interrupted me.

"What is an IGF-1 level?" she asked.

"That's a blood test that measures how much hGH is in your body. But it's not necessary with you, because you'll only be using low doses. I don't use high doses in my patients. Remember, we want to be safe about this."

She seemed satisfied with the answer and so I continued with the remainder of the informed consent, answering questions along the way.

"So how many patients have you prescribed hGH?" she asked.

Wanting to sound experienced and thus add legitimacy, I lied and said, "Dozens." I had only treated about five patients, but I didn't see the need to tell her that. She might begin to worry and then I would lose her business.

"Sounds good," she said. "I guess I'm ready."

"One more thing," I said, still not feeling comfortable. "You should let your primary care doctor know that you're doing this, just so he's aware. And I'm always available to answer any questions, of course."

I did this partly to see how she'd react but also because I truly did want to make sure patients were using the drug safely. She seemed unfazed by the words.

"That sounds good, but can I ask you something? I looked on the web, and of course there was a ton of information on hGH. There seems to be quite a few products that are administered orally. Are they legitimate?"

"No, they're not. It's terrible. I can't believe they haven't been removed from the marketplace."

"Is that so?"

"hGH doesn't work when given orally because none of the drug actually gets into the bloodstream. Anyway, it's unlikely those products contain any hGH, as the drug requires a prescription. So, that's false advertising."

"Yeah, that was the other thing. As I told you on the phone, my girlfriend has been using hGH she got from some guy at the gym. Obviously, since there's no doctor, she's not getting it prescribed. Are you sure it requires a prescription?"

"Absolutely," I said, nodding vigorously. "It's a medication."

""Cause I'm like, 'Whatever you're taking, that sounds kind of scary'," she said, waving her hand.

"And I would wonder about the source of the drug," I added in a stern voice. "What about quality control? Is it coming from Mexico?"

"So, it can come from outside the country?"

I panicked for a moment. I couldn't believe I had told her hGH could be imported. I tried to sound casual as I said, "If you check on the internet, you can definitely see deals from Mexico. Things like that."

"But yours isn't from overseas?"

"No," I said quickly, feeling my stomach knot as I did. "That could be dangerous."

This seemed to reassure Jill, who then said, "I doubt the hGH she's using is from overseas because nothing bad has happened. In fact, she's had great results."

"People usually do," I said. "It's really amazing, actually."

"For me, it's more like an anti-aging thing. That is what I'm looking to use it for."

"And I like that approach, because I believe the western model of medicine is too restricting. We need to focus on sustaining good health. There's a lot of good data regarding anti-aging treatments. Perhaps we can even extend a person's lifespan."

"That was the other thing 'cause I checked on the FDA website, and it says hGH cannot be used for anti-aging."

"It's not an approved indication, but it can be used off-label, based on physician judgment. This is permitted by the FDA so that the lengthy and expensive approval process doesn't need to be repeated for every potential therapeutic use of a drug. And that's legal."

"So, it's no problem even though it's for anti-aging?"

"That's not a problem," I said, believing I was correct. Later, I would learn that hGH was one of only a few drugs that could not be used off-label. In a remarkable example of either recklessness or foolishness, I hadn't researched whether hGH could be used for anti-aging. However, given that I was also importing a prescription drug from China, perhaps it wasn't surprising that regulatory and legal issues were not foremost in my mind.

"For some reason, I thought it was illegal," she continued. "And there was something else. I saw an article in the *San Francisco Chronicle* about that whole thing with Barry Bonds. Something about human growth hormone being strictly regulated. But I guess that's not the case."

I tried not to squirm as I said, "It's strictly regulated. It requires a prescription. You have to—I keep going back to this—you have to be safe about the use of it. But it can be used as part of wellness program. There are many documented benefits of hGH."

"In that case, I'm ready to start," she announced.

My gut instinct was telling me I couldn't fully trust her, so I decided to limit the amount of hGH I would dispense to her. This required another lie.

"I only have a couple of vials in stock," I said, despite a refrigerator full of the drug. "I'm afraid you'll have to return in a month for a refill."

She looked disappointed for a moment but quickly caught herself. "I understand," she said. "But one more thing. I just want to make sure the drug isn't coming from overseas."

"Oh no. I wouldn't do that," I said, the lies coming ever more easily.

"So, it's not from a place like China?"

"No, it's not," I said firmly. But the "China" reference caught me off guard, and I wondered if she noticed my uncomfortable shift in the chair. The uneasiness quickly dissipated after I once again reminded myself the drug was safe, despite where it came from.

"Okay, then I'm ready to try it," she said, appearing satisfied at last.

I nodded and retrieved the vial sitting on the counter. Then I showed her how to prepare the drug for injection. She watched me intently, even asking if she could look at the vial's label, which listed the drug's name, manufacturing date and lot number. George had sent me the labels in a separate package from the drug so that the powdery substance in the vials couldn't be readily identified if intercepted, and I had later carefully placed the labels on each vial.

Finished with my demonstration of the injection technique, I grabbed an alcohol swab and told her, "I'll give you the first injection here so you'll know how to do it."

Her body stiffened slightly, and she said quickly, "That's okay, I'll just have my boyfriend do it tonight. He's a paramedic."

I hesitated, confused over why she wouldn't want the first dose given to her by a doctor.

"Are you sure?"

"I have the instructions you gave me. I'm sure he can do it."

I looked at her quizzically.

"Really, it's okay," she reassured me.

"Okayyy...I guess that's alright," I said slowly. "But only if you're sure he can do it safely."

She smiled and nodded. "Don't worry."

"How about if I demonstrate on myself?" I suggested.

After she nodded. I lifted my shirt and pinched some fat on my belly. Then I cleaned the area with an alcohol swab, buried the needle and injected one unit of Chinese human growth hormone.

"See how easy it is?" I said.

# CHAPTER FOURTEEN

Forever Lithe had only been open for a year and I was already phasing out mesotherapy. I stopped accepting new patients and was in the process of completing treatment courses for patients already under my care.

The botulinum toxin business, on the other hand, was going well, and on that basis, I had decided to incorporate Restylane injections, the other cosmetic procedure George was doing, into the practice. Restylane is a medication composed of hyaluronic acid, a naturally occurring substance found in the human body. It is a large molecule whose unique properties include the ability to hold tightly to water. When this happens, the molecule plumps up, providing volume and fullness to the skin. As such, it is an excellent treatment for filling in the deeper wrinkles on the face, but the injections are also used to give people fuller lips. The procedure was a good complement to botulinum toxin.

I contacted George for a supply of the drug but was disappointed to hear his factory did not manufacture it. So, I was forced to order the drug directly from the US supplier. I'd pay full price, but at least there would be no legal or regulatory issues with its use.

Several months after I started giving Restylane injections, a forty-year-old woman came to the clinic requesting lip augmentation. As usual, I had her read an informational sheet, complete a medical questionnaire, and sign an informed consent. Afterwards, I performed the procedure without any immediate complications. The next day, however, she called in a panic, reporting that her lips were swollen and painful. I scheduled a follow-up appointment and reassured her the symptoms would likely resolve within several days. But when she returned three days later, her lips were indeed excessively swollen, hard and painful. I quickly determined she had suffered an allergic reaction, a known and yet rare side effect of the drug which was unrelated to my injection technique.

The patient was irate, and she called and emailed me daily to complain, even sending multiple pictures of her deformed lips. She threatened to sue, but then backed off when I pointed out that what she was suffering was a known side effect listed on the informed consent she signed. In the end, it took over a month for her lips to fully heal, and I was glad when I no longer had to deal with her anger. However, it would not be the last time I heard from her.

Despite this uncomfortable encounter, I still enjoyed performing the cosmetic procedures. One of my favorite things to do was Botox parties. The most memorable were the ones hosted by a San Francisco burlesque performer. I drove to the first party with a nurse whom I'd hired to help me. The location was a basement apartment in the middle of a dicey section of the city. I walked in to find an androgynous bevy of twenty-something burlesque performers waiting for me. Colored light bulbs lit the space, funky fabrics covered the walls, and incense burned in every corner. I fleetingly mused that perhaps, after administering botulinum toxin and Restylane, I was to be sacrificed.

One of the first patients I treated was a lovely transvestite named Kaye, who wanted lip augmentation. I filled the upper lip first and then gave her a little bit in the middle of the lower lip, just to provide a hint of poutiness. I handed her a mirror afterwards for a look. She pursed her lips several times as she stared, before breaking into a radiant smile.

"I love them!" she exclaimed. "Thank you so much." Then she hugged me and planted a big kiss on my cheek. The coarseness of her two-day-old beard blended well with her stale tobacco breath.

"You're welcome," I replied, pulling away as tactfully as I could.

She then proceeded to dance around the room, showing off her new assets to the others. Soon afterwards, as alcohol made its rounds, the mood of the party participants progressively improved. Meanwhile, my nurse and I were busy performing injections in the corner, near one of the burning candles.

Midway through the event, a woman in her sixties came over to me as I was arranging supplies. She told me she was there solely for the entertainment value of the evening. I wanted to tell her I was basically there for the same reason. Within minutes of meeting me, she startled me by talking about sex.

"Do you masturbate, doctor?" she asked me.

"Excuse me?"

"Jerk off."

"Yes, ma'am, I do."

"Are you happy with your orgasms?"

"Aren't we all?"

She smiled in a grandmotherly way.

"I mean really happy?"

"Perhaps you should explain."

"Well, most men when they please themselves, they do this." She bent her knees, thrust out her pelvis and pulled her head back. Then, she grabbed her imaginary penis and began a furious simulation of masturbation.

I looked around and saw only mild interest among those standing nearby.

"That's not the way to do it," she said. "The man has to lie down and slow down. He has to get to know his penis better. And he should become friends with his prostate, too."

I nodded my head, wishing she would go away.

"I can show you the right way, doctor."

"Right here?"

"No, of course not. We'll go back into the bedroom."

"Thank you so much for the offer, but I should probably get back to the injections. Do you have a card or something?"

She placed a gentle hand on my shoulder and gave me a benevolent look. Just as I was becoming really uncomfortable, she handed me her business card. I thanked her, slipped it into my pocket, and got back to business.

Near the end of the party, one of the patients told me he worked at the Supperclub, a restaurant in San Francisco where patrons are served dinner in bed while watching continuous live performances on stage.

"You should be in the show," he suggested.

"What do you mean?"

"You can inject Botox on stage."

Seemed reasonable.

"Why don't you come tonight?"

I showed up at the restaurant at eight, and was immediately taken into the dining room and directed to the most desirable table. For the next two hours, they brought me course after course of food. I was even given a massage by a professional masseuse. Finally, it was my turn to perform. The lighting was poor and so before going out, I put a tiny drop of correction fluid just below each injection site. I ended up injecting four dancers on stage. A smattering of applause and muted confusion from the patrons ended each treatment, and I was glad when my "performance" ended.

Afterwards, I was invited to a post-party in the bowels of the building. There were four or five couches set up in a huge semi-circle. Loud dance music played on the speakers. The lighting was again dim, and I could not readily distinguish male versus female. I'm not sure it would have been much easier to do in broad daylight. Very quickly, the atmosphere became sexual, and I could see pairings (and more) happening around me. Then, directly across from me, at the end of a black leather couch, I saw a naked man with an erect penis who appeared to have a powdery substance spread over the top of his member. I soon found out why when another

176

man, using a straw stuck in his nose, removed the powder with a single pass. I decided that was my cue for departure, and I thanked my host, just as he was putting his pants back on, for a memorable evening.

Future Botox parties would prove to be less salacious, thankfully. But what great fun I was having! And, unlike what I experienced at the hospital, these patients were almost all happy, satisfied and appreciative. And that even included the ones that weren't having blow snorted off their penises.

While I was getting busy with cosmetic procedures, Lance and I continued to have far-ranging scientific discussions about age-related and aesthetic therapies. In doing so, we distracted ourselves from our main goal of solving the problem of hair loss. Never was this more evident than when we got interested in the skin-damaging effects of ultraviolet radiation. With some research, we discovered a company in Australia that was investigating the use of melanocyte-stimulating hormone (MSH) injections to produce sunless tanning.

Since MSH is a peptide, we could make it using our protein synthesizer. All we needed were the ingredients (amino acids), the recipe (the correct sequence of amino acids), and Oliver running our manual peptide synthesizer. Three weeks later, we had enough to supply Lance and me for about six weeks. The timing was perfect; it was the middle of winter and I was rather pale. Once we purified and sterilized the peptide, we mixed the powder with sterile water for injection.

We decided to start treatment simultaneously so that we could compare results. The drug was self-administered once a day, but after three days I did not notice any color change and wondered if Oliver had screwed up the synthesis. After waking up on the fourth day, I looked in the mirror and could see a faint tan. By the fifth day, it was clear I was getting darker. On day ten of treatment, I looked like I had just returned from a two-week vacation in the Caribbean. At fourteen days, I was embarrassed by how dark I was.

But then I noted a problem: I was now looking like a freckled leper. All the freckles on my body had gotten dark and stood out noticeably, especially on my face where they looked like age spots. I discarded the remaining drug down the bathroom sink. It took two months of daily Retin-A treatment to finally get rid of the ones on my forehead. By that time, I was quite content with paleness, but the experience rattled me. I had taken vanity to another level. Insecurity about my appearance had caused me to inject homemade chemicals into my body and rub an untested solution on my scalp.

But I didn't have time for a full-scale epiphany. I was too busy working full-time at Cade County during the day and operating two cosmetic clinics at night and on the weekends. In between, I was still involved with Follicle Research and my effort to become famous and wealthy. Juggling these commitments meant I routinely went to bed around two and woke up at six-thirty. Sometimes I would fall asleep at the dinner table, until Jessica's gentle prodding on my shoulder would send me bolt upright.

"What time is it?" I would blurt out, thinking that I had been asleep for hours and had missed something. Jessica, who had not yet learned how to tell time, would shrug her shoulders.

So tired and distracted had I become that once when she asked to go for a walk, I returned from my bedroom with the Baby Bjorn strapped across my chest. Jessica, who was now three and had grown out of the baby carrier two years before, gave me a puzzled look.

"Why are you wearing that, daddy?" she asked.

"I have no idea," I replied as I sheepishly removed the thing.

I simply didn't have enough time for everything, so sometimes I'd take Jessica along with me to the Forever Lithe clinics. While she sat in the corner playing with her dolls, I injected illegal Botox into unsuspecting patients.

"She's so cute," they would coo, faces freshly full of tiny needle holes.

My foray into anti-aging and Botox and mesotherapy also served to further delay the development of our peptide. We still hadn't conducted even a small clinical trial, and we didn't have the money to do so. Realizing this, Lance worked his substantial contact base until eventually found a powerful entertainment law attorney in Los Angeles who agreed to broker a business arrangement with one or more of his wealthy clients.

Once the attorney signed a non-disclosure agreement, we conducted a conference call with him, during which we emailed him Before and After pictures. He seemed genuinely excited and told us he would be speaking with several of his clients over the next several days and would get back to us. He sent an email the next day telling us to "stop wasting time with small players/venture guys and get a real deal done that can meet your objectives." He emphasized that a "real deal" would require proof and that "pictures will never be enough when it comes to writing checks and entering into agreements."

The email finally convinced Lance of what I had been telling him all along: we needed proof of effectiveness from a clinical trial. In addition to focusing Lance, the email also gave us hope that funding would soon come. One week later, however, we received another email from the lawyer with a decidedly different tone. He had performed a background check and discovered Lance's chiropractor license had been revoked ten years previously for failure to report one count of a felony theft conviction and one count of misdemeanor theft. He also discovered Lance had committed multiple acts of insurance fraud. He was irate about the lack of disclosure and immediately terminated our relationship.

I was flabbergasted and angrily called Lance.

"I don't feel like bringing those skeletons out," was his response.

I hung up on him and immediately started my own background check. As I did, I couldn't believe I had never done anything more than a superficial Google search on Lance, especially when I soon discovered even more troubling information. One of the most disturbing was a letter to the editor of the website where I first learned about the hair peptide. It was from one of the doctors quoted in the article I read that day in my home office and which prompted me to contact Follicle Research. In the letter, the doctor reported that the quotes attributed to him were "general, theoretical and hypothetical statements about hair regrowth treatments in general and not related to products made by Follicle Research."

I called Lance back to confront him.

"I don't remember the exact details of the conversation," he said, stumbling. "He might have been talking about our peptide or maybe not. But what difference does it make really, Max?"

"A whole fucking lot," I replied.

"Look, it's academic whether he said it or not. You and I both know the peptide works."

He was technically right. Except for FR-2's failure, I had seen my own excellent hair growth results, in addition to the results experienced by Lance and several others. And I knew the science was legitimate, even if Lance wasn't entirely honest.

"Is there anything else you're lying about?" I asked.

"Nothing else," he said, but I didn't believe him. After all, he was a steroid and hGH dealer to professional athletes and had a criminal record involving deceit. At that moment, I realized I should probably bail out of the partnership. With Lance's history, it would be impossible to get significant funding, and I was certainly not generating enough money in the Forever Lithe clinics. But I also realized that despite Lance's dishonesty and shady past, the hair peptide was a legitimate example of innovative, sophisticated science. There was nothing fake about that, nor the patent that had already been filed by Lance on our behalf. I couldn't imagine giving up on something so revolutionary. I told myself that all I had to do was keep a close eye on Lance and everything would be fine. On and on went my deluded rationalizations.

But little did I know the bad news was just starting.

During morning hospital rounds one month later, I received a call from Lance.

"Uh...umm...Max," he stammered. "The feds intercepted one of my packages containing hGH."

I nearly dropped the phone.    Lance was breathing quickly as I made my way outside.

"What happened?" I said, my heart pounding as I found a spot under a large oak tree.

"There was a package that was delivered to a friend of mine and it had some hGH from China. Five minutes after it was delivered, some federal agents raided the house, and took the hGH and some other things."

"Other things?  Like what?"    I already knew the answer, and didn't expect the truth from Lance.

"I don't think it's going to be a big deal," he deflected.

"Sounds like a big deal to me.  Did they arrest you?"    I started shaking as I thought about the hGH webpage on my Forever Lithe site.

"No. I wasn't there at the time, but my car was in the driveway. They found some stuff there too."

My head was swirling. I knew the "stuff" was anabolic steroids.    But I was still worried about the hGH.

"Yeah, some of those things could cause problems for me," he said, seemingly to himself.

*Was he going to jail?  Was this the end of Follicle Research? Could I be in trouble?*

"What happened with the hGH?" I asked him, realizing I needed to get hGH off my website right away.

"My friend told the investigators it was for him. They believed him because the packages had his name on them. So, I should be okay."

I didn't know what was fact and what was fiction. I waited before speaking, trying to consider all possibilities. I looked up and saw one of my patients in a hospital window. Admitted with liver cirrhosis, he looked particularly yellow in the natural light shining in. I moved behind the tree so he couldn't see me, and asked Lance, "Have the feds talked to you?"

"Briefly, because of some of the things they found in my car."

The withholding nature of his end of the conversation would have annoyed me more had I not been so concerned. I wondered if they were coming after me next.

"Did they find hGH in the car?"

"Some. But don't worry. I have an attorney and the hGH was for legitimate purposes. You know that."

I didn't know that, but this was not the time to dispute it. He was doing a poor job of lying. I suspected it was a bigger bust than he was letting on. My mind raced back to all those cryptic cell phone conversations I had overheard. That must have been about "the stuff." How big was his operation? Was he a major player in the underworld of performance enhancement drugs in professional sports? I prodded him for more information, but he refused to say more.

"My attorney will probably be calling you. He's just going to confirm that the hGH was for medically-related reasons. You know, hormone supplementation. Things we talked about."

The liar was asking me to lie for him. But, I told myself, he had given me an incredible opportunity, and I needed to support my partner.

"I'll talk to him," I replied, but he had already hung up.

Several days later, I received the phone call from Lance's attorney. He informed me that Lance had not been arrested but that the feds wanted to question him about the use of hGH.

"I'm just calling you for routine confirmations," he said.

I had no idea what that meant, and his nonchalance both irritated and alarmed me. I wondered if they were trying to use me somehow.

"You know that Lance is interested in hGH for supplementation purposes only, right?"

"Right," I said hesitantly.

"And that that use is perfectly acceptable within the medical community?"

"Uh, huh."

"You know he wasn't actually prescribing hGH but rather was working with physicians who were."

"Of course."

"Have you ever seen Lance give high doses of hGH to anyone?"

"No."

"And you're a good friend and business partner of his, correct?"

"Yes."

"Have you ever seen him distribute anabolic steroids?"

"No."

I squirmed in my chair and again reminded myself Lance needed my support. My statement was true, but I knew he was distributing the drugs.

"Are you aware of the benefits of low dose hGH?"

"Very much so."

"And so you think it's a legitimate treatment for wellness?"

"I do." I began to wonder if the conversation was being recorded. Everything was getting a bit too big and scary for me.

"I think that's all we need for now. Thank you for your time. I don't think anything is going to happen with this. The feds just wanted some general information. I used to be a federal prosecutor so I know these guys pretty well. Just in case, can I call you again if the need arises?"

"If you need to," I said weakly.

The attorney never called me again. And since Lance never spoke again about the issue, I assumed the whole thing had faded away. But it shut down Follicle Research for a good two months, as Lance seemed preoccupied during that time, so much so that I rarely spoke with him.

In the meantime, I called my website designer and asked him to remove all references to hGH. I decided I would discuss hGH with patients only if they raised the issue. I would, however, continue to move towards creating a wellness medicine and anti-aging clinic. If I was low-key and responsible with my use of hGH, I wouldn't get busted like Lance, who was importing large quantities of hGH and using high doses for performance enhancement. My use of the drug was legitimate and legal, so everything would be fine. I still considered the source of the drug to be a minor issue.

I just needed to keep plodding along until we developed more proof of the peptide's effectiveness. The threshold was so close; certainly, I could hang in there until that time.

I hadn't heard from Jill Monroe in several months and so I decided to contact her by email to let her know I had received a new shipment of hGH.   A week later, I heard back from her in an email.

"I'm just spending too much money these days, if you know what I mean!" she said.   "I'm doing some freelance work in Phoenix and should have a few extra bucks within the next week…any chance you can hold onto a month's supply for me?"

"No problem.   Just let me know," I responded.

Two weeks later, she sent me another email, asking to place an order.

I waited a week before responding, as I was still uncertain about her.   But in the end, I decided to sell to her.   I simply couldn't resist making money from the transaction.   I had compromised so much of my integrity by that time that just one more small thing—small at least in my mind—wasn't that big a deal.

But it would turn out to be a very big deal, and my next contact with Jill Monroe would be under dramatically different circumstances.

I hadn't heard from Lance since his bust two months earlier.   Then one day he sent an email.

Hi Max,
How is everything??  I'm okay.  How's your Mom??
The other thing seems to be fine…
The hair product is awesome…I have been using it for just over 2 months and it's better than ever.

Finally, we have enough for some other people. I have your address here from before…so I'm sending out like 4-6 months for you. You have to get started on this.

Also, Jeffrey Hersk from Discovery Channel is starting treatment. Tommy introduced him and he is stoked.

Max…we have some awesome things to talk about in the hair growth sector…call when you have time…or I'll call.

It's been too long…let's get this thing going again.

Thanks.

Lance.


So instead of supplying peptide to perform a clinical trial showing effectiveness and safety, it seemed that Lance was now making the drug for various well-connected people. Although doing this made some money for the company and massaged Lance's ego, it didn't move us toward our goal of demonstrating proof of concept in a controlled study. I was fed up with the two years of dithering, and so I wrote Lance an email.


Hi Lance,

I definitely don't want to lose our friendship; I think highly of you as a person and would like to maintain contact.

I would like to get some things off my chest though.

I think you are a brilliant mind and have generated many ideas but you lack focus and organization. We needed to figure out a specific objective and how to achieve it instead of bouncing from one hypothesis to another. We could have done so much with the original peptide in the last 2 years. It's a bummer, really.

Now, I need to get my financial life in order and purchase a house. I'm going to turn 40 in 6 months and need to stop paying rent. I can't participate in speculative pursuits anymore. I need to make cash, basically. I would like to continue working with you but my time is so limited right now and I need to focus my efforts on things that bring me money now. More than anything, I want Follicle Research to succeed.

I'll talk with you soon.

Max

I needed time away from Lance and Follicle Research to collect my thoughts. I felt I was mixed up in something that wasn't right, and I was tired of it. I couldn't trust Lance to be truthful or to stay on track with the peptide. And on top of these issues, I was injecting Chinese medications into patients.

By now, my divorce had been finalized, and I had come to terms with the fact Alice had a new family. I even had developed a good relationship with her husband, Jerry. In my own family, Mom was doing well after her bone marrow transplant, and I had gotten into a nice rhythm with Jessica, with our relationship deepening as she matured from toddler to kindergarten student. I had even started to calm down a bit at work, although I still wasn't completely happy at Cade. For the first time in three years, I experienced some clarity of thought, and I began to realize just how deep I had waded into the abyss. Then one day, while I was playing with Jessica, something happened that brought an end to my involvement in Follicle Research.

We were playing Zingo, a game like bingo where each player competes to cover all the squares on his card first. Midway through the first game, Jessica said, "Daddy, you have lots of hair on your hands."

"What are you talking about?" I asked, looking down. And then I saw that my knuckles did look hairy. I remembered noticing it a few months previously, but I reassured myself I was just imaging things. It couldn't be from the hair peptide, I reasoned then, because that would mean the drug was getting into the bloodstream. And so, I forgot about it—or, more accurately, ignored it—until Jessica's comment.

The next day, I asked my nurse if my hands looked hairy and with some hesitation, and after chuckling at me, she took a close look and agreed. Beginning to panic, I pulled up my sleeves and looked at my forearms. They also looked like they had more hair. When I got home that night, I removed my shirt, went to the bathroom and grabbed a hand mirror to look at my back. When I saw hair there, I panicked.

*No doubt about it. It's the hair peptide.*

Lance and I had always assumed the drug's effect would be limited to the scalp. But the fact that I was growing hair on other parts of my body meant we were wrong, and this was a huge problem. So, I called Lance.

"Yeah, I noticed the same thing," he replied when I told him of my excess hair.

"Did you ever think of telling me?" I asked, incredulous.

"I didn't think it was a big deal."

"Bullshit. You know it's a big deal. Growth of hair in places other than the scalp means the drug is getting into the bloodstream.    That means it could be unsafe, and, therefore, useless."

"I don't think it's unsafe."

"How can you possibly know that?"

There was no response.

"Now, the peptide *has* to be studied in a more formal manner, with well-controlled clinical research studies. And we can't call it a cosmeceutical anymore."

"I'm not going through the formal FDA approval process," Lance replied.    "That would take years."

"We have no choice."

"Let me get back to you," he said, sounding panicky. Then he hung up.

I slammed my cellphone down and went directly to the bathroom.    I took out the remaining ten containers of hair peptide from the drawer and stacked them on the counter.    Then I poured out the contents of each one.    I would never use the peptide again.

I stopped responding to Lance's many emails and phone calls and cut off all ties with him.    Lance's last email acknowledged the end of our relationship:

Hi Max,

Hope all is well. We are just getting back from Mississippi coast. My 84-year-old mother was living on the coast that was devastated. She is fine. I will only be back to Charlotte on Saturday. From your lack of response to my emails and phone messages, I can only guess that you want no further contact with me. When you have time, please send the Follicle Research corporation papers and info to my home in Charlotte, as I wish to continue. Hope all goes well with you.

Lance

I would talk with Lance only one more time. In that final, brief conversation, I was both angry and scared. And my life would never be the same after it.

# CHAPTER FIFTEEN

The doorbell just kept ringing on that beautiful fall day, disturbing my last-minute packing. Although it could have been the cabbie, something deep inside told me something was wrong. Something *felt* wrong. And that's why, I think, I moved so quickly to the stairwell to open the door. Less than a minute later, I was handcuffed right on the sidewalk in front of my own house, surrounded by hyped-up men.

When Agent Jurgenson finished with the cuffing and Miranda rights, he spun me back around to face him. Pointing with his left hand to a piece of paper he held up in my face with his right hand, he informed me he had a search warrant for my apartment. And then the men in black began gliding past me, into my apartment. When the last one had passed, Agent Jurgenson tapped on my handcuffs and said, "Let's go upstairs to talk." He then guided me, handcuffed and helpless, up the stairs. I was now a guest in my own home.

When I reached the top of the stairs, I could see that the agents had already dispersed throughout my apartment and were beginning their search.

Agent Jurgenson directed me to the living room. After I sat on the couch, he asked one of his men to remove the handcuffs, warning me not to "try anything funny" once they came off. I was then handed a document to read.

The first page was an order for "any U.S. Marshal or any other authorized officer" to arrest me and bring me to the "nearest available United States Magistrate or District Court Judge."

Turning to the second page, I read:

"I, the undersigned complainant being duly sworn state the following is true and correct to the best of my knowledge and belief. On or about April 24, 2005 in Alameda county, in the Northern District of California defendant did knowingly distribute and possess with intent to distribute human growth hormone for use in humans other than the treatment of a disease or other recognized medical condition, where such use has been authorized by the Secretary of Health and Human Services, in violation of Title 21 United States Code, Section 333(e)."

I had been busted for hGH.

"You have been charged with a felony."

Jurgenson was talking to me while taking things out of his bag—a pen, legal pad, various papers—and making himself comfortable. He gestured in the direction of the document I was holding.

"Maximum penalties: 5 years in prison, $250,000 fine, 3 years supervised release." But I could scarcely take any of it in. Just words on a page to me.

Attached to the document were fifteen additional pages of an "affidavit in support of criminal complaint". It was written by one Jane Attwood, "Special Agent for the United States Food and Drug Administration, Office of Criminal Investigations," and it presented a summary of the evidence against me, also including a description of hGH and its medically-approved uses. The scope of the investigation overwhelmed me. They had gone through my trash, performed surveillance on my apartment and offices and intercepted packages addressed to me containing hGH from China. But it was the description of my interaction with an undercover agent, caught in detail by the wire she was wearing, that really rattled me, even though the actual transcript of the conversation was not in the document.

I did my best to read carefully the meticulous description of my criminal behavior, but in the end, I resorted to skimming through the text, unable to focus on the unsavory details. My attention was blurred by a whirlwind of images from my past, and it was the incongruity of these images with the document in front of me that seemed to lift the shades to allow the sunlight of reality, legality and morality back into the room.

Somewhere in the middle of my epiphany of the obvious, one of the agents came into the room and asked me if there was any hGH in the house.

"Yeah, in the freezer."

Without a word, he turned towards the kitchen. As I watched him walk away, I realized Chinese botulinum toxin was also in the freezer and would be easily found. As he disappeared, I called out to him,

"There's some Botox in there as well."

Silence filled the room. And then footsteps. The agent was back.

"Is that from China too?"

"Yeah."

I hung my head as the agent and Jurgenson exchanged satisfied glances. My cell phone, which was sitting on a table near the stairs, started ringing.

Repeatedly.

After the third call, Jurgenson asked one of the agents to grab it. He brought it into the room and said the call was from Craig Sams, who was the chiropractor from whom I'd rented my office space in San Francisco. I would discover later that he was calling to warn me that federal agents had raided my office there. Unknown to me at the time, simultaneous raids were also taking place at my Oakland Forever Lithe clinic and my office at Cade County.

Surprising me, they asked if I wanted to take the call.

"No, thanks."

By that time, the phone had stopped ringing. The agent then started looking through my text messages as he slowly walked out of the room, making clear that my property was now the US Government's. As he left, he nearly bumped into a portly middle-aged man walking in. The man came right over to me and Jurgenson introduced him as a "Special Agent of U.S. Customs and Immigration." Reflexively, I stood to greet him, shook his hand and told him, "nice to meet you," before realizing the absurdity of the gesture.

I sat uncomfortably for a few minutes while Jurgenson and the agent whispered between themselves. Clearing his throat, Jurgenson turned to me and announced he would be reading my Miranda rights again. No less shocked this time around, I sat fidgeting as I listened. Upon completion, he passed me a piece of paper that stated I understood my rights.  He then asked for me to sign it.

As I did, he asked, "Would you like to have an attorney present for questioning?"

For the first time, I felt I had a modicum of control.  I wanted to hold onto it, and so I hesitated for a minute. Somewhere in a small section of my brain still forming rational thoughts, I remembered that, if arrested, one should never answer questions from law enforcement without an attorney present.  As I sat there thinking, I could hear agents combing my apartment for evidence, which they would quickly find on my computer and in the unlocked file cabinets.  I had not attempted to hide or disguise anything, and they already had the hGH and botulinum toxin.  Figuring that an attorney couldn't help me under the circumstances, I decided to tell them everything.  I figured my honesty and willingness to cooperate might even work in my favor.

"No, that's not necessary," I answered.

Jurgenson looked surprised.  He glanced at the other agent sitting next to him, and then he pulled another piece of paper from his briefcase.

"Can you sign this form, please?"

"Waiver of Rights," it read at the top.  Underneath were two questions:" Do you understand each of these rights?" and (2) "Understanding each of these rights, do you now wish to speak to the police without a lawyer being present?"

The form scared me. It seemed too formal. I preferred just having a conversation. The reality of the situation had not fully penetrated my consciousness.

"I'd rather not sign it."

"But you'll still talk with us?"

"Yes."

"Are you sure?" Jurgenson seemed confused.

"Yep."

Shrugging his shoulders as he looked at the other agent, Jurgenson said, "Let's begin, then."

Jurgenson then asked me a series of general questions about Forever Lithe, like when I started the business, how many patients I saw, what my business hours were, how patients paid me, etc. This went on for about ten minutes before he again pulled out the attorney waiver form.

"Are you ready to sign this now?"

I figured since I was already talking, my signature was merely a formality at that point.

"I guess."

Jurgenson then said he and the agent needed to have a discussion in the adjacent room. I could hear their whispers twenty feet away but could not discern the words. Every fifteen seconds or so, Jurgenson would peer around the door to check on me, nodding. I realized I was still holding the paper with my signature. Feeling like it was dirty, I shoved it onto the coffee table in front of me.

I noticed my palms were sweaty and so I rubbed the sides of my thighs to dry them. In doing so, my right hand passed over something in my pocket, and I remembered I had placed two Vicodin there in case my bad knee started to hurt on the cross-country flight. Realizing the pills would numb my senses, I quickly pulled them out of my pocket, popped them into my mouth, and swallowed. No one noticed, which gave me a small measure of satisfaction. Now all I had to do was get through the next twenty minutes until the high started to kick in. I knew I'd still be able to function with the drug on board. I'd done it before.

Shortly thereafter, the men returned to their previous seats. Jurgenson announced that he wanted to talk about my involvement with hGH. I took a deep breath.

His questions were deliberate and specific. He wanted to know how, where, when, and why I imported hGH from China. I gave him all the details in whatever depth he desired. He scribbled furiously in his legal pad. I suspected it was the easiest and most fruitful interrogation of his career. However, despite all the detail I provided, I withheld one vital piece of the puzzle: Lance. I was protecting him. Later, after plenty of time for reflection, I would not feel any obligation to continue to do so.

Jurgenson was also interested in the number of packages of hGH I had received from China. At this point, the US Customs agent interrupted and asked if I received every package I had ordered from China. I told him that a couple of shipments were seized by U.S. Customs and that I attempted to track down the seized parcels by contacting both the Post Office and US Customs officials. He seemed aware of this, nodding his head when I emphasized that I made multiple calls in an attempt to obtain information about my held shipments.

"These were illegal shipments, you're aware?" he asked.

198

"Had I known they were illegal, I would not have been calling to ask about them."

He shook his head in disbelief. Since I had never considered the act to be illegal, I certainly did not figure it was worthy of a felony charge. My silent self-flagellation for my ignorance was interrupted by Jurgenson asking if I knew it was illegal to use hGH "off-label." This was my chance for some redemption.

"hGH is no different from other prescriptions and so it can be used off-label," I told Jurgenson.

"That's not correct," he said firmly.

I shook my head in disagreement.

In response, Jurgenson began dialing a number on his cell phone. This was followed by a discussion of the issue with another person, who confirmed there were no off-label indications for hGH. Satisfied with the answer, he ended the call and informed me of my mistake.

Humiliated and scared, I just sat there silently, praying that the experience would end soon. And indeed, it did, for the plunder of my apartment was now complete and Special Agent Jurgenson was satisfied that I had answered all relevant questions. I was informed that I would be taken to the San Francisco federal building for fingerprinting and photographing and for an appearance before the judge. Remarkably and irrationally, I had been hoping they would simply ask their questions and then leave.

I caught a glimpse of Jurgenson's wristwatch. It was 11:46. Two hours had passed.

"Just one more thing before we go." Jurgenson said. "How do you feel about what you've done?"

My response caused Jurgenson to pull out his notebook again and scribble down the answer, later found in the last line of his filed report:

"Kepler stated that he could not believe that he was stupid enough to do something like this and that he felt ashamed and humiliated."

# CHAPTER SIXTEEN

As we stood to leave, I could hear the men in black making their way toward the stairs. One was carrying my computer. I caught his eye just as he was walking out, causing him to stop.

"There's too much data on the hard drive to download it all right now. We'll take it in and copy it and then return it later." Without waiting for a response, he started down the stairs once again, reinforcing my growing awareness that my property was no longer mine.

As we headed to the stairs, Jurgenson got a phone call saying my transportation was delayed, so I was directed back to the couch to wait. When I sat down, I glanced around my apartment, wondering when I would see it again. By that time, several of the agents had filtered back into the room. One sat next to me on the couch while several others milled around, looking at my pictures lined up on the fireplace mantle. An older man picked up a picture of Jessica, examining it for a minute or two. Annoyed by the intrusion, I wanted to knock it out of his hands. The man sitting next to me, apparently noticing my discomfort, turned to speak.

"How big is that TV?"

"Uh, um, fifty inches," I replied.

"How much was it?"

"Three thousand."

"How do football games look on it?"

I sat back, more relaxed. I loved that television.

"Great. It's high definition. It seems like you can see individual blades of grass. Totally different experience."

The agent seemed impressed.

"The resolution is 720p, which gives a remarkable picture. Almost like you're there."

The other men left the fireplace to join us in admiring the television. The remote was on the table.

"Go ahead and turn it on," I offered to one of the agents.

And suddenly, I found myself sitting in my family room with five federal law enforcement agents watching a documentary on Yosemite in high definition.

We had been watching for about five minutes when Jurgenson came into the room to announce the car had arrived and turned off the television. I immediately stood up and one of Jurgenson's assistants led me down the stairs, through the front door and gate, and onto the sidewalk in front of my apartment. An unmarked car was parked across the street with two young female agents in the front. Jurgenson and the man at my elbow walked me across the street and to the passenger's side of the car. I scanned the street to see if any of my neighbors were watching and caught sight of my elderly neighbor looking down on me from the second floor of her home. Her bewildered expression added to my humiliation; she had brought me homemade cookies when I moved in two years earlier, and she always greeted me as "doctor" whenever I saw her.

When we arrived at the car, the man let go of my elbow and Jurgenson announced almost apologetically that I would have to be handcuffed for transport. And so, directly across the street from my apartment, in the bright light of high noon and with five or six feds and my neighbor looking on, I was asked to turn around and put my hands behind my back once again. The clicking noise of handcuffs tightening around my wrists seemed to echo off the houses lining Duncan street. I tried making sense of the moment but I couldn't. I wondered what Greg would think when I didn't arrive at the airport, and even more, I wondered what he would think when he found out why.

Jurgenson opened the door for me, cupped the top of my head with his hand and gently guided me into the back seat of the cruiser. His kindness gave me brief comfort. As he pulled the seatbelt across me, he asked in a quiet voice if I was okay. Unable to speak, I nodded my head slightly and with that the heavy door of the sedan closed around me. The cruiser quickly pulled away from the curb and suddenly Jurgenson was gone.

Almost immediately, I began weeping. For a few moments, the only sound inside the car was the sound of my sniffles. Then the driver asked the woman in the passenger seat, "So this is the first year you'll have three weeks?".

"Almost three weeks. Nineteen days."

"Are you going anywhere?"

"Probably Hawaii with Tom."

After several minutes, the woman in the passenger seat pulled out some tissue and turned to wipe my eyes for me and hold the tissue to my nose as I blew. I thanked her for that simple act of kindness. She didn't hear me, though, because she had resumed her conversation about Hawaii.

The dire situation seemed to heighten my senses, for I noted how they spoke, their facial expressions, body language, their hair. I could feel the purr of the engine and hear the squeak of the brakes. I looked out the window and noted the blue sky and the interesting faces on the street. The people seemed so alive and so far away. I saw things I hadn't noticed before: certain stores, the bright red of stop signs, the quality of the roads, the acceleration of a car.

We went down Duncan, turned right onto Dolores, and quickly turned right onto Cesar Chavez.

I started crying again. To stop, I needed to distract myself. My attention turned to my wrists, which were already aching from the handcuffs.

"The wrist joint, also called the radiocarpal joint, is an ellipsoid joint formed by one of the forearm bones (the radius) and the articular disc proximally and the proximal row of hand (carpal) bones distally," I recited to myself.

We turned left onto South Van Ness and took it all the way into the Tenderloin District.

"And the carpal bones...there was a mnemonic we used in medical school to memorize them...what was it? Some Lovers Try Positions That They Can't Handle. Scaphoid Lunate Triquetrum Pisiform Trapezium Capitate Hamate." I smiled slightly at the memory.

We turned right onto Golden Gate Avenue.

"The joints of the finger include metacarpal phalangeal, proximal interphalangeal and distal interphalangeal."

My thoughts were interrupted by our arrival at the federal building, where we found street parking. We sat there for about five minutes until Jurgenson approached, opened the door and asked me to get out. Suddenly, I found myself standing handcuffed on a sidewalk in downtown San Francisco. Jurgenson's colleague again took me by the elbow and the four of us started walking. Curious pedestrians stared while cutting a path around us.

After half a block and too many stares, I put my head down and tried focusing only on the sidewalk under my feet. My concentration was interrupted by a sharp turn to the right and before I knew it, we were going through large glass doors. Inside, people were waiting at a security checkpoint. We detoured around them, hesitating only long enough for Jurgenson to flash his badge for the guard. Once through, Jurgenson and the elbow man peeled away. It would be three months before I would see Jurgenson again.

One of the female agents placed her hand on my elbow and we continued on our way through an expansive lobby filled with attorneys in suits, federal marshals with holstered guns, other law enforcement personnel of all types and building employees. In a nearby elevator, I stood in handcuffs next to the federal agents and people in suits as background music played. One of the attorneys could not help himself and stole a look at me. His gaze was quickly averted when we made eye contact. Mercifully, the ride came to an end and we quickly left the elevator. We then proceeded through a series of locked doors that beeped and clicked open with a swipe of a badge. The heavy clanking of each door behind us created the sensation that we were entering a fortress.

Finally, we reached the inner chamber, a small room where I was signed over to a slightly built, middle-aged man with a stony expression and a gruff voice. With a cheery "good luck," the two female agents removed the handcuffs and were off. I looked up and saw a sign on the wall that read "booking."

The man directed me to stand in front of a gray screen for my mug shot. I stared at the camera, waiting for my picture to be taken. The flash of the camera stunned me momentarily, and when I recovered, the man was pointing impatiently at a chair, telling me to sit down. He then instructed me how to position my hand to obtain the best fingerprint, but I was preoccupied with trying to assimilate the moment and I misheard him and screwed up the first one. Not happy with having to repeat his instructions, he was more forceful when he grabbed my hand the next time. One by one, the tip of each finger was rolled over a black ink pad and then placed on a piece of paper.

The man then asked me to step into a small room, approximately four by seven feet in dimension. Once inside, another heavy door was closed behind me. Thick glass windows extended all around the room, starting halfway up the wall and going to the ceiling. I had the sense that I might asphyxiate in the room, as the walls and ceiling squeezed in and down on me. I was relieved when I spotted an air vent in the ceiling to my left. The room was barren, except for a small ledge protruding a foot from the wall with a chair tucked underneath. I began pacing. I pressed the index and middle fingers of my right hand to my left wrist. My heart rate was over one hundred beats per minute.

I paced and paced. It was the only thing I could do that felt productive. Images, but not rational thoughts, filled my head. My daughter's face, my bleeding head when I tripped into a wall when I was eight years old, the crowd at my college football games, the beautiful candles at my wedding, my freshman dorm room, the young patient I saw in clinic one week earlier with swollen wrists. They flooded my consciousness, like names in a spinning Rolodex, there and gone in an instant. My breathing felt fast and my hands unsteady and I didn't know what to do other than pace. I started reviewing the physiology of the heart. Cardiac output, stroke volume, sino-atrial node, atrioventricular node, QRS complex.

The only certitude I grasped was that my life as I knew it was over. Nothing would ever be the same. Ever.

I was left there for a long time. I don't know how long, though, because my perception of time had changed. At some point, the door was unlocked, and I stumbled out in a haze of confusion. I was told they were taking me to see the public defender.

It took me awhile to figure out they were talking about an attorney.

# CHAPTER SEVENTEEN

The federal marshal escorted me out of the inner sanctum of the building into a more heavily populated central area, where elevators took us to the public defender's office. The secretary nodded her head expectantly when the marshal announced my name incorrectly (Keebler, as in the cookies), and pointed us in the proper direction. We passed into a large, open corner office with windows for walls, affording a one-hundred and eighty-degree view of San Francisco. Part of me wanted to crash into one of the windows and fall to an early death. As I contemplated this, I noticed a man standing to greet me.

He was a tall black man with refined features, a well-groomed beard and a friendly demeanor. With a smile, he shook my hand and introduced himself as Michael Greer. Turning to my escort, he gave a quick nod, which sent the marshal on his way. He motioned to a soft chair in front of his desk.

Instead of returning to his chair, he sat on the corner of his desk, one foot touching the ground and the other dangling. His physical proximity was comforting; he was the first person that day who seemed to be on my side. I sank into the comfortable chair.

"I'm one of the public defenders here. Since you don't have an attorney, I've been assigned to you. I can continue to be your attorney or you can hire your own."

Seeing no reaction from me, he glanced behind at a paper sitting on his desk. Picking it up, he began to read aloud.

"You have been arrested on a single felony charge, which is a serious matter, of course." He seemed a little embarrassed about stating the obvious and gave me a sympathetic look. "I will represent you on your initial appearance in court today. It will be a very brief hearing where they will read the charge and then the judge will ask how you would like to plead. You will say 'not guilty.' Afterwards, you'll be permitted to go home."

My hands, grasping the chair arms tightly, trembled.

"However, you'll have to return to court in one week to post bail. Someone needs to come with you. Someone who will vouch for you that you'll come back to court."

I knew it would have to be Dad. Mom could never do it. She valued integrity and honesty above everything. It would take her more than the intervening week to come to terms with my arrest.

"You'll need to surrender your passport at your next court appearance, and you will not be able to travel anywhere outside of the Bay Area. The exact boundaries will be discussed with you by your parole officer."

I lowered my head, closed my eyes and stopped listening. I was startled when I felt Michael's hand on my shoulder.

"Are you okay?"

In the midst of my world unraveling, he provided a measure of calm. Looking up at him, I could see that he was about my age. I imagined under different circumstances we might have found ourselves talking at a cocktail party or other social gathering. In his office, however, the dynamic was decidedly different.

"We should go now," he announced.

Stumbling to my feet, I followed Michael out of his office, down the hallway and to the elevators, where we stood waiting.

"They recently upgraded these elevators," he offered as I pawed mindlessly at the linoleum with my shoe.

Next, I found myself standing in the front of a courtroom, staring at a federal judge. Apparently, they had been waiting for us because as soon as we arrived, a clerk began speaking, reading the charges.

I felt like I was watching a movie. A federal judge was talking, telling me I had been charged with a felony. A felony. And from the look on his face, he took what he was saying seriously. How did this happen? I was so out of place here. As these thoughts raced through my head, Michael nudged me on the arm.

"I'm sorry. Yes."

"Your Honor," Michael reminded me in a whisper.

"Yes, Your Honor. Excuse me."

The judge gave me a slight smile. I reached into my pocket for the Vicodin but then remembered I had already taken them. I felt completely overwhelmed and helpless.

"In that case, how do you wish to plead?"

I looked to Michael, who mouthed the correct response.

"Not guilty, Your Honor" I said. The words sounded like they were coming from someone else. It seemed as if things moved so rapidly in the courtroom. Everything was confusing.

"Your plea will be so entered into the record. You will be released from custody on your own recognizance, but are ordered to appear in one week, on October 19, 2005, at 10:30 am to post bail. Do you understand these stipulations?

"Yes, Your Honor."

I stood there motionless until Michael pulled on my arm, guiding me out of the courtroom and into the hallway. I couldn't feel my legs as I walked. Once outside, Michael handed me his business card, turning it over to show me he had scribbled the date and time of my next court appearance on the back.

"There's one thing before you go. The press is likely to get hold of the story. Human growth hormone is a popular topic right now. If you are contacted by a member of the press, do not speak with them under any circumstances. Do you understand?"

I nodded.

"Will you be okay?"

I was already thinking about my name being in the morning paper. Everyone would see it, and then I would want to run away. Everything in my life was going to be destroyed.

"Come on, let me walk you out."

*Where would I possibly go?*

Released from the building, I headed in the direction that seemed easiest. And kept walking. Through the city, I

211

kept walking. Past faceless pedestrians, down unknown streets. It might have been two miles or maybe five, but by the time I reached my front door, the sunlight was fading. I stood in the spot where the men in black had earlier handcuffed me, paralyzed with fear that the men were still in my apartment or would be back soon. It was somewhat reassuring that Jessica's sock was still on the stairs. I tried to slow my breath and think. I reached into my pocket and realized I didn't have my key.

I walked around back, jumped the fence and kicked in the door. Poking just my head inside, I stood there listening for a minute or two.

"They're gone," I assured myself.

I walked slowly and quietly, almost on my tiptoes, listening to every squeak and moan of the stairs as I ascended. I paused only briefly to scoop up the sock, squeezing it tightly against my chest. When I reached the top, I listened again. Reassured no one was there, I started pacing. The apartment looked different, smelled different.

I moved to my bedroom and saw clothing scattered over the bed, the drawers from which they were pulled still open. Only the sock drawer had contents, and I dug into the back for my stash the agents had somehow missed. With great satisfaction, I pulled out the wad and started counting the hundreds. When I finished, I stuffed the bills into my pocket.

In my home office, the steel file cabinets, previously full of documents related to Forever Lithe, were sitting open and empty. Pushing the top drawer closed, I found a cut-out newspaper ad in the back of the lower one.

"Professional Botox For Less!"

It was my best ad and had brought a fair amount of business. I looked at my picture on the right side of the ad and remembered when the photographer came to my office. He had suggested I put on a white doctor's coat and hang a stethoscope around my neck.

"That's a great deal you're offering on Botox. I paid almost twice that for a doctor just down the street. Making any money?"

"Well, it's just an introductory offer to get the practice going," I managed to stammer.

"Yeah, that makes sense."

The picture, like the Botox, felt like a fraud. Real doctors don't inject their patients with illegal drugs.

I quickly crumpled the ad and knelt to throw it in the trash can under my desk. While doing so, I noticed cords dangling from the back of the desk where my computer had been. Like the rest of my life, it had become the property of the US Government.

I stood to walk out of the room, kicking at a Forever Lithe pamphlet on the floor. I headed into my daughter's room, which appeared untouched, the only place of purity in a corrupted home. I stood there for a few minutes, looking through the window at the Birds of Paradise blooming in the backyard.

I needed to get my cell phone. The last time I saw it, a government agent was reading my text messages. I found it sitting on the kitchen table, and after powering on the device, I noticed several waiting voice mails. My hands shook as I attempted to dial the mailbox number, resulting in several failed attempts before finally connecting.

The first message was from the chiropractor whose call I hadn't taken. He sounded breathless and nervous.

"Yeah, uh, Max. Been trying to call you but you're not picking up. A bunch of guys from the FDA or federal marshals or something came to the office and served me a search warrant. Then they went through all your stuff. They took all your vials of Botox out of the freezer. Just wanted to warn you in case they're looking for you. I hope you're okay. Give me a call."

The second message was from a secretary and friend from Cade County Hospital. For the previous eight years, our offices had been across the hall from each other. In a long-winded message, she said three men had shown up at hospital security, presented a search warrant and asked to be taken to my office. They were escorted there by the hospital chief of security, a woman I had once dated for a short time. Reluctantly, she had unlocked my office door, and they spent the next thirty minutes collecting various files and documents.

By the end of the message, she was almost crying.

"What in the world's happening, Dr. Kepler? Is everything alright?"

The last three messages were from Greg. Annoyed in the first message, he was obviously concerned by the third.

"Ummm, Max, I don't know what happened but it doesn't look like you made it on the plane and your phone has been turned off. I'm going to leave the airport and head home, but please call me when you get the message."

I ended the call and leaned against the kitchen counter. I needed to let a few people know what happened. I decided I would contact Greg first. He was my best friend and had always been supportive during difficult stages of my life, all the way back to when I became ill with Wegener's Granulomatosis.

He picked up on the first ring.

"Max, is everything okay?"

"Not really," I barely managed.

"What the hell happened?"

"I. I. I need…help. I'm in big trouble. I got arrested today."

"What are you talking about?"

By then I was whimpering. Not crying. I wasn't even capable of crying anymore. I could only whimper, like an injured dog on the side of the road. I tried to collect myself.

"Importing human growth hormone and Botox from China."

"It was illegal?"

"Yes."

"Oh, man."

There was silence.

"I need help, Greg. Please help me."

"I'll do everything I can. Are you at home?"

"Yeah."

"Just stay there, okay? Stay right there. I'm going to make some calls and will get back to you in an hour or so."

Then he was gone. I held the phone to my ear.

"Greg…Greg?"

I was alone again. I needed to move. I began pacing the hallway again. I realized Dad and Danny still had hGH. There was no doubt the feds would be closing in on them. I needed to warn them before they were busted. But how could I contact them without the feds knowing? I was certain they had tapped my phone and were monitoring my e-mails. I wandered into my office, trying to figure out a solution. Then I saw the fax machine.

I grabbed a blank piece of paper and wrote down a message in large, capital letters.

"GOT ARRESTED TODAY FOR IMPORTING BOTOX AND HGH FROM CHINA. OUT OF JAIL BUT HAVE TO GO BACK TO COURT IN ONE WEEK. THEY KNOW YOU AND DANNY HAVE HGH. DESTROY IT ALL IMMEDIATELY. DON'T CALL ME. THE PHONE IS TAPPED."

After I faxed the message, I texted him, "Sending you a fax right now. Very urgent."

Then I waited for a response. Five minutes later, a fax came through.

"NOT GOOD, MAX. NOT GOOD. WILL TAKE CARE OF HGH. WILL CALL LATER. WON'T TELL MOM YET."

I sat there imagining the panic Dad must have been experiencing in that instant. I couldn't believe I had exposed my family to my reckless behavior. I began whimpering again, felt lightheaded, and sat down. I started rocking forward and back, holding my belly with crossed arms. A short while later, I began to feel pathetic and forced myself to stop.

I still needed to tell Alice. How was I going to explain to her I'd been arrested for a felony drug charge? Alice, a woman with a medical degree from one of the finest institutions in the country, who came from a family full of

216

graduate degrees. I decided it would have to wait until morning. It was all too much for one day.

Instead, I went into Jessica's room and stood at the window until the darkness completely enveloped the Birds of Paradise.

# CHAPTER EIGHTEEN

I told Alice the next morning. She didn't say much. She didn't ask why or how. She didn't chastise me or get angry. Instead, she asked if I was okay and when I told her I thought I might die from an anxiety attack, she offered to write a Valium prescription. And then she urged me to set up an appointment with my psychiatrist. It was the closest I had felt to her in a long time.

Since I had taken a week off to visit Greg on the day I was arrested, I had plenty of free time. I spent most of each day isolated in my apartment, numbly watching television, flipping through channel after channel, never able to focus on one program for long. Brief walks around the block or to the corner convenience store for a soda were my only respites from the apartment. I did not read, work out or visit friends. I went three or four days without showering. I never even considered it. Without an appetite, I began losing weight.

Time became irrelevant. I longed for the darkness because that would bring sleep, but then I would lie awake in bed. I soon discovered I could fall sleep on the couch with the stereo playing. It was though I was playing a trick on my mind, telling myself I wasn't really going to bed, I was just going to lie on the couch and listen to music. Terrible dreams, most often of Jessica being present during the raid, would wake me.

Four days after the arrest, I still had not spoken with Mom. Dad had told her the day after the arrest, but I never asked for her reaction nor did he offer it. We both knew she would be devastated, and that realization made me sick. Most of my life had been one continuous proud moment after another for her, as evidenced by the Max Kepler shrine she had created in a spare room at home. There, she hung my diplomas from college, graduate and medical schools, along with various awards, such as the Alpha Omega Alpha certificate for being elected to the medical school honor society, all-league awards for baseball, basketball and basketball from high school, college scholarship certificates, and a plaque commemorating my induction into the Boon High School Hall of Fame.

More than ever, I needed Mom's support, and so I decided to call her. I began pacing the hallway of my apartment as I dialed the number. The phone rang many times before she answered. By that time, I was nearly hyperventilating.

"Hi Max," she answered in a hollow voice, caller ID giving me away.

"Hi Mom. How are you?"

"Umm…I'm okaaaay," she lied weakly. "What's up?"

"I need someone to come back for the next court hearing."

I already knew her answer, but I had to ask.

219

"I think Dad's going."

Her voice was distant. Indifferent.

"Okay."

Silence.

I was too ashamed to cry.

"What are you doing now?" she asked.

"Nothing much. I have to go meet with some people in the hospital this afternoon."

I walked into the kitchen and saw the empty Tupperware containers still on the countertop, botulinum toxin and hGH long gone.

"I'm so sorry, Mom."

"Okay."

Dirty dishes were piled in the sink. I could smell the unemptied trash nearby. I moved away.

"Well, just wanted to give you a quick call. I gotta leave in a little bit. Talk to you later."

After hanging up, I curled up in a fetal position on the couch and began shaking. It was the loneliest moment of my life.

It occurred to me everything would be easier if I weren't alive. I had no intention of killing myself—even considering it nauseated me—but the abject longing for a complete break from reality made death seem, at least theoretically, preferable. The feeling lingered briefly before I realized such thoughts were absurd. I loved life and my child way too much to do such a thing. I forced myself to sit up, and I stayed there, leaning forward with elbows on knees staring into space until the tears ran dry. And then I prayed that thoughts of death would never come again.

Although emotionally spent, I needed to get ready for a meeting that had been arranged with members of hospital administration, the Chief of Staff and head of security. I quickly showered, dressed and jumped into my car. As I drove down Highway 101 to the hospital, I dreaded the thought of seeing the people at the meeting, especially Nancy Stillings, the CEO. When I accepted an offer of employment at Cade County Hospital three years previously, it was partly in response to Nancy, who had just been hired. We had talked for almost an hour during my initial job interview.

"I'm trying to change the culture of this place. To do that, we need good people. You're the type of doctor and person I want at this medical center. I have a good feeling about you, Max," she told me.

It was both a compliment and a challenge, and I spent the next year and a half of employment trying to prove the accuracy of her comments. In the process, we had developed an excellent professional and personal relationship. But now I had turned everything upside down, and I began feeling increasingly anxious as I drove. I reached into my pocket, pulled out a Valium, and swallowed it. By the time I reached the hospital, the effect had kicked in, and I felt more in control.

I parked on a nearby side street and entered the hospital through Shipping and Receiving and used the freight elevator. When I arrived at Nancy's office, the door was closed. The secretary, seated across the hall, greeted me warmly and told me they were "just finishing up a quick pre-meeting."

Several minutes later, the door opened and a grim-faced Nancy emerged.

"Come on in, Max," she said, barely making eye contact.

The five meeting participants were sitting around the conference table, watching me carefully. No one stood to greet me, although several murmured "hello." As I sat down, Steve, one of my partners and the Chief of Medicine, mouthed "Are you okay?" I nodded and he gave me a faint smile. Nancy sat down and cleared her throat.

"Max, we called this meeting to discuss what's happened. We have some real concern regarding the seriousness of the allegations. We understand you've been arrested for importation of drugs. But we don't have any specific details and were hoping you could tell us more."

Tears began to form but I squeezed them away. I would not humiliate myself further. Taking a moment to compose myself, I didn't dare look at anyone's face. I needed to imagine I was talking about someone else.

"There was an arrest for importing human growth hormone from China."

I heard a rustling sound and then silence.

"What were you doing with the growth hormone?" Nancy asked.

"It was being used in my private cosmetic practice."

"Were you using it on any patients at the medical center?"

"No, of course not."

"Why were you using it?"

"As part of an anti-aging regimen. It was being used in low doses in a small number of patients."

"Were you receiving the shipments from China here at the medical center?"

222

"Yes."

Sighs pierced the air. Nancy's face went taut.

My ears were ablaze. I started to feel lightheaded again. Nancy looked at hospital counsel, who nodded.

"Max, we're concerned about the negative publicity your case could bring to the hospital. We have an obligation to think about the institution as a whole. It would not look good if the press found out one of our doctors was having illegal human growth hormone from China shipped to the hospital."

"I understand."

"I'm afraid I'll have to suspend your contract until the matter is resolved. You will not be permitted to work here, nor will you be able to be on the premises without a valid reason. You'll need to surrender your hospital badge. Do you understand?"

"Yes."

"I don't want to do this, Max. I want you to know that. Also, I want you to know that we're not revoking your privileges, because then we would have to report it to the Medical Board of California. We're simply suspending your contract."

"I completely understand," I replied. "Thank you."

"Are you going to be okay? You're not looking so good."

"I think I just need to go home."

As I stood to leave, a cacophony of "take cares" and "hang in there's" filled the room.

I was walking down the hallway when Nancy called after me.

"Max, I need your security badge."

Returning to her, I fumbled to unclip the badge from my belt, and in the process, it fell to her feet. We both reached down simultaneously, nearly bumping heads before I could retrieve it.

"I'm sorry," I said, as I handed the badge to her.

"So am I."

My second court appearance would take place one week after my arrest. I expected Michael to be my attorney, but Greg insisted I find the best criminal attorney around. He had done some research for me and narrowed the list down to three law firms. At the same time, one of my partners at the hospital suggested a fourth. I made appointments with all four.

My first meeting was with the attorney recommended by my partner. He was an older, established San Francisco attorney, whose office was on the fifteenth floor of a large office building downtown. After checking in with the receptionist, I was led to a large conference room stacked with rows of legal books. Shortly after I was seated, the attorney appeared in the doorway. He was tall, with big feet that swung out to the side as he ambled over to me. He was accompanied by a young, female paralegal.

In a big, blustery voice, he introduced himself and shook my hand too hard. Then he slid into an overstuffed chair, placed his elbows on the armrests and leaned back into nonchalance. His paralegal dutifully assumed a position to his right and I sat a short distance away, on the other side of her.

"So, what kind of trouble have you gotten yourself into, son?"

One month previously, I would have never allowed such condescension. Now, I was just glad someone might be able to help, and so I spent about ten minutes summarizing my predicament. When I finished, he squeezed his chin between his thumb and index finger several times, staring off into space for a long time. He turned to me with a look of feigned empathy.

"I can do it for one hundred thousand dollars," he announced.

I believe he expected gratitude.

"Is that for everything?" I indulged.

"Yeah, everything," he replied, glancing at his paralegal.

"Can I think about it for a couple of days and give you a call?"

"Of course, but don't wait too long, as other cases might come up and right now I have some extra time for yours."

"Will do," I replied, tempted to give him a thumb up and a wink. Instead, I shook his hand and hurried on my way. His name was crossed off the list before I reached the elevator.

Next, I arranged a meeting with a new firm consisting of two young attorneys. Both had graduated from Stanford Law School and were already highly regarded despite their brief careers. They insisted on conducting the meeting in my apartment, and they arrived looking like the odd couple. One was overweight and poorly dressed and the other, dressed in a dark blue pinstriped suit and expensive shoes, looked like he worked out twice daily. Over the next thirty minutes, they took turns explaining how they would approach the case and why I should choose them. As I watched them, I realized they expected my case would garner media attention and therefore serve as a springboard for their practice. And although I appreciated their enthusiasm and skill, they were simply too young and inexperienced.

I then visited a female attorney whose office was in a small, nondescript building in the Cow Hollow section of San Francisco. She answered the door personally when I knocked and took me into an office with old carpet, a couple of half-alive plants, several books and an outdated computer. Wearing jeans and a casual top, she had a demeanor that was similarly low key. She maintained eye contact during our entire visit.

"I'm so sorry you're going through this," she kept repeating as I told her the story.

By the end, she had formulated a legal strategy, which she articulated very clearly, frequently referencing legal precedents as she did. She never mentioned her rate, and I probably would have been satisfied to have her as my attorney, but I wasn't certain she was the best. And with the predicament I was facing, I needed a great attorney, not just a very good one. Before I left, I asked her to name the top criminal defense firm in the area, and she came up with Arguedas, Cassman and Headley. It was one of the firms Greg had recommended.

I called the next day to make an appointment with Cris Arguedas. She was on vacation so they suggested I meet with her partner, Ted Cassman. My initial reluctance dissipated after I read his background information on their website. Educated at Stanford University and Berkeley Law, Ted had joined the firm in 1984 and over the years had been involved in some high-profile cases.

In 1987, he wrote the winning briefs in U.S. v. Merchant, a case before the United States Supreme Court. He had been recognized by "Best Lawyers," a rating service of outstanding lawyers as determined by peer recognition and professional achievement. He was said to be an absolute bulldog for his clients, and one with an impeccable memory for details. I was anxious to meet him.

The law offices were in a warehouse section of Oakland, which I thought odd for such a high-powered firm. Later, I discovered they were about to move into a new location in Berkeley. I checked in with the receptionist who promptly guided me to Ted's office upstairs.

Ted was sitting at his desk staring at the computer. He quickly stood up, and I discovered a wisp of a man wearing an over-sized dark suit. His hair was sparse, with the most substantial portion being a tenacious tuft on top resembling a clump of overgrown weeds. But he had a warm smile, blue eyes and a demeanor so gentle that I was immediately put at ease. He shook my hand and asked me to sit down as he returned to his chair.

"How can I help you, Max?" he asked.

He lifted his eyebrows after I told him about my arrest. On the wall behind him, there was an autographed photograph of a professional football player who had been one of the athletes receiving performance-enhancing drugs from the BALCO lab busted by the feds. I had read that Ted had represented him admirably, essentially getting him off.

"Do you have a copy of the indictment against you?" he asked.

I handed it to him, and he spent less than five minutes reading through it.

"Has any member of the press attempted to contact you?"

"No."

"That's good. Make sure you don't talk with them."

I nodded.

"Let's start by getting some basic demographic information, and then you can give me a summary of your behavior that led to the arrest."

I spent about thirty minutes describing the sequence of events, intermittently stopping to compose myself. Ted was patient and reassuring, telling me to take my time. He took notes during the entire session and agreed to take the case once I finished.

"You should know my hourly rate is five hundred and fifty dollars per hour," he said almost apologetically.

"I understand," I replied, without even thinking about the number. Desperation had changed my perspective on many things.

"This will be a costly case to defend, and so I'll need a retainer of twenty-five thousand dollars," he said. Even as he was asking for money from me, I found Ted likable, and I felt he'd take care of me.

"I barely have two thousand dollars in my account right now, but I'll get you the money." I felt dizzy as I realized my destiny was no longer in my hands. I had given up the divine privilege of self-determination, and the result was that I felt utterly lost. Whatever power degrees and accomplishments had earned me was now obliterated.

"Can you get it to me by the next court date in five days?"

"Yes, I will." I knew I could use my credit cards for cash.

Ted slid a piece of paper containing the fee agreement across the desk and asked me to sign it. He also signed it, made a copy and gave one to me.

"Let me walk you out," Ted said. When we reached the front door, he told me, "Try to get some rest. Work out, if you can. I'll call you tomorrow."

I didn't want to leave. Ted made me feel protected and safe. But he turned away, and so I walked out into the day, grasping the agreement and feeling a thread of hope.

In addition to the retainer, I would be required to post a ten-thousand-dollar bail at my next court appearance. And, as expected, the court required someone to accompany me to the bail hearing to personally guarantee I would make all future court dates.

Dad flew into San Francisco the day before the date. He looked weathered and tired, struggling to pull his suitcase off the conveyor. He had lost some weight as well, but when he saw me, his eyes lit up and he came right over to give me a prolonged hug. I stifled tears by reminding myself of the challenge ahead.

"How was the flight?" I asked as I tossed his bag in the trunk.

"Good."

We didn't speak again until we were on the freeway.

"Playing much golf?" I asked him.

"Yesterday was the first time I've played in a week."

Dad normally played golf every day.

"How'd you do?" I asked him.

"Decent," he replied, and then with renewed energy he continued. "So, you remember the fifteenth hole? The par 4, with the dogleg to the right and the pond on the left?"

"Yeah," I replied, feigning interest.

"Well, I pulled my tee shot and the ball ended up about a foot from the water. So, I get over there and realize I can't stand on dry land to hit my second shot. The only way I can do it is to stand in the water. So, I take off my shoes and socks and everyone is looking at me like I'm crazy. But I wasn't about to take a penalty shot. There was money on the line."

It was the middle of the day and traffic was light. I could see the blue water of the San Francisco Bay beyond Dad. Soon we would be passing Candlestick Park. Dad was still talking; I was still nodding.

"So, I get into the water and I'm lining up the shot and I notice the wind…"

But my mind was somewhere over the Bay and after another five minutes of trying, Dad gave up, and we spent the rest of the ride in silence.

As we pulled into my driveway, I saw Jessica's stroller in the garage. I had not seen my daughter since the arrest; Alice had wisely kept her away. I had become obsessed with the possibility that she could have been home during the raid.

"Just stop it," I would tell myself. "It didn't happen."

I would pray silently, thanking God for preventing her from being a witness to that day's events. I wanted to believe the Government had shown mercy and waited until she was safely at school. Believing this humanized them and made them less scary. Even so, nightmares of Jessica witnessing the arrest continued.

Additionally, I struggled with the fact that despite my responsibilities as a father, I had nonetheless engaged in illegal behavior. It hadn't seemed to matter that I had a young child whom I adored. I had always felt truly blessed to have my daughter. Given that, the irresponsibility and selfishness of my behavior was mind-boggling to me. Why hadn't I considered the potential effect on her? I had placed the most important obligation of my life in jeopardy, and the knowledge of that made me physically sick.

Terrible as I felt, I knew I had a choice. I could either succumb to self-pity and perpetual anguish, or I could suck it up and start being the father my daughter deserved. In the end, it was an easy decision; all I had to do was look into her beautiful brown eyes or hear her sweet voice say, "I love you, Daddy," to know I could never expose her to the emotional turmoil I was undoubtedly going to experience in the upcoming months. There would be no repeat of the mistakes of my father by taking out my unhappiness on her. My daughter would not feel responsible for her dad's emotional well-being. In fact, she would never even notice a difference in my behavior if I could possibly help it. My commitment was complete, and it was this early decision that would provide at least a hint of stability in my newly chaotic life.

# CHAPTER NINETEEN

The bail hearing was to be held in the United States District Court for the Northern District of California on Golden Gate Avenue, just a few blocks from City Hall in San Francisco. Ted arranged for us to meet in the cafeteria on the third floor before the hearing. He wanted to discuss the preliminary strategy for defending the case.

From a distance, the Federal Building appeared to be just another tall office building in the big city. But this fortress of federal law and order was far from ordinary, a fact emphasized by the large concrete barricades hastily erected around it after 9/11. We wove between them to reach the main entrance, where Dad and I stood and stared. The building looked inordinately large from this perspective, and I felt diminished in its presence.

"Come on, let's go," Dad encouraged me.

Ted was already seated at one of the cafeteria tables when we arrived. He greeted us warmly and after we sat down, he told us the court appearance would be brief and procedural only. What he wanted to discuss was my defense.

"I've had a chance to look through the case a bit since we met in my office four days ago, Max. The defense is complicated by the fact you spoke freely with the investigators the day you were arrested, without an attorney being present. Everything you said during that session will be used against you in a criminal trial."

I lowered my head in embarrassment at the apparent stupidity of my actions.

"Can't you say the statement was made under duress?" Dad suggested.

"No, I'm afraid not. Max signed two different documents authorizing the interview and was read his Miranda rights twice."

Dad sighed.

"Additionally, they have the evidence seized during the raid. Will they find anything important?" Ted asked me.

"They will find everything. I made no attempt to hide anything. It's all there."

"Including documents or references to the importation of hGH from China?"

"Yes."

"Payments for hGH?"

"Yes. I mean it when I say everything." Already, I felt like I was talking about another person. Again, I wondered how I had wandered so far off track.

Ted stroked his beard as he stared straight ahead. He gritted his teeth and then cleared his throat.

"This is a bit unusual, so we're gonna have to take a different approach. Since you're basically caught, the best strategy is to continue to cooperate fully with the Government. By doing so, perhaps we'll be able to negotiate a settlement before going to trial."

I nodded. It seemed like a reasonable approach, but what the hell did I know?

"This means you'll definitely be convicted of a crime. There is no way of negotiating a settlement without pleading guilty."

"Will I lose my medical license if I plead guilty? I don't want that to happen. *That can't happen.*"

"That's something we'll worry about later. Right now, we should focus on preventing a trial and keeping you out of prison."

Dad was silent. My heart started pounding, and I felt it hard to breath. At an adjacent table, two federal marshals were having breakfast. I could see the badge on the waist of the bigger fellow whenever he reached for his coffee. I kept staring at the badge as Ted kept talking.

"You'll need to get letters of support from as many people as possible," Ted informed me.

"But then people will know I'm in trouble," I said.

"I think we're past that stage now," Ted said gently.

I dreaded the thought of asking for letters. I didn't want to make people uncomfortable, and I knew some of them would be concerned about how the Medical Board would perceive them if they wrote a letter of support for a suspected felon.

"Max, I also need to tell you that I have been speaking with the Government and they are considering filing additional charges against you," Ted continued.

"Are you serious? For what?"

"They can file felony charges for every Customs violations. How many illegal shipments did you receive from China?"

"Maybe eight or ten."

"Each one of those is a felony. You've already admitted to those crimes."

"Oh, my God," I said, barely able to contain my emotions.

"I'll do my best to convince them not to file more charges."

Ted's voice sounded distant. "Please. You have to," was all I could manage.

"I'll try. But there's more bad news. The assistant US attorney told me she doesn't want you practicing medicine again. She doesn't think you're fit to be a doctor."

I put my head in my hands. Dad wrapped his arm around me. I wanted to scream or cry. Instead, I sat silently, my mind racing, trying to find a way out. A way to deal with it all. Ted was quiet now, waiting for me to compose myself.

Suddenly, I remembered my obsession with war stories. Not necessarily with war itself, but rather, the soldier experience, and how it was the ultimate test of a human being. It challenged every dimension of human existence: love, hate, fear, kindness, evil, hope, tragedy, loyalty, violence, greed, fairness. I had always regretted that I never had an opportunity to prove my mettle under such extreme circumstances. But maybe my current crisis was my chance to do just that. And with that thought, I began to reformulate my predicament, for although I wasn't technically at war, it was clearly my time to fight. Maybe I had even subconsciously created this situation for just such a challenge. I would deal with the psychology of such a warped possibility later. For now, what mattered was that I had a fighting strategy.

"We're not gonna let them do that," I told Ted. "We can't let them. This is bullshit. Now I'm pissed."

Ted looked at me warily.

"Calm down. Being pissed will not be helpful," he admonished me. "You need to show remorse. Now, let's go to the hearing."

We entered the courtroom on the fifteenth floor. There were other hearings going on and so we sat in the gallery for ten minutes before my case was announced. Dad accompanied Ted and me to the lectern in the front. The charge was read, including maximum penalties.

"How do you wish to plead?" the judge asked me.

"Not guilty, Your Honor," I said in a firm voice. Dad seemed to be shrinking by the second.

"In that case, you'll be required to post bail in the amount of ten-thousand dollars. Is someone here with you to pay bail and guarantee your attendance at future court appearances?"

"Yes, Your Honor," Ted said. "Max's father, Lawrence Kepler, is here today."

"Good morning, Mr. Kepler. By your appearance today, are you willing to take responsibility that your son Max will attend all future court hearings?"

"Yes, Your Honor," Dad said in a weak voice.

As I watched Dad, I couldn't believe I had put him in that position. I couldn't imagine how I'd react if I were in his position, how disappointed and upset I would be. Yet here he was, standing tall in a federal courtroom, supporting his son.

"Thank you," the judge replied, and after confirming the next court date on January 12, 2006, the court adjourned.

As I followed Dad out of the courtroom, I watched him stumble over a fold in the carpet and nearly fall, bracing himself against one of the gallery benches. His hands were shaking as he reached for the door in the back. The courage he'd summoned for the court appearance had deserted him.

Once we were safely in the hallway outside, Ted informed me that he had scheduled an appointment with my probation officer at eleven.

"Probation officer?" Dad asked, now looking ashen. I put my hand on his elbow, and Ted nodded.

"They're located on the tenth floor. You should make your way over there now. I'm going back to the office and will call you tomorrow. We have a lot of things to discuss."

"Thanks for helping my son," Dad said as he shook Ted's hand.

After Ted disappeared into the elevator, Dad turned to me.

"That's enough legal stuff for me today, Max. I'll wait for you in the cafeteria."

After escorting Dad to the cafeteria, I headed back upstairs to Pre-trial Services on the ninth floor. I checked in with a secretary who slid a packet through a slot in the heavy glass window separating us.

"Fill out these forms."

The paperwork took almost thirty minutes to complete. I had to provide an extensive biographical sketch and contact information for a variety of people, including family and friends. There were questions as to whether I had ever been convicted of a violent crime, if I owned a gun, had I ever used illegal drugs, how much alcohol I drank. I listed the surgical scars from my seven right knee surgeries as my only identifying marks. I wrote "physician" as my occupation. Somehow thinking it would seem less intimidating, I said I weighed two-hundred and fifteen pounds, ten less than my actual weight. Later, when the parole officer showed up at my apartment with a gun strapped to his waist, I realized the absurdity of that maneuver.

I returned the finished paperwork and spent several minutes considering the need for a parole officer. Shortly thereafter, I was taken into a nondescript office halfway down the hall. There I met Richard, who introduced himself as my Pre-trial Services Officer. Fully expecting a tough guy, I found instead a warm, welcoming man.

"Please have a seat, Max. How are you doing?"

"Okay, I guess."

"Let me tell you a little about the mission of Pretrial Services and my particular role. I am here to help you through both the pre-trial and trial period."

I almost smiled. A federal law enforcement person was going to help me? It seemed unlikely.

"Pretrial Services maintains a position of impartiality within the criminal justice system. You have not been convicted of a crime and so we do not treat you like a criminal. I am not your parole officer. I am here as a resource as you go through a difficult time."

I relaxed a little at that.

"My role is to ensure you make all of your court appearances and comply with the conditions of bail. I can help answer questions you might have about a process that can be scary and confusing. We are an independent entity and not affiliated with the US Attorney's office."

I was still trying to differentiate him from a parole officer.

"I will come by your house to check in every few weeks. But first, I wanted to go over some of the requirements of pretrial release. It's important that you understand these completely because violation of any of them could result in bail being revoked."

I had to make all court appearances. I could not commit a crime, use drugs, or miss my scheduled appointments with Pretrial Services. I could not travel without permission outside the Northern District of California, which was comprised of fifteen counties. To get permission, I would have to submit a written request two weeks in advance. In that request, I would need to state where I was going and why, how and with whom I was traveling, the name of the person I was staying with, and the exact dates of travel.

After I signed a contract listing the probation requirements, Richard shook my hand and gave me his card.

"I've written down the date and time of my first field visit to your home. It should only take about fifteen minutes."

Over the next ten months of biweekly visits, Richard became more like a helping friend than a minder. I even stopped noticing his gun. But I was still never fully comfortable with a federal law enforcement agent coming

239

into my apartment, a fact reinforced the time Richard visited while Greg was staying at my place.

On that day, I was taking a shower when Richard showed up, and Greg let him in. When I came out of the shower, towel wrapped around my waist, I found the two of them sitting stiffly in the living room, Greg looking uneasy.

"Hey, Max," Richard said cheerily. "Just came by to see how you're doing."

"Doing the best I can, Richard," I replied. "Be right back." I went to the bedroom and quickly dressed. When I returned, I sat on the interrogation couch next to Greg. I had given it the nickname several weeks after the first session with Jurgenson.

"Looks like you've been working out," Richard observed.

I had been going to the gym daily, finding it was an effective, albeit temporary, stress reliever.

"Just wanted to remind you the next court appearance is in January," he said.

I nodded. Ted had already told me this. Apparently, the purpose would be to formally acknowledge the case would be going to trial and to set a date for its start. I was hoping it would be cancelled, not only because I hated being in that courtroom but also because that would mean Ted was effectively negotiating a settlement. He still had three months to work on it.

"Will you be going back to work anytime soon?"

I had no answer to that question, since it wasn't up to me to decide.

Hospital administration had made it clear I had no chance of returning to work until the legal issues were resolved. Despite my suspension, the Chief Medical Officer of Cade County, a man named Dr. Sang-Ick Chang, had continued to maintain contact with me. A fellow Harvard graduate five years older than me, he was a short, stocky Chinese man with a round face who could be domineering with staff and with anyone who crossed him or disagreed with him. And he could be draconian. At one point, he had even tried to break up our medical partnership, a group that had been together over thirty years, because he wanted to create a different physician structure at the hospital.

We had never had a particularly close relationship, although we were always cordial. So, it was surprising when I found him contacting me several weeks after my arrest to see how I was doing.

"Fine, I guess," I said, feeling very uncomfortable. I couldn't imagine he had any empathy for me. I always envisioned him as a hardline rule-follower and guessed he had nothing but contempt for my actions. I waited for him to reveal the real reason for the call as we engaged in small talk. But it never came, and suddenly he was saying, "I'll talk to you soon," before hanging up. Baffled, I sat there contemplating the conversation, deciding finally there must be some angle he wasn't telling me about.

But he called me the next week, and then the week after that he came to visit me. On that day, I met him at the bottom landing of my stairs. It was eight o'clock, and he was on his way home from the hospital. Despite having a wife and two small children waiting for him, he made time to stop to see me.   The expression on his round face was softened and his eyes gentle.

"Hi, Max," he said as he entered, reaching for a hug. I awkwardly returned the gesture.

"Thanks for coming," I said.

"I just wanted to check on you and tell you personally I'm thinking about you.   I want you to let me know if there's anything I can do to help you."

Pushing back tears, I stood there feeling touched by his kindness.   Sang began telling me about what was happening at the hospital, trying to make me feel like I was still part of the team.

"We miss you at the pharmacy and therapeutics committee meetings," he said.   "With no one to chair the meetings, nothing gets done."

Sang stayed a while longer, and when he left I gave him another hug, this one more exuberant and heartfelt.   At that moment, I stopped trying to interpret his actions and just accepted them for what they appeared to be:   an attempt by one human being to provide unconditional support for another.   Later, I would find out just how much I would have to rely on that support to save me from disaster.

For now, Richard was still in my living room.

"I guess I'll head out now," he announced.   Greg sat glued to the couch.   Once Richard was gone, he turned to me.

"I didn't realize you had a parole officer," he said quietly.

"Probation officer," I corrected him.   "Did you forget I've been charged with a felony?"

242

Greg shook his head. Although baffled and disturbed by what I'd done, he was still there for me. Married and with a child at home and his wife pregnant with another, he still found time to fly three-thousand miles to see me on a regular basis. And that was in addition to all the phone calls he made just to check in. He was demonstrating the true meaning of the term, "best friend."

Despite visits by my probation officer, my inability to work, the shame of being charged with a felony, and the uncertainty of what would ultimately happen to me, at least I now had plenty of time to spend with Jessica. And I took full advantage of it, engaging in various activities with her that previously I was too busy for. And in the process, I felt even closer to her and even more determined not to fail her. My deepening relationship with Jessica seemed to ground me, and I would discover that my connection with her would carry me through many difficult moments in the months ahead.

Nonetheless, my emotional state was still precarious six weeks after the arrest. I was convinced the Government was watching me, and I kept expecting them to return at any time to raid my house. If I heard a strange noise, I imagined they were out there, watching, waiting. I decided to catch them in the act and so I placed my trash in a precise location, with the contents in a particular order. Then I'd wake early the next day before the garbage truck came, go down to the sidewalk and examine the trash for evidence of tampering, which I never found. While driving, I watched cars in my rearview mirror to make sure I wasn't being tailed. At all times, I refused to speak about the case in any detail on the phone, certain the Government was listening.

I asked Ted in an email on November 20, "What are the chances my phones are being tapped?" He responded, "Much less than someone is reading your emails! Call me."

"I think they're watching me, Ted," I told him by phone.

"Are you sleeping, Max?"

"Not really."

"You need to get some sleep. And stop worrying about the Government. They already have more than enough evidence."

In the meantime, I had to find an attorney to represent me before the Medical Board. Ted arranged a meeting with Gordon Fanning, a well-respected attorney who had been practicing law for thirty years and knew members of the California Medical Board personally.

I met Gordon in the main conference room of his office complex near San Mateo. He was in his late sixties and overweight, to the point where he seemed to waddle as he walked. His cherubic face was friendly but his demeanor was a bit gruff. I thought he seemed more like a general contractor than an attorney. His speech was brief and halting, and I could not imagine him making any memorable courtroom speeches. But he had contacts and that, as I would learn, is sometimes worth more than talent in matters of the law.

He had not reviewed the legal documents I sent him, and his unpreparedness and lack of responsiveness to my inquiries was something I would later have to get used to. I spent the first ten minutes watching him flip through papers I had sent him two weeks previously, his heavy breathing the only sound in the room. As I waited, I began timing his breaths so that I could calculate his respiratory rate. At least that would distract me from the fact that my confidence was waning with each passing minute. When he finally finished, he stacked the documents into a neat pile and cupped the two upper corners with his hands.

"You're facing two main problems with the Medical Board: premeditation and violation of the ethics clause. You knew the drugs you were using were illegal, but still used them, and you lied to patients about the source."

"That's not entirely true."

"Regardless, I think there's a fifty-percent chance that you will have your license revoked."

"That can't happen," I said firmly.

"I know that's difficult to hear, but I just want to give you an honest appraisal."

I felt faint. I stood up and started pacing the room. It felt as if a band was being tightened around my chest.

Gordon looked concerned. "I'll give you a few minutes," he said, before leaving the room.

I nodded and then started talking to myself after he left. "What am I going to do? Mom will be a mess. What am I going to do? I have to find a new career. I will be completely humiliated. Everyone will find out. I'll never see my patients again."

Then the instinct to fight took over, and I began to feel angry. I stopped pacing and stood waiting for Gordon to return.

Minutes later, he came back, lifting his eyebrows when he saw me.

"Take a seat, Max, and try to relax."

I managed to make it over to the table and sit down, but my fidgeting hands betrayed my nerves.

"Do you feel any better?"

"Not really," I answered.

"Nothing is going to happen with the Medical Board right now. We won't even report it to them until the criminal case is over."

I breathed deeply.

"You need to concentrate on your current case and try to get the best possible outcome. The lesser the sentence, the more likely you'll keep your license. A felony conviction would make it difficult for you."

I could take no more of his gloomy prognostications.

"Thank you for your time," I said, standing to shake his hand.

"Sure," he said, taken aback by my abruptness. "Let me know if you have any questions."

I nodded and quickly walked out of the conference room. By the time I reached my car, I started to feel sick, and it took me ten minutes of sitting behind the wheel before I could drive away.

My thoughts were everywhere on the ride home. I needed help, a calming influence, and so I called Mom and told her I had met with Gordon.

"What did he say?"

"He said there was a fifty-percent chance I would lose my medical license," I barely managed.

Mom gasped.

"Oh, Max. I'm so sorry. You probably never thought that was possible."

"Mom, I know you're mad at me. I know I let you down. But I need your support."

She took a deep breath and sighed.

"You know I'll be here for you.   Would you like me to come out there for a week?"

"That would be great."

"I'll find a flight right away."

Two days later, I picked her up at San Francisco International. I was relieved that she looked healthy. She gave me a big hug, and I cried in her arms for a minute or two. Then I wiped away the tears and picked up her suitcase. For the first time, I felt like I truly had the courage to face it all.

But I needed more help with my emotional state, and so I started seeing my psychiatrist again, even though it was a struggle to pay him. I had begun therapy with Dr. Steele two years earlier at the suggestion of the couple's counselor whom Alice and I had been seeing. He had been a help to me through the separation and eventual divorce. In his early sixties, tall and thin, with curly white hair, Richard Steele was a brilliant man, full of insight and advice. He often quoted literature, and sometimes he seemed more like my guru than my therapist.

His office was in an old Victorian on California Street in San Francisco. My appointments were at seven in the morning and, depending on the season, it could still be dark outside when I sat down in the cozy chair across from him. The walls were lined with his own paintings, usually abstract combinations of various color themes. They felt comfortable, as did I when I settled into a session. For a while, there was a certain painting behind his chair that blended perfectly with his voluminous grey hair. Sometimes as I sat looking at him, I wasn't sure where his curly locks ended and the painting began.

Although I had told him of my cosmetic business, including my use of Botox and hGH, I had never revealed the source of the drugs. When I first told him of the arrest, he was stunned. He wanted to know why I never told him about the importation.

"You never asked," was my excuse.

"There was a reason you never revealed this to me."

"Obviously, I knew it was wrong."

"We're going to take some time to look at this."

And we did. At least four or five sessions on that issue alone. The use of Botox and hGH and the failure to tell my psychiatrist I was using illegal drugs meant I had violated both ends of the doctor-patient relationship.

Dr. Steele suggested an antidepressant, but I refused this, as I wanted to experience the full emotional impact of my behavior. I felt it was necessary for true change to occur. I had even stopped taking Valium.

Dr. Steele helped me manage my overwhelming guilt, but he was never successful in ridding me of it. That was a task that I would have to complete alone.

In my sessions with Dr. Steele, I realized I had made my life progressively more complicated over the years. Now, I had a distinct desire to unwind that, to return to my childhood when my character flaws had not yet developed, and life was innocent and simple.

I often thought about when I was a kid playing baseball. If I concentrated hard enough, I could smell the leather of my mitt, feel the smoothness of the bat in my hand, sense the perfect tightness of the cap on my head, hear the sweet sound of a well-struck ball. I could see the faces of Tim, David, Todd, Danny and all the other neighborhood boys as we rode our bikes in formation to the baseball field each morning. One of us would carry the bat, and another, the ball. All of us hung our mitts from the handlebars.

Baseball was the magnetic pole around which our lives revolved. We started playing when there was still snow on the ground in early spring, hurrying home from school to get in a few innings. Then we would play nearly every day during spring and right through the humid Ohio summers.

When we weren't playing a game, I would toss the baseball with Dad or practice using the various contraptions he had built for me. Sometimes my parents would allow me to go to a convenience store nearby with Tim, my oldest friend and neighbor whom I had met the first week we moved to Ohio when I was ten. We had first encountered each other over a toad someone had discovered in the grass. Within thirty minutes, his dad was pitching baseballs to us in the back yard. At the convenience store, we'd buy baseball cards and sweets like Necco Candy Buttons or Bit-o-Honey's or Pop Rocks. We'd tear open our baseball card packages, anxious to see if we got one of our heroes from the Cincinnati Reds, guys like Johnny Bench and Pete Rose and Joe Morgan.

At night, after showering and putting on my pajamas, I would lie on the family room floor next to Dad, all the windows in our non-air-conditioned house open, listening to Joe Nuxhall and Marty Brennaman broadcast the

Cincinnati Reds' game on the radio, while the crickets chirped and the fireflies glowed outside.

Right after the arrest, my desire to recapture the feeling of childhood was so strong I decided to go to a batting cage to hit baseballs. For the next several weeks, I drove thirty minutes every two or three days so that I could put on a dirty helmet, grab a beat-up bat, and swing at baseballs tossed by a machine. In those moments, I was twelve again, hitting home runs in Little League at the field behind the local church on Fisher Drive, my parents watching from lawn chairs nearby. They would smile proudly at their all-American boy with the big bat and the happy smile as he ran triumphantly around the bases.

But then the pain of my blistered hands and aching shoulders would snap me back to reality. I wasn't that boy anymore; I was a thirty-six-year-old man facing a felony charge and possible prison time. No number of trips to a batting cage were going to erase that. And so one day, in the middle of a twenty-pitch cycle, I simply dropped the helmet and bat on the ground and drove home, never to return. It was time to grow up.

# CHAPTER TWENTY

The preliminary hearing was scheduled for January 6, 2006, and Ted was furiously trying to negotiate a settlement with the Government before it occurred. As discussed in the federal building cafeteria, he would argue that I had been truthful, cooperative and remorseful, hoping it would sway the Government. He was also trying to dissuade them from filing the additional ten felony charges. If he failed, I was clearly in serious trouble, as they already had an airtight case against me.

Amid these efforts, the federal prosecutor informed Ted that the Charlotte FDA office was investigating Lance's role in a steroid and hGH distribution ring and was interested in what I could add to their investigation. Ted saw this as a golden opportunity, which he outlined to me on the phone that evening.

"I think you took part in these criminal acts because of Lance," he told me. "He's an unethical person who held power over you and used that power to influence you to participate in bad behavior. You were mesmerized by him."

"I was mesmerized by his intellect, that's true. But he didn't make me do anything."

"No. This was a bad character. You would not have done these things without him."

"Uhhh...okay...not sure that's completely true."

"Do you want to go to prison?"

"No."

"Well then we're going to have to rely on a little more than your likability and admission of guilt."

"But implicate my partner? Is that right?"

"You have no choice, unless you want to go away for a while. Remember your daughter."

I spent the rest of the evening mulling over his words. It was a reasonable strategy. Lance had not been truthful with me, and in some cases, he had used me. For example, several times he had shipments of hGH sent to me because he said he was going to be traveling and didn't want the drug to spoil. It didn't make a lot of sense at the time, but now that I had a chance to reflect on it, he clearly was trying to hide it from US Customs. He had other shipments from China routed through me as well, and although I didn't open them, I now suspected they contained anabolic steroids. Then, after he was busted, there was that call from his attorney asking me to essentially lie for him.

Given all this, I decided to go along with Ted's strategy. But I was worried the Government would not find value in what I had to say. I didn't have much incriminating information about Lance, mostly because he had kept important things from me. And of course, I hadn't bothered to ask many questions.

I rationalized my decision to speak about Lance to the Government by reminding myself I would be unable to provide any additional information beyond that found in the emails I exchanged with him, and the Government already had those. So, if Lance went to jail, it would be based on evidence other than what I could provide. And my cooperation would surely draw favor with the US attorney's office.

After Ted informed the Government I'd be willing to cooperate, they agreed to meet with us for a proffer session whose purpose was for me to provide information about the investigation. The Government's offer of a proffer session was great news, as it was well-known that these sessions were a prelude to a plea bargain agreement. It was Ted's first big victory on my behalf.

Ted felt that the proffer offered another advantage, telling me, "I think it will be helpful when they meet you because right now they have a certain notion of who you are. A face-to-face meeting will personalize the issue."

The meeting was scheduled for a Thursday, six weeks after the arrest. Besides Ted and me, the Assistant United States Attorney (AUSA) Kirsten Lawry and the FDA agent who had coordinated the investigation, Marissa Long, would be present. For a day or two, I actually pondered whether I could settle the affair on my own. My life experience taught me that rules were adjustable, according to person and circumstance. Maybe it could be as simple as, "Hey, come on now. I'm Max Kepler. I'm a good guy. I made a mistake, but I didn't hurt anyone. I guarantee I'll never do something like this again. Can we all just forget about it?"

But I was living in a pipe dream.

In advance of the meeting, Ted sent a letter to Kirsten, "introducing" me. The document, meant to soften Government defenses, consisted of a summary of my life, admission of guilt, and acknowledgement of my cooperation with federal law enforcement agents.

"They're gonna be tough on you," Ted reminded me before we went into a conference room enclosed entirely by glass. As we approached, I saw two young women sitting inside. The one on my right looked familiar to me, but I couldn't quite place her. The other one was a stranger. Both stood to greet us as we entered; the woman on the left introduced herself as AUSA Kirsten Lawry. She was young, fit, fairly attractive and seemed friendly enough, given the circumstances. I thought it good she was female. The other woman identified herself as special FDA agent Marissa Long.

"I think you know me as Jill Monroe," she then added.

I nearly dropped the folder I was holding.

Once everyone was seated, Kirsten spoke first.

"As you know, Dr. Kepler, this session is being conducted pursuant to a proffer. Its purpose is to gather more information regarding your activities over the time in question. If you're truthful, your words cannot be used against you in a criminal trial, but they can be used to pursue further investigational leads. Thus, it is in your best interests to be truthful here. Although we can take notes, this session will not be recorded."

Ted already had his laptop out.

"The fact that we're having this session does not mean we are negotiating a plea bargain agreement. In fact, the government can provide you no assurances whatsoever that this session will benefit you in any way."

I looked at Ted quizzically.

"This is just a formality," Ted reassured me.

"We might ask questions regarding a related federal investigation of a person of interest. It is important you are truthful in your answers in that regard as well. Do you understand the conditions of this proffer?"

"Yes."

"Please take the time to read this proffer agreement and let me know if you have any questions."

She slid the document across the table, and I tried to read it, but it seemed like Chinese. I could feel the hot stares as I looked for help.

"Don't worry about what it says," Ted said. "Just sign it."

When I was done, I returned the agreement to Kirsten, who then nodded at Marissa.

"Very well," Marissa said, straightening her notes. "Let's start."

Over the next thirty minutes, she asked questions I had already answered on the day of the raid, and I wondered if they had even taken the time to read Jurgenson's report or go through the seized evidence. But then I realized they were trying to first establish credibility by checking my answers against information they already had. Their subtle nods or facial expressions revealed their intentions. Once through, Marissa slowed down when she reached details of hGH shipments.

"Did you receive every shipment of hGH you ordered from China?" she asked.

"No, two of them were held up by Customs," I replied.

"Do you remember the dates?

"February and April of this year."

"Was it hGH or Botox and how much were in the shipments."

"It was hGH only. I don't remember the exact number of vials, but I can check my records and let you know."

"How were the shipments labeled?"

"I don't know. They were seized."

"Fair enough. How were the other shipments that you actually received labeled?"

"Zinc powder samples. No commercial value."

"So, you intentionally had them mislabeled to reduce the chance they would arouse suspicion?"

"Yes."

"How many vials were in each package that was seized?"

"There were one hundred vials in the first package and one hundred and fifty in the second."

"What did you think happened to the vials?"

"I wasn't sure. I kept calling Customs to inquire about them."

"I'll tell you what happened to them. They were sent to the FDA Forensic Chemistry Center and results confirmed that the vials contained hGH. The February 15, 2005, and April 28, 2005, seizures totaled more than 1,650 doses."

That seemed like a lot. I wondered how they came up with that number, but my brain had no room for rapid math calculations.

"Do you understand the rules regarding the use of prescription medications in the United States?"

"Generally, yes."

"Then you know that only medications from FDA-approved facilities can be prescribed to patients in the United States?"

"I think I knew that."

"Was the hGH and Botox you imported from China from an FDA-approved facility?"

"I doubt it."

"Let me remove any doubt. I checked with the FDA Office of Chief Counsel in Rockville, Maryland, and they confirmed there was no Chinese company which has FDA approval to market and distribute any hGH product within the United States."

The line of questioning continued for over ninety minutes. All details regarding hGH and Botox were discussed, including total number of shipments, Chinese contacts, method of payment, shipping of drug across state lines, etc. They asked what I said to patients, how many patients were treated and whether any had side effects.

Kirsten occasionally interrupted, primarily to clarify certain answers I had given. She seemed to have trouble with some concepts, frequently mixing up hGH and Botox. I already had pre-conceived notions about her intellect after doing a background search and discovering she had not attended a top-tier law school. Nonetheless, her questions were the most upsetting, which quickly negated my snobbish opinion of her.

"What did you tell patients about the origin of the Botox and hGH?" she asked.

I looked down and hesitated. The room seemed inordinately quiet.

"I told them it was from the United States," I said, keeping my head down.

"So, you lied to your patients?"

I looked up at Kirsten. My eyes moistened as I nodded.

"How do you feel about violating the trust of your patients?"

I grabbed a tissue from a box Kirsten had pushed towards me.

"Terrible," I whispered.

Kirsten and Marissa nodded. I saw a glimmer of sympathy on their faces.

"Will there be anything else?" Ted asked.

"No. Thank you," Kirsten said.

It took all my energy to stand up. I wanted to fall to my knees in supplication, apologizing endlessly, but I knew that would result in nothing but scoffing. "Of course, he's sorry," they'd say. "They all are when they're caught." But in that moment, I felt as sorry as I could ever imagine someone feeling. I looked at Kirsten, dressed in professional attire, looking every bit the lawyer, and realized the entire point of her job was to prosecute people like me. I felt embarrassed such resources were being used that way. I had become a parasitic drain on the system, and I was as sorry for that as I was for the behavior that landed me there. I started to say something to her, felt that I should, but couldn't imagine how to say it or even what to say. Instead, I turned towards the door.

"Take care," I heard Kirsten call after me.

The session drained me, and I wanted to go home for a nap, but instead I drove down to Cade County for a scheduled meeting with my partners to discuss the progress of my case. Each of them had been forced to work harder to cover me in the three months since I had been arrested, and I could sense they were beginning to lose a little patience with the uncertainty. Despite that, they agreed to keep my position open until my return, whenever that might be. Several of them even checked in several times a week to see how I was doing, and each had written supportive letters on my behalf, which Ted had submitted to the Government. If that wasn't enough, they intermittently exerted pressure on hospital administration to make sure my contract was not terminated.

When I arrived, I found the door locked, and after punching in the code, I walked in to find them already assembled. The room grew silent, and everyone looked at me uncomfortably.

"Hi," I said. "Remember me? Max Kepler?"

That seemed to loosen them up, for suddenly they all stood up in unison to greet me. Each came over to hug me and say a few brief words.

I found a seat at the end of the table, and once everyone had settled down, my heart began to race. I felt so out of place that I nearly got up and walked out.

"How you holding up?" Lou, the oldest member, asked me.

"As good as can be expected, I guess."

They looked skeptical, which made me more anxious. Just that morning, I had weighed myself and noted I had lost fifteen pounds.

"I guess you guys are wondering how long this is going to take."

"We'd just like to get a general time frame," said one of the cardiologists.

"I know that," I answered. "Believe me, the waiting is the one of the toughest things."

"Three months, six months, longer?" our young oncologist asked.

"The simple answer is that I just don't know."

"What's your best guess?" asked Adita, a kind and gentle Indian woman who was one of our hospitalists. Adita had gone to medical school in India and subsequently was married in the traditional arranged manner. The newlyweds then moved to the U.S. and started a family. She was deeply religious, and I often wondered what she thought about my immoral behavior.

"It could be over in a week or six months," I answered. "At this point, there's no way of predicting."

Adita looked disappointed. She probably was the most impacted by my absence, in terms of an increase in her workload. This made me feel terribly guilty, of course, but there was nothing I could really do.

"I'm so sorry, Adita," I said.

She waved her hand at me and smiled warmly. "We'll just have to deal with it," she said.

I wanted so much to give them something and so I sat thinking of possible solutions.

"I'll ask my attorney whether a letter from the group asking for a more definitive timeline will help. Perhaps the letter could describe the hardship my absence has created, both for you guys and the patients. Maybe then they will give us a better idea of when the whole thing will end."

"That's a reasonable idea," Lou said. "Another idea is that we hire a temporary person to fill your position."

"The problem with that is that no one will take a temporary job if we're unable to tell them how long they'll be working," Steve pointed out.

My guilt was reaching its zenith. I didn't know whether to try to save my job or relinquish it.

"I think," I said, "that you need to decide what constitutes a reasonable amount of time to keep my position open. I will defer entirely to you for that decision. I want to say unequivocally that I hope to return to the group and would be very disappointed if that did not happen. That being said, I want you to know that I'll respect whatever decision you make."

"We were discussing just that issue before you arrived. We fully support you and will wait as long as we possibly can."

I fought to keep my emotions in check.

"I can't begin to tell you how sorry I am. I know I've let you down."

Then I stood silently, unable to continue. Reassuring words washed over me. I felt a hand on my right shoulder. I marveled that people could be so good.

"I don't know how I can ever repay you guys. At times, I feel like such a burden."

"We're here for you. Call whenever you need someone to talk to," Lou said.

"Thank you," I said. The day was too much, and I just wanted to get home.

"All we ask is that you keep us informed, Max," Lou said.

"I will. Promise." I gave them a forced grin.

Then I opened the door and headed for the freight elevator for my stealthy escape.

Within a month of the proffer session, Kirsten had decided not to pursue additional charges. Although I had an amazing attorney in Ted, the decision was more a consequence of favorable circumstance. As it turned out, the Government agency investigating the case was the FDA, which focuses on drug violations. The FDA was concerned more about my illegal use of hGH than its importation. If the investigating agency had been U.S. Immigration and Customs (ICE), they would have focused on my Customs violations, and, in that case, I would have been hit with felony charges for each of the ten times I imported hGH or Botox into the US.

I wasn't satisfied, though.

"I want the single felony charge dropped or reduced," I told an incredulous Ted.

"I've never seen that happen in a federal case, and I doubt it will happen here," he said, clearly trying to be patient.

"I don't care. It has to happen."

"Whatever you say, Max," he said dismissively.

"Ted, don't tell me it can't be done. People have telling me shit like that my whole life."

"I'll do my best," he said.

I dropped the topic for the moment, but after that I would intermittently remind him, hoping over time it would become a reasonable possibility in his mind.

Sometimes, I resorted to email, once telling him, "I understand there is a low likelihood of this happening, but this is what I have to expect will happen. Even if you find this delusionary, please suffer me gladly. I've faced similarly low odds before in my life and overcame them."

I didn't yet know that Ted did not require any additional motivation. Over time, I would discover just how ferociously Ted fought, and how personally invested he was in my case. Psychologically, it helped me to know that. And in turn, I tried to show him who I was: a good man with a three-year-old daughter, loving parents, family, and friends, and a career in the balance. And so, I would send him brief e-mails with a picture of my daughter or an anecdote about my life. Sometimes it would be a one-liner like, "Please always remember that a day in court for me is not just another day, regardless of how routine it might be to you." Other times, I would ask about his family or something else about his life. It was not disingenuous or conniving; I wanted ours to be more than a business relationship, like we were partners in a journey. Maybe even friends.

Ted continued to work hard on Kirsten. He was charming and warm, and his effervescent personality and sincerity made him eminently likable. I knew this could have an impact on people, and sometimes I would fantasize how his non-confrontational discussions with the AUSA were benefiting me.

"This is a good guy," Ted would say. "You don't want him to stick him with a felony. It won't accomplish anything. He has too much to offer society. All that training and expertise would be wasted."

I believed Kirsten would eventually come to believe it. I just wished *I* could believe it as well, but my level of shame was simply too overpowering.

While my attorney and I were bonding, the scheduled start of the criminal trial was approaching. The government submitted a request to the Court for a delay "because Mr. Kepler has met with federal authorities and is cooperating in continuing investigations with the goal of reducing the severity of the charge(s). This cooperation involves investigations in other districts and therefore requires coordination with other United States Attorneys and law enforcement agencies, which has caused delays."

Although the decision was mostly a judicial formality, it did provide some hope, especially when we heard Kirsten wanted to meet for another proffer session. I hoped the Government was starting to realize I was a minor player, having treated only five patients with low-dose hGH over a one-year period. Perhaps their interest was shifting towards gaining useful information about Lance. Maybe I could get off entirely.

But there was still the issue of the botulinum toxin, and I worried the Government would turn their attention there, particularly since I had treated many more patients with this drug. Then I saw a news article about a doctor who injected himself and three others with illegal botulinum toxin and was sentenced to three years in prison. Although all the patients, except the doctor, experienced whole body paralysis from the injections, the news still shook me up and so I immediately emailed the article to Ted. I couldn't wait for his reply so I called.

"Did you get the article I just emailed?"

"Yes. Why did you send it?"

"It's not a good environment for my case right now. Can we delay?"

"There's nothing to do, Max. There will always be these issues."

But I was a mess, and so I started taking Valium and resorted to sleeping on the couch again with music playing. Once again, it was the only way I could sleep.

The news wasn't all bad, however. Several days later, Ted learned that FDA agent Marissa Long (aka "Jill Monroe") had accepted a job in the private sector. Her departure meant that the investigative point person who had coordinated the investigation leading to my arrest would be gone, leaving the case to a new agent. It was unlikely this new person would welcome handling a case already investigated. This could cause a loss in the Government's momentum, and Ted sensed a golden opportunity for the second proffer session requested by the Government.

That session took place a little more than three months after the arrest. I met Marissa Long's replacement, an intimidating white man with a perpetual scowl, at Ted's office the day before. On the day of the proffer session, he was running a few minutes late and so Kirsten, Ted and I waited at the conference room table for his arrival.

"I hear you're a swimmer," Ted said casually to Kirsten. She blushed.

"Where did you hear that?" she asked.

"Mr. Williams," Ted said, referring to Kirsten's boss, the US Attorney for the Northern District of California.

"He told you that?"

Ted nodded.

"Well, yes, I do love it. I swam in college, and I continue to compete."

"What strokes?"

"All four, but now it's mostly freestyle since I've gotten into distance swimming. Right now, I'm training for a triathlon." Kirsten smiled proudly.

"Serious stuff," Ted said.

"It is, but I've had to cut back because my shoulder's been hurting. So, that's been disappointing." Her voice trailed off.

I sensed an opening. "Does it hurt when you do this?" I asked her.

She watched as I reached behind my back.

"Kinda."

"How about this?" I continued, demonstrating another movement.

Mimicking me, Kirsten cupped her shoulder with her left hand and attempted to make a large circle with her right arm, wincing in pain when the arm got above her head.

"Definitely."

"That's what I thought. Mind if I take a look?"

She looked at Ted, who remained expressionless.

"Sure."

I walked around the table and stood behind her, putting my hands on her shoulder.

"Just relax and let me move your arm. Tell me when it hurts."

I extended her arm to the side, rotated her hand so that the thumb was pointing down, and then slowly raised the arm above her shoulder.

"Now," she said, as her arm reached a position parallel to the floor.

At this point, the DEA agent arrived and stood in the doorway, looking bewildered.

Paying no attention to him, I repeated the motion several times, along with other maneuvers. When I was finished, I guided her arm back to its resting point.

"You have a rotator cuff injury, but I don't think it's torn."

"What can I do about it?"

"Anti-inflammatories like ibuprofen, rest, physical therapy. Sometimes cortisone injections can be helpful. I can give you the names of several rheumatologists in the area."

"I'd appreciate it very much."

I returned to my seat and smiled slightly as I looked at Ted, who simply sat blank-faced. My satisfaction quickly soured when I realized Kirsten had seen my expression. And so had the DEA agent, who began drumming his pen on the table as he stared at me. I wanted to tell them I was simply happy that I could be a doctor again, even if only briefly, but instead I remained silent, aware that Marissa was ready to start the session.

She began by repeating the same instructions given at the previous meeting and then asking me to sign the form again.

"As you know, Marissa has left the FDA for private practice," she said. "I thought we could start by quoting part of her investigative report."

On April 13, 2005, during a conversation with me, Kepler again affirmed that he was a "huge fan of hGH"

267

and that many cosmetic benefits could be gained by injecting hGH, including weight loss. He stated that he was able to obtain wholesale prices for the hGH he provided to his patients because of his background in pharmacology. He stated several times that hGH required a prescription. He stated that his hGH was not from overseas, and he could offer his hGH for less than other sources because of his contacts he had in the pharmaceutical industry. He stated that everyone who had ever used hGH would provide a positive testimony as to its results.

Kepler offered to provide hGH to my friend, even though the friend lived in Baltimore. Kepler stated that "she just needs to fill out the paperwork," and stated that he could Fed-Ex his hGH anywhere. Kepler offered to extend a discount to me, if I could provide new customers.

When she was finished, Kirsten looked at the DEA agent, who placed his pen back into his front pocket and smiled. Any sense of control I felt previously from giving Kirsten medical advice had now vanished as she began her questioning.

"Dr. Kepler, I find it hard to believe that, despite having doctorate and medical degrees, you didn't know there were no off-label uses of hGH."

I hesitated before saying, "I don't know what else to say to convince you, but it's true."

She raised her eyebrows and turned up her palms like she was catching rain. She looked at Ted and shook her head. Ted shrugged, as if to say, "I know."

She spent the remaining time asking detailed questions about botulinum toxin, covering some of the same ground from the previous interview, looking for inconsistencies in my story. She didn't find any, however, since I had been truthful then and was being truthful now. My challenge was keeping my emotions in check.

As the discussion proceeded, I began feeling removed from the illegal behavior being discussed. It was as though I were speaking of another person; it seemed easier and less shameful when I could successfully compartmentalize my actions. Still, I was relieved when the questions finally stopped.

"Thank you for your time, Dr. Kepler," Kirsten said.

I nodded silently, too embarrassed to say something like, "You're welcome." I was also disappointed, having hoped for something more positive from the session than a mere "thank you." I looked meaningfully at Ted, who was casually putting away his laptop. "Do something!" I wanted to yell.

Kirsten was checking her calendar. I stared at her, hoping to discern some hint of her thoughts. Ted stood up, put his bag on his shoulder, and straightened his tie. When Kirsten looked up, he surprised me by saying casually to her, as though discussing the weather, "We would like to move towards a settlement."

Then he gave her a smile.

Kirsten smiled back. "That's not possible right now until there is more progress in the other case."

Ted nodded his head. "What's the expected timeline there?"

"Right now, it's indefinite," she said.

"Okay...I see," Ted replied, as he tapped me on the shoulder to leave.

As I stood up, he looked at Kirsten with another smile and said, "Since this could drag on indefinitely, how about we drop the charges for now? You can always re-file them later."

His easy delivery made his suggestion seem so plausible that it took Kirsten a moment to decipher it. She tilted her head to the side and searched Ted's face. He simply stared back with that same affable smile. The DEA agent had stopped going through his paperwork and looked at Kirstin, waiting for her answer.

Slowly, Kirsten's face broke into a smile and she laughed.

"Now, Ted. I don't know about that," she said playfully.

"Come on," Ted said, keeping it friendly. "Why not? It would take away the time pressure and, as you know, you can always re-file later."

He grinned. The moment had happened so subtly that I found myself not only awed by Ted's skill, but also suddenly hopeful. Kirsten kept staring at Ted, clearly considering his suggestion, but then her eyes dropped and she said in a firm voice, "I'll have to think about it, but I doubt we'd do it. Let's be in touch over the next week or so."

"Sounds good," Ted responded, chipper as usual. "Thank you."

"Of course, Ted," Kirsten said, standing. She then looked at me and as she said, "Take care," I again saw sympathy in her expression and imagined her opinion of me had shifted. Perhaps I had reason to hope.

"You too," I said.

# CHAPTER TWENTY-ONE

In our proffer discussions with the Government, I agreed to travel to Charlotte to meet with the FDA agent investigating Lance. It would prove to be an expensive trip, since Ted would need to come along and I would have to pay his five-hundred-and-fifty-dollar rate from the moment he left his home until he returned nine hours later. In addition, I would have to cover airfare and all expenses, such as meals and cab fares. But I felt I had no choice so I decided to consider it an investment in my future.

We landed in Charlotte around three in the afternoon. A short taxi ride later, we arrived at the Charles R Jonas Federal Building and went to the tenth floor, where a DEA agent with a gun holstered to his waist greeted us in the US Marshals office. I stared at the gun as we followed the man through a series of locked doors to a conference room. The Charlotte AUSA attorney, a middle-aged woman with a stern look, was already there when we arrived. Also present was a Special Agent from the Office of Criminal Investigations (OCI), an agency that assists the FDA in conducting and coordinating criminal investigations involving violations of the Federal Food, Drug, and Cosmetic Act, the Federal Anti-Tampering Act, and other related federal statutes. He also carried a gun.

I grew up hunting in southwestern Ohio. Dad taught us how to use a shotgun, clean it, and be safe with it. But our guns were used for shooting animals. The handguns the agents carried were designed for shooting people. Given this, I found it difficult to feel comfortable around these armed Government folk.

Once introductions were made and everyone was seated, the Special Agent asked me to sign an attestation that all of my answers would be truthful. My hand shook as I signed the paper and slid it back. With that, the session began. He was the first to speak. His beginning flurry of questions established basic information about my initial contact with Lance—how we communicated and the like—creating a lull before the more difficult questions began.

"Has Starling ever mentioned that the US Postal Service and FDA seized several parcels containing hGH?" the Special Agent asked.

"He told me that shipments sent to a friend's house were seized and that the 'Feds' did it," I replied.

"Has Starling ever mentioned that an order of hGH that *he* ordered was seized?"

I remembered the conversation with Lance and later with his attorney regarding the bust.

"No. He said the order was for a friend."

"So, he told you the hGH was for someone else?"

"That's correct."

The agents looked at each other and shook their heads. We all knew Lance had lied.

"Has Starling ever mentioned that Postal Inspectors and/or the FDA executed a search warrant at a house owned by Terry Folsom, located in Charlotte, North Carolina?"

"Lance never talked with me about details of the seizure. He just told me a package had been intercepted at a friend's house. I also spoke with his attorney, who gave me almost no details of the event."

"His attorney called you?" the AUSA asked. "Why?"

"I think he was trying to gather support for Lance."

"Did you supply it?"

"Not really. I just kind of agreed to everything he said."

"How many times did you talk with him?"

"Just once."

The AUSA scribbled some notes. The Special Agent resumed his questions.

"When did you first realize that Starling was involved in hGH?"

"During a business trip we took to Dallas several years ago, but he never shared any specific details. He told me he was selling the drug."

"To whom?"

"He never told me."

"Did he mention any names at all?"

"He said he knew of some professional athletes that used hGH, but he never actually said he was supplying them with the drug."

"So, he never gave you names of pro athletes that he sold hGH or any other drugs, such as anabolic steroids?"

"No.   He never told me specific people to whom he supplied hGH."

The Special Agent nodded to the AUSA, who picked up the questioning.

"Do you know Starling to be married?   If so to whom?"

"He said that he was divorced from Terry Folsom, a veterinarian with whom he shared custody of their daughter."

"He told you he had a daughter?"

"Yes."

The AUSA shared a smile with the Special Agent.

"That's not his daughter," she told me.  "He was never married to Ms. Folsom, and they do not share custody. That's her daughter."

My mind raced back to all the conversations we used to have about our daughters, including the shared sentiment of how privileged and thrilled we felt to be fathers.  It was a point of connection between the two of us and strengthened our friendship.  I couldn't believe he had deceived me about that, and I struggled to maintain my concentration.  But I had no choice, the questions kept coming.

"Did Starling ever ask you to order hGH for him?"

"I did place one order for five-thousand dollars' worth. Since I owed him money for supplies he had purchased for our company, he thought this might be a reasonable way to pay him back."

"What was the date, origin of shipment, method of shipment, shipping destination, method of payment, description of contents of package?"

"I'll have to check my records and get back to you. But I always paid with Western Union and the packages were usually labeled as, 'zinc powder samples, no commercial value,' by our Chinese contact."

"Were there times Starling had his orders of hGH shipped to you?"

"Yes, there were two times in which Lance told me he was out of the country and asked me to receive shipments so that the drug wouldn't spoil. When he returned, I shipped the packages to him."

"Did you or Starling ever use any types of codes when discussing hGH?"

"We did, but only for convenience. We used "G" and "GH", but not any other terminology."

"How did Starling routinely distribute hGH to his clients other than in person? If methods include FedEx or any other type of commercially available shipping methods, what was the account number, and who opened up the account?"

"Lance once told me he had shipped hGH by Fed Ex, but never gave me any additional details."

"How did you acquire the contact information for ordering hGH?"

"Through an unrelated business trip I took to China."

"During your relationship with Starling, what other drugs besides hGH were discussed ordered, purchased, distributed or acquired? Please provide details surrounding each drug."

"I'm not aware of any specific drugs that Lance was distributing."

"Starling never told you he was selling anabolic steroids to athletes?"

"No."

"Did you ever receive shipments of anabolic steroids from China on behalf of Starling?"

"Not that I know of, although there were several shipments of an unlabeled powder that I received, and then sent on to Lance."

"Please give the dates of those shipments."

This had happened only twice and so I had no trouble remembering the information. After I provided the dates, the three questioners talked among themselves for several minutes. When they finished, the Special Agent resumed the questioning.

"Who was your hGH contact in China and how many shipments were made?"

Knowing that they had copied off my hard drive the many Yahoo chats I had had with George, I didn't hesitate to answer, telling them George's full name and informing them that I had ordered hGH eight times from him. "Two of those orders were seized by Customs," I continued. "I have prepared a spreadsheet giving all the details of those eight orders."

I handed over the Excel spreadsheet that Ted had prepared, and the Special Agent looked it over briefly before placing it in a folder.

It was the AUSA's turn. She wanted details of the partnership Lance and I had.

"We didn't purchase things together, split profit or solicit customers together. We were not in an hGH or steroid business together. I never ordered, nor did I ever possess, anabolic steroids, at least that I was aware of. I ordered hGH ten times, as you can see on that spreadsheet, and then I used the drug on five patients, two family members and myself. I prescribed hGH in my Forever Lithe practice."

"Did you ever hear of a website called HGHonline.com?

"I have never heard of this site," I said, before quickly asking, "Was Lance using it to sell hGH?"

The Special Agent interrupted before the AUSA had a chance to answer.

"We can't discuss that," he said.

The AUSA began writing notes, so the Special Agent picked up the questioning.

"How many patients or clients will be able to say they received one of the products from Lance Starling?"

"I have no idea."

"What assets does Lance Starling own?"

"I don't know. I think a boat, a house, some cars and maybe some property in Colombia."

"Are you aware of any business that Lance had in Colombia?"

"No. Did he have one?"

"We can't discuss that."

"Are you aware of Lance being connected to organized crime in any way?"

I looked at the AUSA closely, trying to decipher if this was a joke. But her face was intense as she waited impatiently for my answer. "No," I said slowly, looking at all three of the people across the table. "Should I be scared?"

Their faces were expressionless. I turned to Ted, and he patted me on the back.

"Let's not worry about that right now," the AUSA said, but I had already started doing just that. Panicking might be a better description, as I wondered whether Jessica might be in danger. I was partnered with a man who had ties to organized crime? Had my greed made me that blind? I felt myself starting to lose my composure as the questioning resumed.

"What assets do you own jointly with Lance Starling?" the AUSA continued.

I had checked out.

"Dr. Kepler, are you still with us?"

I cleared my throat and forced myself to settle down. "Sorry, yeah, some laboratory equipment, I guess."

"Nothing else?"

I shook my head. The Special Agent then looked at his two colleagues and saw they had no more questions.

"Thank you, Dr. Kepler, for your time. We'll be in touch if we need anything else."

"What about the organized crime thing?" I asked.

"Dr. Kepler, we cannot discuss specifics of other investigations. The important thing is for you to continue to tell the truth."

The trip home was long, partly because our flight was delayed, but mostly because I kept replaying the details of the interview in my head. From the questions and the body language of the Government people, I felt I had reason to be nervous about my safety and Jessica's, should I ever have to testify against Lance in the courtroom.

I asked Ted about it during dinner in the airport, as we waited for our delayed flight.

"I don't know any more than you, Max," Ted replied. "I wouldn't worry too much about it, though. Lance is not going to prison based on your testimony. You simply don't have that much information."

His words made me feel better, and I relaxed for the rest of the dinner, which Ted paid for. Ted always seemed to know how to settle my nerves. He felt like a father figure, friend and attorney all rolled up into one. And he always seemed empathetic, something I never expected from an attorney.

He was also sensitive to the financial difficulties I was facing, which were substantial. The trip to Charlotte alone cost over six thousand dollars, and I had already paid Ted fifty thousand in other legal fees. Fortunately, my parents and Greg had given me loans after I maxed out my credit cards. As I struggled to pay the minimum amount due on the cards, my credit score plummeted. In addition, my suspension from Cade County was costing me lost salary to the tune of one thousand dollars each working day since the arrest four months earlier.

At one point, I couldn't pay Ted, and he called to discuss the situation.

"Max, we need to talk about money. You are behind now."

"I know, Ted. Can you give me a little time? I have to find another source for funds."

"I completely understand your situation and have been very sensitive to it. I've been careful to minimize my time so as to keep the bills manageable for you. But I do not want to have you owing me money."

"Could I pay you in smaller increments?"

"As of today, you owe us a little over two thousand. I suggest we send you that bill and you pay half of it. Then get the rest here within a month."

Conversations like this were to happen many times, and Ted always worked out a solution for me, even waiving a five-thousand-dollar attorney fee at one point.   This was something I never asked for, and it buoyed my spirits tremendously.

With my financial situation progressively worsening, I needed to find employment, and so I decided to apply for a hospital moonlighting job.  My medical license was still valid, after all.

I started with a place nearby called St. Luke's Hospital, where I had worked several years earlier.  I called a doctor I knew there.

"Great!" he said when I explained my intentions. "We'd love to have you back.  Come by tomorrow and we'll talk about some open shifts you can take."

I met him in the main lobby of the hospital, which was a rundown building located on Cesar Chavez Street in the Mission District of San Francisco, at nine-thirty.  He greeted me with a vigorous handshake.

"Let me show you around, just to remind you of where everything is," he said.

On my tour, I was introduced to multiple staff members as "one of our new docs."  After we were finished, he pulled me into his office.

"When do you want to start?"

"Immediately," I replied.

"Great," he said.  And then holding out a piece of paper, he continued.  "Here are some open shifts over the next month.  Let me know which ones you'd like."

I didn't reach for the paper.  Instead, I said, "I do have a bit of a problem I need to tell you about."

"Okay," he said, with a curious look.

"I'm going through some legal stuff right now. It's confidential but I guess I should tell you."

His smile faded and he put the paper down on his desk.

Hesitating, I continued. "I got into a little trouble with human growth hormone."

"What kind of trouble and how little?"

"Well, I got caught by Customs importing a relatively small amount from China."

He sat contemplating my words. Then he looked down at the resume I had brought with me.

"That doesn't sound like that big of deal," he concluded. "But just in case, you should talk with the Chief of Medicine about it. He's the one that makes the final decision about credentialing issues."

"Alright."

He started shuffling papers on his desk.

"I guess I'll take off now," I said hesitantly. "Thanks for the tour and we'll talk soon."

"Sure thing, Max," he said, without looking up.

He picked up the phone to return a page he'd received.

"The application?" I whispered.

"Sorry," he mouthed. Cradling the phone against his shoulder, he reached into a file cabinet and pulled out a packet of papers. He was answering a question about a patient's high blood pressure when he handed them to me.

I thanked him, but he had already pulled the phone off his shoulder and turned his back to continue the conversation with the nurse. I left the office as quickly as I could and once in the hallway, I considered going home. But I desperately needed a job, so I headed to the hospital library where I completed the application. My stomach dropped when I read one of the questions:" Have you ever been arrested for, or convicted of, a felony?" I reminded myself that the doctor didn't think it would matter and answered the question.

I then dropped the application off with the Chief of Medicine's secretary, who informed me he was gone for the day. Recognizing my name, she assured me he would have it first thing in the morning and that I could expect to hear back quickly. But after a week, there was no word, and so I left several messages with both the Chief and the doctor who showed me around. They never returned my calls, and after a while, I gave up.

After that, I went on a number of interviews at various hospitals in the Bay Area. Each time, the interviewers greeted me with enthusiasm that rapidly waned as soon as I disclosed my arrest history. It didn't matter that I had done excellent work for these hospitals in the past and that my credentials were outstanding. No one was willing to hire me.

Desperate, I turned to Jerry, Alice's husband, a venture capitalist who sat on the board of a large hospitalist corporation in the area. Within an hour of my humbling inquiry, he had set up an interview with their head recruiter. I revised my resume, dressed in a suit and arrived thirty minutes early. After warm introductions, I told the recruiter I was available immediately and willing to work any day, night or weekend shift at any hospital. Then I passed her my resume and watched for the inevitable enthusiasm.

"We can definitely find a spot for you, Dr. Kepler," she said right away. "We think you'll like our hospitalist group. The next step is to get you credentialed so that you can start working."

"That sounds great. In the interest of full disclosure, I just want to tell you I have some legal issues I'm dealing with right now."

"Yes, I heard that from one of our board members, but with your resume, I can't imagine that being much of a problem. You just need to provide details in the application and everything should be fine."

The recruiter sent me off with a handshake, a basket full of smiles, and assurances that, "we'll be in touch in a couple of days." As I left, I took a big sigh of relief. Although I had to ask on bended knee, at least I had a job.

Those few days passed, and then a week, and then two. I left messages for the recruiter. I wanted to ask Alice's husband to intervene, but I realized he had already extended himself enough. Finally, the recruiter called me; her previous friendliness and enthusiasm were long gone.

"Dr. Kepler, we were really impressed with your credentials and I enjoyed meeting you and…blah blah blah blah." I winced as I braced myself for the inevitable. "But there is concern about your legal situation and how that could impact our liability and malpractice insurance," she continued. "I'm afraid that we are unable to offer you a position at this time."

*Fuck you. Fuck all of you.*

"I understand. Thank you," I said politely.

And with that rejection, I had officially run out of options. It was as if I had taken an indelible marker and written "VOID" all over my resume. I was the lame duck doctor, and that reality generated feelings of worthlessness

I never imagined possible. I wandered around in a daze
of despair for two or three days. I couldn't imagine that
a short four months ago I had complained that patient
care was boring and unchallenging.

And then it occurred to me that although no one would
hire me, I could at least volunteer my physician's services
at free clinics. I knew they were desperate for doctors,
and not surprisingly, they jumped at the opportunity to
speak with me. I went on multiple interviews, during
which I revealed the felony charge, and each time I was
summarily rejected.

Around this time, my landlord told me she planned on
moving back into her apartment and gave me one
month's notice. I didn't really mind, as I had never felt
comfortable there after the arrest. However, soon after
starting my search for a new apartment, I discovered
renting would be nearly impossible due to my low credit
score and lack of income. After two weeks of futility, I
started to feel really desperate, particularly since my
daughter stayed with me half of the time.

Then, during a casual conversation, a medical school
classmate informed me his roommates were moving out,
leaving two spare bedrooms. Jeff's house was located in
Redwood City, thirty-five miles south of San Francisco,
which was a fairly long drive away from Alice.
Nonetheless, I had no other options, and so I asked if
Jessica and I could move in. He graciously agreed.

Thankfully, the house was wonderful, complete with a
pool and two hot tubs, and Jessica loved it. Jeffie—my
daughter's name for my roommate--was amazing around
my daughter, and in turn she loved having another person

284

in the house. At the time, Jessica was attending a Jewish preschool (even though we are not Jewish, Alice thought it was the best preschool around), and one day she hid behind the couch when she heard him coming in the front door. Once he entered, she popped her head above the couch and called out, "Shalom, Jeffie!" Jeff almost fell to the floor laughing. In the midst of a very bad time, the house served as our refuge, and I was grateful for Jeffie's generosity and accommodation.

I was also grateful for the continued support I received from my friends and partners. And to my surprise, Alice emerged as one of my strongest advocates. She periodically checked in with me regarding my emotional state, and she gave me slack on issues around which we would have previously quarreled. There were numerous times when she watched Jessica for me, or picked her up when it was my turn, or paid for something that ordinarily would have been my responsibility. Never once did she criticize me. All the while, her life was quite busy with her new husband, her fifty percent custody of Jessica, and a full-time job as a radiologist. She and Jerry even invited me over for dinner several times, invitations that I accepted, even if the evenings proved to be somewhat awkward.

Sometimes, Alice would send me brief messages meant to be helpful in my emotional and spiritual journey through the criminal process. I found particularly illuminating a quote she gave me from Carl Jung, the famous analytical psychiatrist.

"The shadow is a moral problem that challenges the whole ego-personality, for no one can become conscious of the shadow without considerable moral effort. To become conscious of it involves recognizing the dark aspects of the personality as present and real. This act is the essential condition for any kind of self-knowledge."

I spent many sessions with my psychiatrist trying to understand this shadow, to determine whether it represented some fundamental character flaw in me. As I went through this process, my dwindling self-esteem sometimes deteriorated into self-revulsion. Instead of being an asset to society, I had become a liability. American taxpayer money was being used to investigate and prosecute me. I also had difficulty around my violation of patient trust, which I had perverted and manipulated for self-gain. So overwhelming were these feelings, I sometimes wished I would be sent to prison. Not because I felt sorry for myself or wanted martyrdom. Instead, I felt that by serving time, I might be able to achieve some karmic recompense for my sins, and that in turn might take away the guilt and bring peace.

The Government was still pondering Ted's suggestion a month after his dramatic attempt at a home run in the federal building. Trying to capitalize on a possible opportunity, I sent Ted an email after speaking to the hospital CEO.

A few thoughts. Can you ask them again to drop the charges? I fully understand that they will charge me later but in the meantime, I could return to work, something I confirmed with our CEO. I'm asking this because in addition to my financial hardship, my partners are requesting a more definitive timeline. My absence has increased their workload.

If this strategy does not work, would a letter addressed to the US attorney from the partnership describing the current hardship at the hospital and, thus, the need for a clearer timetable for appropriate planning be helpful? For example, if Kirsten says that it will take another 6 months before this is resolved, the partnership could try to find a temporary physician. This is hard to do and might require hiring a permanent person, which would mean I would lose my job. Call when you have the chance.

Ted presented the plan to Kirsten, who said she would take it under consideration. Another two weeks passed by without any word. I called Ted.

"Should we interpret the silence as a decision not to proceed with dropping charges?"

"They're just chewing on it. I will follow up tomorrow when I talk to her about your case and another."

After making us wait a total of six weeks, the Government finally refused our suggestion. Although the chances had been slim, I had nonetheless pinned my hopes on the possibility of getting off and so was of course disappointed with the outcome. My feelings were tempered, however, by the Government's confirmation they were interested in negotiating a plea bargain. This could mean a reduction of the charge to a misdemeanor.

Still, I wanted more, so I called Ted.

"Don't get annoyed with me, but please remember that I want to have the charge dropped."

"Hello to you, too, Max," he responded. "Now come down out of the clouds and join the rest of us earthlings."

By now, I had been out of work for five months. For the first time in my life and at the age of forty, I began checking the classifieds. I came across an ad for Mobile Health Exam, a company that provided medical examinations for clients applying for life insurance. I called the contact number and arranged for a phone interview the following day.

A registered nurse named Sam answered the phone and said he was the physician coordinator. After several screening questions, he asked if I could come in for an interview. I could barely sleep the night before. The interview took place in an ugly warehouse district of San Francisco, in a nondescript building that shook with each dump truck that rumbled past on its way to and from the rock quarry located nearby.

Sam, an exceptionally nice person who looked and sounded two cigarettes away from metastatic lung cancer, interviewed me for fewer than twenty minutes. After making sure I could administer an ECG and draw blood and that I had a valid medical license, he spent most of the time providing information about the company. Afterwards, he offered me the job, which I immediately accepted. Apparently, it was a job even someone with my sordid past could have.

I quickly filled out a one-page job application—which did not include any questions about criminal history, thus absolving me of responsibility of providing the information—before going on my way. Later, I read over the ten-page manual given to me that described the job responsibilities. These included conducting a medical history, performing a physical examination, collecting blood and urine samples and performing an EKG. I would conduct the evaluations wherever the client desired, which was normally at their workplace or home.

Each evaluation took about forty-five minutes, not including driving and parking time, and paid sixty dollars, which worked out to about forty-five dollars per hour. The load was variable; sometimes I would see no clients in a day and other days I would see four or five. In the first four weeks of work, I made eighteen hundred dollars, which was not enough to pay my rent, let alone my legal expenses.

It was a job that a medical student would find unappealing. It did not require any real decision-making, such as rendering a diagnosis or devising a treatment plan, but rather was a simple information-gathering job. In addition, parking in the city was difficult, and I had to lug equipment back and forth. Some clients, upon hearing I was a doctor, voiced surprise that I was doing such a menial job.

Nonetheless, it was work, and I was grateful for the opportunity, right up to the moment I injured myself carrying the heavy ECG machine up a long set of stairs, forcing me to quit. A subsequent MRI confirmed the presence of a herniated disk in my neck, and it would take six weeks of rest, high doses of ibuprofen and an epidural steroid injection before the shooting pains in my arm subsided. I never applied for disability; I felt I didn't deserve it.

After I recovered from my neck injury, a friend told me of the opening of a high-end day spa in downtown San

Mateo. She suggested I look into whether they were interested in having Botox and Resytlane injections done there. Although I had no interest in doing cosmetic procedures anymore, I had run out of options for making money, so I called Ted.

"You want to do what?" he nearly shouted.

"I know," I answered sheepishly.

"I assume it's not from China."

"Of course not. I'm a little desperate, Ted."

"Okay, Max. Let me talk to Kirsten about it."

Surprisingly, the Government approved my request, stating they could not prevent me from doing the procedures since I still had a valid medical license. The only stipulation was that I obey the law. I immediately filed the necessary paperwork with the Medical Board and obtained a business license.

Several weeks later, I attended an introductory meeting held by the owner, whom I had met previously. She was an attractive, twenty-five-year-old woman from a blue-collar background who graduated from a local community college and then went on to get a cosmetology degree. Upon graduation, her father, a plumber who started his own business, decided to buy a spa for his daughter. Newly married to a janitor and without a stitch of business experience, she arrived for the meeting in designer clothing, high heels, and a handful of papers titled "Rules and Regulations." Present at the meeting were a pedicurist, three hair stylists, the receptionist, a masseuse, and I.

After introductory comments, the young owner informed us that all employees would be responsible for cleaning duties, which would rotate weekly. She then passed around the chore sign-up sheet. By the time it got to me, "Sweep Floors" was still available, and so I pounced on it. Then, for the next week, I fulfilled my obligation at the end of each business day. The following week, I was assigned bathroom duty, and after one day of it, I informed the owner I was retiring from cleaning duties, effective immediately. Regardless of what I had done in the past, I still had more to offer than cleaning toilets. She sighed, rolled her eyes, and walked away, her two hundred dollar heels click-clacking against the beautifully-refinished hardwood floors, but she didn't fire me.

Over the next six weeks, five of my ex-patients from the Forever Lithe offices came to see me. They were puzzled by my higher prices, and so I felt obligated to tell every one of them that I had previously used Chinese botulinum toxin on them. I did not, however, tell them that I had been charged with a crime for illegally importing the drug. I couldn't face their possible disappointment and anger, and, anyway, I was now using a legitimate drug. The only disappointment they experienced was the realization that American Botox was not as effective, despite being far more expensive.

Although the location was good, the spa plush, and the patients interesting, the volume was never adequate. I was making about five hundred dollars a week, which was not nearly enough. By now, six months had passed since the arrest and my financial situation had become dire. I needed to find another solution, and I realized it would have to involve something other than doctoring.

After a fair amount of deliberation, I decided to search for a job that utilized my doctorate degree in Pharmacology, eventually deciding on biotech consulting. I already had some experience in this area, as five years previously, my brother-in-law, Jarrett, had hired me to do some work as a member of the scientific advisory board for his hedge fund, and I had enjoyed the work. I figured that if I learned more about both biotechnology and finance, maybe I could do it full-time. Jarrett, who still kept in touch with me and intermittently checked in to see how I was doing, told me he would put me in touch with his contacts in the business world once I was more prepared.

I started by reading a variety of general finance and investing books--*The Intelligent Investor, Security Analysis, Common Stocks and Uncommon Profits, The Interpretation of Financial Statements*. Then I read books that dealt specifically with investing in biotechnology, including *The Biotech Investor's Bible* and *Biotechnology Valuation*. I also spent a lot of time on Yahoo Finance message boards getting an idea of how investors think about biotechnology. Furthermore, I listened to podcasts on the subject and watched financial shows on television. I devoted six hours each day to training for a new career, not only because I needed the money, but because I was beginning to face the fact that I could lose my medical license.

Once I developed some level of comfort in the biotech field, I decided to formally analyze a selected drug that was in the middle of clinical development. I pored over financial reports, studied the scientific data extensively, and talked with scientists and physicians affiliated with the company. I spent a week writing the report, and then emailed it to the CEO of a boutique investment bank in San Francisco whom Jarrett had introduced me to.

Impressed by the analysis and my credentials, and no doubt encouraged by Jarrett's endorsement, he invited me for an interview. The bank was located in a tall office building in downtown San Francisco. I checked in with the receptionist and waited for several minutes before an attractive woman, who identified herself as the CEO's assistant, escorted me to a corner office. On the way, I passed through a large room where rows of young people in business attire sat studying monitors, some simultaneously carrying on excited phone conversations. Compared to the relatively subdued environment of a hospital, the place was alive with energy.

I met with the CEO and another high-level executive for over an hour. Soon, they brought other members of the firm to meet me, including the head of the banking division, the head trader and the head of equities research. All of them were much more assertive and socially confident than most doctors I knew. The conversation continued for another two hours, and I was exhausted by the time I left. No one seemed concerned about my legal difficulties, even though I told the CEO of the matter, and five days later, they invited me for another round of interviews.

On my second visit, they pushed harder, asking specific questions about various biotech companies and drugs in development. Some asked purely financial questions, which was a challenge, given my limited background. I was certainly glad I had studied for the prior two months. Others wanted to know in detail how I arrived at certain scientific conclusions. Later, I was invited to a third interview.

This time, I was told to prepare a portfolio of eight biotech companies that I could discuss in detail. I worked furiously to generate a list, and then I spent long hours studying each of the companies and their drugs in development. When I arrived for the interview, I was taken into a conference room that contained numerous large flat-screen TV's and told I would be having a videoconference with the firm's lead trader, who was based in New York.

The interview went so well that the head of equities research sent me an email the next day telling me that a job offer was forthcoming, he just needed to get approval from a few more people. It was a sell-side analyst position, which meant that I would have to convince clients to purchase certain stocks based on my evaluation of their companies' drugs. I would be a salesman, a highly educated and informed one, but a salesman nonetheless. As such, I would have to offer a biased opinion. Under those circumstances, I couldn't imagine I could be entirely honest. Instead, I would be dealing with shades of truth. I realized I couldn't do that anymore; that Max Kepler had died.

There were other aspects of the job that bothered me as well. The clear objective in all my dealings would be profit; it was the driver of everything. Being a doctor, I was used to a different endpoint: making patients better. Money came as an afterthought. But I desperately needed a job, and I turned to Ted for advice.

"It's nice to know you have options," he answered. "You must be so relieved."

"It's kind of tough to make a decision in the midst of everything that is going on. Realistically, how long do you think it will be before I actually can return to work as a doctor?"

"I would hope within the next month or two."

"It's already been seven months since the arrest. I'd hate to take the job and then leave weeks later."

And so, I never accepted the offer. After what I had been through, it just didn't seem possible. I could never compromise again, and accepting the job felt like I'd be sacrificing my principals for self-gain once again. I called the head of equities research to inform him of my decision. He seemed slightly annoyed but otherwise let me off the hook pretty easily. I was relieved that Ted, upon learning of my decision, said that he agreed with my reasoning.

"Our goal is to get you back where you're needed, anyway," he said.

# CHAPTER TWENTY-TWO

Around the time I turned down the offer from the investment bank, things seemed to have stalled in my legal case. I called Ted.

"If they aren't ready to decide, can you try again to see if they will drop the charges so that I can return to work?"

"We tried that before."

"How about we give it another bid. They can always charge me later, right?"

"Right," Ted responded.

"Doesn't sound like you want to try it."

"It's not going to work, Max."

Afterwards, I gave Sang a call at Cade, looking for help. He was walking to a meeting when he answered.

"Any update on your legal issues?" he asked.

"They're still working on it but we're hopeful that we'll reach a plea bargain soon with a reduction of the charge to a misdemeanor."

"Is there anything I can do?"

"Would you be willing to speak with the assistant US Attorney on the case? That might expedite things."

"I would be delighted to. I am now the Chief Operating Officer, so maybe that will bring some weight to the issue."

Kirsten, however, not only refused to take Sang's calls, she phoned Ted and told him to stop Sang from calling anymore.

"I have all the information I need," she said.

A week later, we received word that Kirsten had been reassigned to another state. This was a potential disaster, as we had worked hard to develop a rapport with her. We could not afford to leave the case unresolved for the next AUSA, who might not be as reasonable. Ted scrambled to arrange one last meeting with Kirsten on Mary 31, 2006, two days before she was to leave. He decided he would present her with suggestions for several different misdemeanor charges that she might find acceptable as part of a plea agreement. That night, he pored through Title 18 of the United States Criminal Code looking for possibilities. While he did this, I sent him an email.

Dear Ted,

Regardless of the outcome tomorrow, thank you for everything you have done and will do for me. There are many people close to me who feel the same way. I'll expect to give Mom some good news tomorrow. If not, I will still pick up my daughter at the usual time. She'll be just as happy to see me, and I her.

Thank you for everything you've done.

Max

For the first time in a while, I fell asleep easily. I awoke early, however, and lay in bed pondering possible outcomes for the day, until the anxiety became too much. I got dressed and went to the gym. Ted called as I was riding the stationary bike.

"Just a second, Ted," I said as I hopped off and moved quickly to a nearby empty stairwell. Still breathless, I asked "What happened?"

"Sorry it took so long to get back to you, but the meeting ran longer than expected. I don't have much time to talk because I have to be in court for another case in five minutes."

"What happened, Ted?" I asked impatiently.

"Good news. We've agreed in principle to a plea bargain involving a misdemeanor violation of 21 U.S.C. Section 331(a), the introduction or delivery for introduction into interstate commerce of any food, drug, device, or cosmetic that is adulterated or misbranded."

"What's that?"

"Just something that I found in my research last night. The Government agreed it would be a reasonable charge to apply to your case."

"No felony?" I asked excitedly.

"None. I expect the misdemeanor will be related to botulinum toxin, instead of hGH, since your use of the former was much greater."

I exhaled deeply and wiped my sweaty face with my T-shirt. I couldn't believe after all the legal maneuvering, I was going to be hit with nothing other than a misdemeanor. Wasn't that the same conviction you receive for a traffic violation?

"So, what's that mean for sentencing?" I asked.

"I am negotiating for a probationary sentence with no prison. You'll have to do community service, probably in the medical field. We'll see about that part. But no prison."

I closed my eyes and breathed deeply. "That's it?"

"Looks like it. The supervisors in the office are reviewing the agreement. I will forward a copy as soon as I get my hands on it for your comments."

"When will it be over?"

"We expect to enter the plea in court on July 13th, at which time the plea agreement will become public. You will then need to report the offense to the Medical Board of California."

I felt so overwhelmed with gratitude towards Ted that I was unable to speak.

"You okay?" he asked.

"I think so. Thanks so much, Ted." I hung up the phone and sank to the floor, staying there until I heard someone enter the stairwell from above. I quickly stood up, put my cell phone into my pocket and left the gym. When I got home, I called Mom with the news.

"You're kidding," she said.

"No, really. Ted did it."

"I can't believe it."

"That's such great news. You must be so relieved."

"You can't even imagine," I said excitedly, before adding, "You must be relieved, too." She didn't respond.

We later learned the Government had chosen hGH instead of botulinum toxin for the charge. They never explained their rationale, but it undoubtedly was related to the political climate regarding performance enhancement drugs.

For purposes of sentencing, the Government utilized The Federal Sentencing Guidelines, a standardized punishment system. My conviction of a Class A misdemeanor normally carried an offense level of six, but because of my cooperation, the Government reduced it to four, a level that called for a sentencing range of zero to six months in prison. Fortunately, the Government decided not to ask for prison time and instead recommended five hundred hours of volunteer work as a physician.

The recommended sentence, however, was not binding on the Court. That meant sentencing would be the purview of the judge.

Ted didn't like that. "You never know what a judge might do," he commented, before submitting a request for a binding agreement. But the AUSA denied it; the judge would ultimately decide my fate.

As part of the plea agreement, I would be required to write letters to each clinic patient explaining that hGH and botulinum toxin were obtained illegally from China and that hGH specifically was not FDA-approved for the intended purpose. This caused me great consternation since, unlike the situation at the spa where I was selective with the information I shared, there would now be full disclosure. Ted tried to get the AUSA to drop this requirement, but the Government refused.

The plea agreement also dictated that I was to pay restitution to all patients. That meant I would have to fully refund every patient whom I had treated with the drugs. Depending on the number of patients I could contact, this requirement could prove to be costly. Regardless, we made no attempt to argue with the Government on this point, as we knew there was no chance for compromise.

Once the plea agreement was finalized, I called our hospital CEO with the news.

"Great news," she said. "Now the next step is to meet with the Board of Supervisors regarding your possible return."

"Why?" I asked.

"They would need to grant their approval."

I was confused. They didn't need the Board's approval to suspend my contract. I couldn't figure out why they needed it to reinstate it. I had always assumed I would be welcomed back as soon as the legal process concluded.

"The Board is scheduled to meet next week," Nancy informed me.

"Do you see there being any problem?"

"Since our last correspondence, members of the Board have voiced concern about your case. They might need some convincing in order for you to return."

"I had no idea. Just let me know the time of the meeting and I'll be there."

"You'll not be permitted to attend. Sang will appeal on your behalf. I suggest you contact him to arrange a time to meet."

"I'll do it right away."

"I want you to know that I still believe in you, Max."

Prior to the formal signing of the plea agreement, Kirsten had moved on to her new position out of state. The last details had been negotiated after she was gone. She would fly back for the formal submission of the agreement to the court. Ted, however, would not be there, as he had scheduled a family vacation for that time. Instead, one of his partners would represent me.

On the court date, I arrived early and sat waiting for my substitute attorney. Kirsten was already there and in a friendly mood.

"Have you gone back to work yet?" she asked me.

"No. The County Board of Supervisors has to approve my return."

"At least your conviction is only a misdemeanor. I have never seen a felony reduced to a misdemeanor while I've been here."

The court clerk nodded behind her.

"Really?" I asked.

"Yes. This is an exceptional circumstance."

I had no idea. I had been disappointed the charges weren't dropped entirely, but now I was being told how lucky I was. I wished Ted were there so I could hug him.

Still, I had never accepted the possibility of a felony conviction. Somehow, I knew it wouldn't happen. And even though the charge had been reduced to a misdemeanor, I did not feel satisfied or victorious. Instead, I still felt sadness and regret and humiliation. I was about to plead guilty to a crime, a conviction that would stick with me for the rest of my life. In codified, formal fashion, I would be acknowledging my immorality.

By now, my replacement attorney had arrived. Young, bright and enthusiastic, she smiled when she introduced herself. Five minutes later, the judge came into the courtroom and I took my now familiar place in the front. The clerk announced the case, and then within a few short minutes I had pleaded guilty and a date had been set for sentencing: October 12, the day I was arrested.

"What a perfect bookend to a nightmare," I thought to myself.

Left unfinished was the matter of my employment at Cade County. To prepare for presenting my case to the County Board of Supervisors, Sang called me in for a meeting.

"Have a seat, Max," he said as I walked into his office. He was grim-faced.

My smile faded as I slouched into a chair. I wondered what had happened to the hug or handshake he usually gave me.

"There is mounting pressure from the Board to prevent your return. It's coming mostly from Jerry Hill, the Board President."

I knew without Mr. Hill's approval, there was no way I was coming back.

"Did they say why?"

"Do you really have to ask that? Maybe it has something to do with the fact you had illegal drugs from China shipped to the Medical Center."

"Oh yeah, that."

He shook his head and frowned.

"Are you having a change of heart, Sang?"

"Of course not. I still support you. I think you're a fine man and an excellent doctor."

I nodded my head in appreciation.

"But you have to understand, by supporting you and arguing for your return, my own reputation is at stake."

I knew Sang aspired to be CEO of the hospital. That dream was gone if I ended up making another mistake.

"I guarantee I won't let you down," I said.

"I know you won't, Max," he reassured me.

I was relieved to finally see the familiar empathy on his face. He then pivoted towards me and continued.

"Now, here's what we need to do. I want you to prepare a document that briefly summarizes your illegal behavior, the punishment for that behavior and the lessons you've learned. Think of things that will sway the Board."

"I'll have it for you tomorrow."

"I've prepared a document of my own that outlines the stipulations and conditions for your return. I want you to review these now and then sign the document. Violation of any condition in this document would result in immediate termination."

I flipped through the pages without reading them and then signed my name. I was willing to return under any circumstances.

One week later, Sang met with the Board of Supervisors. To distract myself, I took Jessica to the San Mateo County Fair. We arrived at eleven, two hours before the scheduled start of the meeting. Jessica, now four and a half, pulled me towards the kiddie rides and chose the miniature roller coaster. We rode it over and over again for the next forty-five minutes, and I spent most of that time worrying. Here, at the last moment, my hope for a triumphant return could be dashed.

After the roller coaster, we spent another hour rotating from the Tilt-A-Whirl to the Berry-Go-Round to the Tumble Bug. When Jessica started to get hungry, we went looking for hamburgers. As we did, we noticed the pig races were starting. Jessica started hopping up and down with excitement.

"Daddy, can we go, please?"

We quickly found seats and then watched in fits of laughter as the tiny pigs tore around the dirt track, their rapidly pumping legs throwing up dirt behind them. At the end of each race, the pigs were given a bucket of slop, which they devoured. Pigs running in circles for a few bites of food mesmerized me, and as I watched one race after another, I briefly forgot the group of people gathered at that moment to discuss my job.

Within twenty minutes, the races were over, and as we made our way out of the stands, Jessica noticed workers had set up a picture booth. We got into line and waited. When it was Jessica's turn, she sat down on a bale of hay and was handed a pig. Just then, Sang called. The commotion made hearing him difficult.

The pig was fidgeting in Jessica's lap, delaying the picture. Jessica looked up, shrugged her shoulders and smiled. I waved at her as Sang spoke.

"The meeting is over. The Board decided to let you come back. Congratulations."

It seemed like someone pulled the relief valve on ten months of pressure, and suddenly I felt pleasantly exhausted.

"I don't know what to say."

Jessica was finished. She didn't want to let go of the pig, so one of the workers gently took it from her. She stood there petting its head.

"The meeting started off poorly. Before I even had a chance to speak, Jerry Hill told me there was no way you could return to the hospital."

I wedged the phone between my shoulder and ear, took out money, and paid the attendant.

"But then I went through your case slowly over the next thirty minutes, emphasizing your value to the medical center."

"I can't believe you did that for me."

Jessica ran to me and took my hand. I pulled her towards an open, grassy area that looked less noisy.

"You're squeezing my hand too hard," she said.

"Sorry," I mouthed to her and relaxed my grip.

"By the time it went to a vote, it was unanimous for reinstating your contract, and that included Jerry Hill."

"How can I ever thank you enough?"

"Just be a great doctor. That's all I ask."

"I'll make you proud, Sang."

"I know you will, Max. See you on Monday."

I picked Jessica up and gave her a big hug. "You're my girl," I cooed.

"I love you, daddy. Can we go on the roller coaster again?"

"Only if we ride the Teacups after that."

That following Sunday night, I laid out my favorite dress shirt and slacks for work the next day. I was so excited that it was difficult to sleep. I woke up two hours early and lay in bed, anxious that I might have lost some of my doctor skills over the ten months away from medicine. Brushing my concern aside, I got ready and left early. When I arrived at the hospital, I entered through the main entrance, since my security badge had been taken by Nancy ten months previously. I went to my office and found it mostly as I had left it, except for some new pens on the desk and several scribbled notes in someone else's handwriting. I pulled open the file cabinet and could see things were missing. I reflected on the story our secretary told me of the day the feds came and combed my office for several hours. The thought made me want to clean up, and so I spent a few minutes doing that, before sitting down for a while.

My doctor's coat was still hanging on the hook by the door. I reached into the pocket, pulling out a billing sheet from October 10, 2005, two days before the raid. Never could I have imagined that as I rounded on patients on that day that several agencies of the Federal Government were making last-minute preparations to arrest me. I reached into the other pocket and pulled out my black stethoscope, the one given to me by a world-famous cardiologist named Kanu Chatterjee. I had received it during residency, after my own stethoscope was stolen in the middle of a Code Blue, as I tried to save a patient's life. Upon hearing about the theft at morning rounds the next day, Dr. Chatterjee, who was also the attending physician for the rotation, pulled his own stethoscope off his neck and handed it to me.

I tried the coat on and found it too big. I had lost nearly twenty pounds since I last wore it. As I looked at my name and degrees stitched just above the right pocket, the familiar feelings of shame started to creep back in. "I am not worthy of this," I thought to myself, before pushing the thought away. It was almost eight o'clock and time for work. I walked down the hallway to the conference room for the usual daily meeting with my partners. Soon people began trickling in, and there were hugs, handshakes, smiles, and encouraging words. Although the previous ten months had tested their patience and loyalty, they had stuck with me to the end, and without their help, things might have turned out very differently. I hoped I could somehow repay them for their remarkable kindness.

As I walked to the wards, I felt tentative and kept my eyes down. I wondered how people would receive me, but soon I was being stopped by various employees, all of whom greeted me warmly. By the time I reached the wards, I was beaming. The hospital looked shiny new and the colors, sounds and smells seemed so alive. It reminded me of the first time I entered a hospital as a medical student, brimming with excitement.

I walked into the nursing station, and the employees there also welcomed me back. I felt a little rusty as I flipped through a few patient charts. Medicine is like a language that way; if you don't practice, you'll lose it. Once I began rounding on patients, however, I felt like I was back where I belonged, caring for the drug addicts and alcoholics and self-abusers of a county hospital. And I soon discovered that I needed the patients as much as they needed me. They were my respite from the chaos in my life. When I cared for them, all my worries and concerns about the outside world dissolved, and I remembered why I loved medicine the first time I was exposed to it.

# CHAPTER TWENTY-THREE

My excitement with being back at work was tempered by the realization that I still needed to notify the Medical Board of California of my conviction. I left two voice messages and sent one email to my attorney, Gordon, without receiving a response. Finally, I asked Ted to intervene, and with his prompting, Gordon sent the required letter to Sacramento, three weeks after I had pleaded guilty in court.

One week later, Gordon received notification from the Board acknowledging receipt of our letter. It had turned into a waiting game. Once the Board opened its investigation, I would start the fight all over again, this time for my livelihood. In some ways, this fight felt more important than the one for my liberty had.

Meanwhile, the Government prepared the letter that I would have to send to all the patients I injected with botulinum toxin or hGH, but before I even had a chance to send them out, I started getting angry messages from patients. Unbeknown to me, the Government had already sent out their own notifications, which included the opening line, "You were a victim of a crime committed by Dr. Max Kepler." Indignant, I called Ted.

"Why is the Government contacting patients?

"They have the right to notify all victims. Remember, Kirsten has left the office. There's a new prosecutor on the case and she's pretty tough."

The first patient response came within days and was among the harshest I received.

Dr. Kepler,

I received your letter today, about the non-approved FDA drugs, you used in my body. I feel as if I were a "guinea pig", as you experimented with my body. I came to you for help, and as a physician, I thought you could help. Now, in hindsight, you did not.

Several weeks back, I received two mailings from the US Court, regarding your upcoming court date, for peddling false medications, to innocent patients. I was not planning to attend, but, after your letter, I might.

Dr. Kepler, do you think that the $400 you are willing to pay me is enough for the pain and uncertainty that these drugs might do to me, my health, my body, and my total well-being?

I called him right away. In addition to his anger about the deception, he was worried about potential adverse effects on his health. I mostly listened to him rant, but I also tried to reassure him that it was very unlikely he would suffer any harm. I told him I was desperately sorry and wished I could do more for him.

310

He ended up hanging up on me, and I never heard from him again.

Soon, other angry patients responded. One of the most cutting messages was handwritten and sent by a sweet, older woman.

I was appalled at your mail.
You should be ashamed of yourself.

There were other patients that were mostly worried about potential harm.

I have been experiencing some weird symptoms that I have gone to my regular doctor for. We ran all kinds of tests and have found nothing so far. I wonder if it could be a side effect. I have been having odd things, like unexplained rashes, headaches, etc. Is there any way to determine what or how was in the injections? It has me more than a little concerned.

This letter bothered me for legal reasons, and after forwarding it to Ted, I called him.

"This is one of the reasons I didn't want to send the letters. It puts me at risk."

"Max, the letter's not what put you at risk."

He was right, of course, and I was ashamed that I had to be reminded of it. Still, I wasn't sure how I was supposed to respond to the patients.

"You figure it out," Ted said, before hanging up.

I never complained again to anyone, including myself, about the messages I got from patients.

There were some patients who rallied to my defense:

311

It is the bloody pharmaceutical lobby that has a stranglehold on our corrupt politicians that is to be blamed for faulting you.

Wishing you the best.

How bittersweet.

I'm thrilled to receive the compensation for the Botox. I think you are a good person and am saddened that you have to go through this. My prayers are with you.

I don't want a refund, as I was always happy with your work and you also gave me great deals for telling all of my friends to come and get injections from you, as well. I hope that you continue to practice medicine and not let one mistake deter you from doing what you like to do. The important thing is to learn from our mistakes, right? I hope all is well with you and I look forward to hearing from you when you decide to start doing Botox injections again.

Thank you for your letter. I had no negative side effects. I don't remember what I paid you but would be happy to receive $300. Let me know if you are doing any Botox work over here with the real stuff.

Altogether, I paid a total of thirty-one patients $14,266.65 in restitution. I had treated at least twice that number, but I didn't have contact information for many of them. So, in a way, I got off easy, something the Government was not happy about, as both the DEA agent and AUSA repeatedly reminded Ted during negotiations for the plea agreement, which made me nervous in advance of sentencing.

Meanwhile, I was working an extra twenty hours each week in overnight and weekend shifts at the hospital to try to pay down my six-figure legal fees. At that rate, I figured it would take me five years to break even. I didn't mind the extra work; it felt like recompense for my sins.

Ted continued to check in with me weekly.

"How are you doing, Max?" he asked one day

"Much better now that I'm a productive member of society again," I said.

"I assume people have been supportive there."

"Ted, people have been so nice. One of my partners even loaned me twelve thousand dollars."

"What?

"He just came up to me one day and said, 'I know you're having a lot of financial problems. I'll be happy to loan you money, interest-free. You can pay me back over the next year.'"

"That says a lot about you as a person, Max."

"I don't know about that, but I felt so humbled by his offer."

"People will forgive you, Max. You need to work on forgiving yourself."

"I'm trying. It's better, but sometimes there will be something to remind me of what I've done and then I go into this emotional spin. I hate those feelings."

"Just try to focus on being a good doctor for your patients and a good dad for your daughter."

"You're right, but I'm dreading the Medical Board. It's been two months since I notified them of the plea agreement, and they still have not contacted me.

"Is that unusual?" Ted asked.

"Gordon said it was, but he also said the Board is very busy. I guess they'll get to it eventually."

"So you just wait?"

"Sounds like it, but I'm getting impatient to get the process going so I can have all of this over with and move on with my life."

"A lull right now is probably good since we still need to return to court for formal sentencing."

Somehow, I kept forgetting about sentencing, probably because the case felt over. The plea agreement effectively served as the end.

In advance of that hearing, the Probation Department would write a "Pre-Sentence Report" (PSR) to help the judge determine the proper punishment. Scheduled to be written by a U.S. Probation Officer named Janet Earles, the report would provide a summary of the case and make recommendations to the judge regarding sentencing, so it carried a lot of weight. I had hoped that Richard, the friendly probation officer who visited me regularly, would write the report, but apparently only a special division of Probation, which included Ms. Earles, was trained for such a thing.

Ms. Earles, a middle-aged woman with a face snarled into a perpetual look of dissatisfaction superimposed onto general annoyance, ushered me into her office without standing or shaking my hand. She went through my background in detail, down to inquiring about a failed relationship from ten years prior. The meeting lasted several hours, and I did my best to give a good impression.

On my way out, she reminded me that sentencing was scheduled for October 12, 2007. One week before that date, Ted called me.

"Janet Earles left a voicemail this morning that she will not have a report ready in time and needs an extension."

"That sucks. I want to get this over with."

"I know, but there is nothing we can do about it."

"So, when will sentencing be?"

"The problem is the judge, who does not normally sit down here in San Francisco. Turns out he won't be back 'til after Christmas."

"That's another four months."

"And I told them it's too long, so the judge suggested we do it on the phone. We would congregate – you, me, Ms. Earles and the prosecutor – in the courtroom, and the judge would be on the phone."

"It would be nice to be able to look in the eyes of the man who is sentencing me."

"Don't worry, it will be fine that way. It's scheduled for November 13th or 20th – at 10 a.m. We're waiting to hear from Ms. Earles."

But when Ms. Earles contacted us again, she reported the court date had been delayed again until January 5, 2007, which would be six months after I had plead guilty. The lack of closure was starting to drive me crazy. The only good news about the delay was that the judge would at least be in the courtroom that day.

While we waited for the sentencing date, Robert Gotling, an analyst with the Central Complaint Unit of the Medical Board of California, called Gordon requesting an update on my legal case. Gordon informed him sentencing was scheduled for January and that the expected punishment was community service and restitution to patients. Mr. Gotling thanked him for the information and then ended the conversation, without any hint regarding the Board's intentions.

A month passed without a word and so Gordon called Mr. Gotling on December 11, 2006.

"Remind me again of the criminal sentencing," Mr. Gotling said.

"Five hundred hours' community service and about fourteen thousand dollars' restitution payment to patients."

"That sounds like enough punishment for us," he said. "I think we can close the case."

"Is that so?" Gordon asked.

"We'll close the file. Just send me a copy of the plea agreement."

Gordon, shocked by the news, immediately memorialized the conversation in a letter which he sent to Mr. Gotling that day.

Inexplicably, the Medical Board granted mercy. But it seemed too easy, and I again felt guilty and, surprisingly, maybe even a little disappointed. At least by going through an investigation, I might have had some psychological exculpation.

Two days later, Ms. Earles finally completed the PSR. When I reviewed the report, I saw that it was a potential disaster because of the mention of mesotherapy and victim injury. It stated that I had not registered my mesotherapy cocktail with the FDA, nor had I obtained a new drug application or an investigational new drug application. As such, I was injecting an unapproved new drug into patients.

Ted's response, with my input, was firm:

The paragraph about mesotherapy should be deleted in its entirety because it is irrelevant, misleading and prejudicial. Three of the drugs that Dr. Kepler used in the mesotherapy treatment were FDA approved for other purposes and therefore, unlike hGH (which is expressly prohibited except for specified purposes) appropriate for doctors to prescribe for off-label purposes. Lecithin was the only drug in the treatment that was not FDA approved. Dr. Kepler wrote to the FDA inquiring whether it could be prescribed off-label. The important point is that by the time of Dr. Kepler's arrest, the government was not asserting that his mesotherapy treatments were unlawful.

Ms. Searles had also included information regarding two patient claims of injury. One was about the anxious male patient who received mesotherapy and complained of excessive swelling, and the other one was from the woman who suffered an allergic reaction to Restylane. Calling them "victims", Ms. Searles noted that she had enclosed "startling photographs" of the woman's swollen lips.

In our response, we pointed out the woman had a rare, but known, allergic reaction to the Restylane, which was an entirely legal drug. As such, there was no criminal behavior involved in the episode. Additionally, the patient had denied having any allergies, which later turned out to be misinformation. Regarding the mesotherapy patient, he suffered nothing more than the usual amount of post-procedure swelling expected with a higher dose of medication, a dose he requested. We argued that including information about these two patients "would be prejudicial and irrelevant" to my case.

Despite our protestations, Ms. Earles refused to change the report. The decision was puzzling, if not infuriating. We were left with no recourse other than the sincere hope that the judge would better understand the irrelevancy of the information. But it did make us wonder whether this was an attempt at circumventing the plea agreement so as to bring about a more severe punishment.

I suspected the new AUSA had something to do with it, telling Ted, "This seems like vigilante justice, federal prosecutor style."

"She does feel like you got off pretty easy. As you know, there's other information in the PSR regarding the government's investigation that I was unaware of. This happened because we negotiated a settlement of your case before you were formally indicted and therefore before we received any discovery – including the investigation reports. Then the prosecutor gave those reports to the probation office. And I must say, some of the information in those reports, as reflected in the PSR, makes it even clearer that we were very fortunate to get the deal that we did."

"I understand that, but the fact of the matter is that even though I got a good deal, I should be sentenced according to the relevant facts."

Guilty as I felt, I was still determined to fight for myself. I couldn't imagine simply allowing the Government to do whatever they wanted, even if I was fully responsible. There was just no way I would lie down; I had spent a lifetime doing the opposite. This wavering between semi-righteous indignation and profound guilt and humiliation would continue.

"We'll work on making changes to the report, but the judge should go along with the plea agreement. Try to remember the balanced summary Ms. Earles included at the end of the PSR."

It read:

Given that Kepler has no prior record of criminal conduct, and what he stands to lose in terms of his livelihood as a physician, future criminal behavior is unlikely. These circumstances point to the need for the sentence to provide the defendant with needed correctional treatment. In an effort to balance all of these factors under 18 U.S.C. Title Code 3553(a)(1) -(7), a sentence of three years' probation and five hundred hours of community service is recommended.

With the completion of the PSR and the decision of the Medical Board to drop the case, my fourteen-month nightmare was effectively over, and just in time for the holidays.

I took Jessica back to Ohio to celebrate. I held off on telling my parents the great news. It was the most excited I had ever been about going home. Mom picked us up at the Cincinnati International Airport, her effervescent smile making her easily distinguishable among the others who had gathered near the terminal to welcome passengers. Jessica spotted her first and ran ahead and into her arms. Holding Jessica in one arm, she gave me a firm hug with the other, telling me, "I'm so happy you're home." I buried my chin into her shoulder.

"So am I," I said.

That night, my brother and his family joined us for a Christmas Eve feast of prime rib, mashed potatoes, roasted asparagus and salad. The dinner table was typically chaotic, with Jessica acting silly with her two young cousins, my brother telling us of his adventures as a pilot and my sister-in-law sharing cooking tips with Mom. No one mentioned my legal issues, and I was happy to simply sit back and remind myself of the good fortune in my life.

Once dinner was finished, the children broke away from the table to play upstairs, and I retrieved a bottle of champagne that I had brought with me, pouring everyone a drink. Since our family rarely drank alcohol, this drew some curious looks.

"I'd like to make a toast," I announced, raising my glass. Dad looked completely confused. "I know the last year or so has been a nightmare for everyone."

Mom cleared her throat. My sister-in-law put her hand on the table and fingered her fork.

"But finally, there is some good news. First, the probation department has agreed with the prosecutor's sentence recommendation. That means my punishment will be five years' probation and five hundred hours of community service. No prison."

"Thank God," Dad breathed. Mom's eyes remained on the table.

"And even better, the Medical Board has decided to close the case. They're not going to perform an investigation."

"Woo hoo!" my sister-in-law yelled.

"Awesome," Dad said.

Mom sat silently, tears starting to form. Then she got up and started towards the kitchen, nearly tripping over the leg of a chair. I could hear her washing dishes a short while later. I looked at Dad, who shrugged, and then downed his champagne in one gulp. It was the most alcohol I had seen him drink in ten years. Over the next hour, I methodically worked my way through the rest of the bottle on my own, trying to forget about my upset Mom in the other room. I knew she found the good news nothing but a tremendous relief and saw no reason to celebrate a good outcome to something that should have never occurred in the first place.

The next day, we exchanged Christmas gifts. It was a particularly boisterous Christmas, although I noticed Mom looked older and seemed quieter than usual. I asked if she was okay, and she gave me her ever-present smile and reassured me everything was fine. But we both knew the year had been particularly hard on her, and as I watched her, I felt sad and guilty. She caught me looking at her at one point and gave me a smile before coming over, putting a hand on my cheek and kissing me.

"Merry Christmas, Max," she whispered.

That night, I received an email from Ted. "Hope you had a wonderful Christmas with your family. And Happy New Year. It will be great for you, I know."

The next day, Sang sent me a brief email:" Happy Holidays, Max. We are all grateful to have you back among us, and I wish you and your family the best in the year to come. Let's pray that this all goes away for good."

# CHAPTER TWENTY-FOUR

On January 3, 2007, two days before sentencing, I called Ted.

"Court is at 9:30 on Friday, correct?" I asked.

"That's right."

"Is there anything else you need from me?"

"Nothing. It shouldn't be a big deal."

Sang called the next day.

"Let me know how it goes."

"I will. Thank you for all your support, Sang."

"No problem, Max. Good luck tomorrow. Are you taking the day off?"

"Just the morning for the hearing, which should be very brief. Then I'll be here in the afternoon."

"Make sure to stop by afterwards."

Late that afternoon, an ex-girlfriend invited me to meet her for a drink in San Francisco. This seemed like the perfect opportunity to keep my mind occupied and so I gladly accepted. Plus, we had not seen or talked to each other for over a year, and it was a chance to relax with someone who hadn't an inkling of what was happening in my life.   And I wasn't about to tell her my drama now, especially since it was effectively ending in little more than twelve hours.

At eight-thirty, we met at a lounge called the Redwood Room, a swanky San Francisco landmark located in the Clift Hotel. We nestled into one of the overstuffed, red velvet couches and ordered a round of drinks. On large plasma screens located throughout the bar were videos of human models staring into the camera, subtle moves of their body or intermittent blinks betraying the fact these were previously recorded live images. I remember the first time I discovered the live art here ten years earlier, finding it both curious and creepy at the same time.

I was excited to catch up with my friend, and before I knew it, it was eleven-thirty and my head was swimming from the four drinks I had consumed. Realizing I shouldn't drive home, my friend suggested I spend the night with her in the city.   I readily agreed, and since I lived thirty minutes away and needed to be in Federal Building by 9:30 in the morning, it made sense for me to go directly to the sentencing from her apartment.   But that meant I would have to wear the same clothes, which included a lime green dress shirt Mom had given me ten days earlier for Christmas. I wondered whether the shirt's brightness might be too exuberant for a federal judge, but quickly reassured myself that the judge would not base his decision on my clothing.

Taking up a spot in a spare bedroom, I set the alarm clock on my cell phone for seven in the morning. Then I lay down on my back and smiled as I stared at the ceiling. My odyssey was now just ten hours from its conclusion.

The thought brought me comfort, and I faded away into sleep, awakened six hours later by the alarm. By now, my head was heavy from the alcohol, and I lay there for a little trying to collect my thoughts. Then suddenly, I was afraid and anxious again, and my palms began to sweat. I pulled myself out of bed and headed for the shower.

I arrived at the Civic Center Plaza underground garage thirty minutes early and spent some of the extra time sitting alone in my car, trying to loosen the tangled knot of thoughts and emotions in my mind. I considered calling my parents—they hadn't called me so I figured they had forgotten the date of my sentencing—but then decided I would contact them afterwards when it was all over.

Once I had made my way to the Federal Building, I hesitated before walking through the front door, so as to collect myself. After going through security, I took a series of escalators to the cafeteria on the third floor where I grabbed my favorite breakfast—eggs, bacon and toast— but I lost my appetite and left it untouched. Within ten minutes Ted arrived, dressed in his usual dark suit, smiling and energetic.

"How long will we be in the courtroom?" I asked, noticing that my hands were shaking.

"Maybe twenty minutes," he said.

I relaxed a bit at that. I would be back at work seeing patients by noon.

Ted glanced at his watch. It was 10:20.

"Time to go."

When we got to the courtroom, it was absolutely quiet, with church-like pews for the gallery and dark wood for the walls. We walked down the aisle and sat next to each other in the front row to wait, each passing second marked by the swinging arm of a stately grandfather clock.

Finally, a clerk came in to announce the case, followed by the judge. He was wearing a flowing black robe and had a perfectly-groomed, gray-speckled beard and a thick head of hair thinning at the temples. He seemed inordinately large to me. His face was expressionless and he wore small round eyeglasses. He glanced at me as he walked to the bench, but mostly he kept his eyes lowered. I tried to imagine him in a more relaxed context—maybe watching his grandchildren play in the park—without success.

Showtime.

"The United States of America vs. Max Kepler," reverberated against the hollowness of the chamber.

An entire country was against me.

Then the judge spoke.

"This is the time set for judgment and sentencing. I have had an opportunity to review the plea agreement, the pre-sentence investigation report, the documents submitted by both parties and, also, Mr. Cassman's sentencing memorandum."

He asked if there were any additional documents he needed to review and both attorneys told him "no." The judge then noted that the US Attorney's office, Ted and the probation department were all in agreement to the applicable total offense guideline range, the criminal history category and the sentencing. This acknowledgment seemed like a good sign, and I was reassured.

326

He then asked Ted if he would like to make any statements on my behalf. I expected Ted to say no, as he has already told me in advance that further comments or pleas from us could be viewed unfavorably at this late stage.

"I believe the Court has everything before it," Ted replied and I figured that was the end of his response. But then he continued:

"I would just note that Mr. Kepler...Dr. Kepler... is a tremendously talented and bright medical doctor who is committed to the health of his patients and to helping people, and his good intentions got all twisted up and misdirected in this matter. It's a terrible and unfortunate circumstance. He immediately did everything right to rectify the situation and to cooperate with the authorities, and we are here before this court asking the court to follow the plea agreement."

Ted's statement led me to believe that he was now uncertain that the judge was planning to follow the agreement. I started shaking again, so much so that my "no" was barely audible when the judge asked if I had any statement to make on my behalf.

The judge went on to say that "the court is satisfied that the agreement of the parties may now be approved," but immediately pointed out that the plea agreement was non-binding. The assistant US attorney confirmed this, while I wondered why the judge needed affirmation the plea agreement was non-binding. Just a formality, I hoped.

He continued:

"I received these documents yesterday and spent most of the afternoon reviewing them closely. One thing I noticed is that one delivery of hGH to Dr. Kepler, for the record, totaled more than 1,650 doses."

Just as it did in the proffer session, the 1,650 doses sounded like a lot, especially the way he said it, slowing his speech and speaking louder.

"I also note that a computer search of Dr. Kepler revealed that he was the founder of Forever Lithe and that he created a procedure called mesotherapy."

This had me puzzled. I was not charged with a crime regarding my use of mesotherapy. But the judge's next statement alarmed me even more.

"The court would note that this was an unlicensed non-FDA approved use of hGH."

Wait a minute. The judge thought I was using hGH as part of mesotherapy?! That was completely false.

He continued his erroneous summary of the case.

"It would appear from the victim impact statements, which I will get to in a moment, that Dr. Kepler never told the victims that he was--that these were non-FDA approved procedures."

Doctors use medications for non-FDA approved indications all the time. This is because it would be too time consuming and costly to obtain approval for every possible use of a drug. Furthermore, doctors are not legally or ethically obligated to tells patients when they are using a drug for a non-FDA approved indication. Finally, Restalyn was clearly FDA approved for the way I was using it. The judge then turned to my interaction with the undercover agent.

"I would note also that during the April 5th, 2005 phone call with the undercover agent, Dr. Kepler indicated that the next step after speaking to the agent was to meet, get to know her and establish a trust relationship."

The judge stopped, took off his reading glasses, looked up from his papers and with glasses dangling from his right hand, waved them angrily in my direction as he said, "This court recognizes that type of language is language used by drug dealers when they try to contact potential purchasers of narcotics!"

He was calling me a drug dealer. I felt my whole body begin to shake.

Slowly and deliberately, he put his glasses back on, picked up his papers, and began reading again, informing the court that I sold the undercover agent five unlabeled vials of hGH for one hundred and sixty dollars while I listed all the potential benefits of the drug, then repeating that they were non-FDA approved procedures and again demonstrating that he was confusing mesotherapy with hGH dispensing.

Next, the judge informed the court that after I had told the agent that I could ship the hGH anywhere, she had asked me point blank whether the drug was from China and I had answered, "Oh no. I wouldn't do that. That is a risky endeavor. I mean, you just don't know about the quality. This is something you inject into your body. It's not just like taking a tablet. So, that's a little dangerous if you don't know the source. You don't want to do that. Definitely not. That's not a good idea." He then listed my education and training, making the point that I knew exactly what I was doing, before announcing that he would read the victim impact statements.

*Not this. Please not this.*

There were only five patients that received hGH and none of them had experienced any adverse effects. But the judge was not talking about hGH now. Again confusing the issue, he was back to other aspects of my practice that were irrelevant to what I was there for.

First, he read a statement submitted to Ms. Earles from the anxious male patient who had undergone mesotherapy. "As a result, I experienced severe swelling around my abdomen. My waist increased by three to four inches. The swelling took a very long time to fully subside, two to three months. I phoned Dr. Kepler often during this time frame as I was experiencing tremendous anxiety. My anxiety was so intense that I had significant acne break out all over my face. This period of months was the most difficult I have experienced to date."

The judge then went on to discuss the woman who suffered an allergic reaction to the Restylane I had injected in her. She had sent in the photographs she had shown me and he proclaimed them "shocking."

I was stunned. How could he get it all so wrong? I was in a federal court of law where truth and facts are supposed to be paramount, but instead I was entangled in a web of confusion and misplaced anger.

"This is about human growth hormone!" I wanted to shout.

But the judge was on a roll now, practically yelling out, "Dr. Kepler, perhaps you didn't listen to the Hippocratic Oath when it was administered to you, but I will read one part of it. 'I will prescribe regimens for the good of my patients according to my ability and my judgment and never do harm to anyone.' You have not only done harm to these patients and others, but you have abused the trust of this nation. You were given a position as a Harvard undergrad with a full scholarship. You took the place that somebody else could have had, that seat. You went to Boston University. You went to UCSF. You were afforded every possible opportunity that this nation can offer someone, and your response is to have done this to unsuspecting victims. The court is more than just shocked. It is outraged. The court has also read 18 United States Code Section 3553, Imposition of Sentence, has reviewed the factors to be considered in imposing the sentence and takes each and every one of those facts into account when sentencing you in this matter."

At this, Ted interrupted, "Your Honor…"

"Excuse me," the judge shouted as he pounded his fist on the desk. "I wish to finish. You can comment after I'm done."

"The court will sentence the defendant to six months in the custody of the Bureau of Prisons. Thereafter, a one-year term of supervised release."

The words washed over me without effect. I was numb. But then it hit me. Bureau of Prisons!

I put both hands to my head, trying to keep it from splitting apart.

Ted then asked for permission to speak, which the judge granted.

"I would like to try and unwind this a little bit because the Court has issued an order and I have heard it loud and clear and, obviously, Mr. Kepler has, too. That order was based, at least in part, on what I would suggest are misapprehensions of the facts that were before the Court. And so in the normal course of things, it's my experience that if the Court intended not to follow the recommendations, you would give us an opportunity to address the Court's concerns, and so I would like to do that now."

The judge pointed his finger, indicating that Ted could continue.

"We understand what the Court has said about the nature of Mr. Kepler's conduct, and I know that the Government has treated this matter very seriously and that the probation officer did, too. And, obviously, from the defense perspective we have, too. There were hundreds of patients that came in to see Mr. Kepler, and the Court has before it two complaints."

"But what I wanted to focus on is the two individuals that the Court was so concerned about that did respond. The first one was the mesotherapy, and for clarity, I hope the Court understands that's a separate issue from the Botox and the hGH, the conduct to which Mr. Kepler pled guilty, and specifically what I will call victim number one, because the court raised it that way. That individual received mesotherapy and didn't receive Botox or hGH and is not a subject of the offense conduct in this case at all. Secondly, and perhaps even more importantly, the photographs that the Court referred to involved Restylane treatment of the lips to that individual. There is no allegation of any kind that anything was wrong with the Restylane that he used in his treatment. Dr. Kepler has worked at great length with that individual to assist her and to rectify the situation, but it was Restylane."

"I'm familiar with it."

"And that's in her statement. So those injuries that were sustained and that were the specific focus of the

Court's concern are unrelated to the offense conduct in this case."

"Anything further, counsel?"

Ted then went on to speak about my immediate acceptance of full responsibility for my conduct and my extensive cooperation. He spoke of the physical custody of my daughter that I shared with her mom. And that I was still practicing and that I had learned my lesson.

"He is a remarkably talented individual who has a great deal of opportunity to benefit this society and this world and his patients and he's doing so, and the order that the Court has imposed would interfere with that. So, I'm asking the Court to reconsider, for the reasons I have set forth."

The assistant US attorney then informed the judge that mesotherapy and Restalyn were indeed not part of the plea agreement but that, from the Government's point of view, the mesotherapy cocktails were not an approved use and were in violation of law. Now it was the assistant US attorney making erroneous statements. She did go on to confirm my cooperation with the Government and that that had played a role in being granted the misdemeanor agreement instead of a felony charge under the Food, Drug and Cosmetics Act.

Ted added that I had traveled to Charlotte to assist with an investigation, but by then, I had checked out and was thinking only of Jessica and being away from her for six months. Suddenly, I realized I would have to fight for myself and for her.

"May I say one thing?" I asked the judge.

"No, Max," Ted interjected before the judge had a chance to answer.

333

Ted then asked for permission to speak with me privately. He pulled me aside a few feet from the lectern where I emphatically told him that I could not be away from my daughter. Ted had a pained expression as he searched for a way to salvage the moment.

Just then, the judge asked the assistant US attorney, "What's the position of the Food and Drug Administration in regards to sentencing of this defendant?"

Huh? The judge was asking how the FDA would sentence me? Isn't that something he should have worked out before walking into the courtroom?" He was second-guessing himself now.

Equally surprised by the question, the assistant US attorney hesitated before answering.

"Your Honor, I don't know that the agency has a position on sentencing. Typically, it doesn't take a position on sentencing. It was aware of the plea agreement and did not object to it."

The FDA agent confirmed this for the judge. Ted reminded the agent that the previous assistant US attorney had the plea agreement approved by superiors in the FDA.

A glimmer of hope. It was clear the US attorney's office, the pre-sentencing department and the FDA all supported the original plea agreement. Perhaps the judge would recognize his error and modify his judgment.

We returned to the lectern and Ted addressed the judge.

"Your Honor, Mr. Kepler wanted to—but I know the Court is aware of this. He wanted to explain to you the hardship that the Court's sentence would impose on his daughter."

"I understand that," the Judge replied.

"Can I say something else to him?" I asked Ted.

"No," came the reply.

The judge began speaking again.

"I'm sure everyone understands the circumstances, that it is a difficult position, but after having read everything before me and after having looked at the victim impact statements and looked at the pre-sentence investigation report..."

"No sir..." I pleaded reflexively, reaching out towards the judge.

"...the Court believes that to reflect the seriousness of the offense, to promote respect for the law and provide just punishment for the offense, that the Court's sentence will stand..."

"No..." I blurted once more, my outstretched arms trembling.

"And that the defendant will be ordered to do six months in custody."

But he wasn't quite finished. He wanted my medical license too.

"I will order that the Government, within 48 hours of receipt of the transcript of these proceedings, submit it to the California Medical Licensing Board, and I order that a copy of this transcript be made part of the record. The Court stands adjourned."

And with that, the judge's gavel came down. He stood up, gathered his robe and walked out of the courtroom.

# CHAPTER TWENTY-FIVE

When the door closed behind the judge, the courtroom once again became silent, until the assistant US attorney began gathering her papers. She looked at me briefly, a mixture of kindness and concern on her face, before walking out of the courtroom. Next to me, Ted paced slowly in a tight circle, eyes narrowed and focused on the carpet.

"What just happened?" I asked in disbelief.

"Apparently, the judge decided not to follow the plea agreement."

"I don't understand. Why?"

"I'm not sure even he knows."

"Now what are we going to do?"

"There's nothing we can do. When you agree to a plea bargain, you agree to accept whatever sentence is handed down."

"But what will I do about Jessica?"

Ted just looked at me blankly. I turned and started wandering out of the courtroom. I could hear him behind me. When we reached the hallway outside, he grabbed my arm.

"Wait here," he said. "I'm going to talk with the assistant US attorney."

And then I was alone in the institutional desolation of the long hallway. As the shock began to fade, fear and panic set in.

"What am I going to do?" I kept repeating to myself. "What am I possibly going to do?"

I decided to call Alice. My fingers were numb as I clumsily dialed the number.

"How'd it go?" Alice asked right away.

I couldn't speak.

"What happened?" she implored. Her tone had turned worried.

"The judge sentenced me to six months in prison."

"What are you talking about, Max? I thought there was a plea bargain. What happened?"

I wanted to crawl into a space where I could neither feel nor cause any pain.

"The judge decided not to follow the recommended sentence. He brought up a lot of shit that was wrong and not related to the case. It was terrible, Alice. Just terrible."

"So do you have to go to prison right now?" she asked through tears.

"I have ninety days to report."

"Please, no! What about Jessica?" she asked.

"I don't know. I need to go," I sniffled.

"What are you going to do?"

"Go to work."

As I hung up, I saw Ted returning. His face was intense and he was taking quick, determined strides. He began speaking even before he reached me.

"I spoke with the AUSA and told her I'm going to request a continuation of the sentencing hearing. The judge did not give us adequate opportunity to respond to his concerns. And those concerns formed the basis of his deviation from the recommended sentencing. He did not follow judicial protocol."

"A continuation? Is there such a thing?"

"There has to be," Ted said defiantly.

"But do you think that will work?" I asked him.

"If he's fair, he has to grant us a continuation."

"I think we just saw that he's not," I said, but Ted was not really listening.

"I need to go back to the office now and start working on this before the judge has a chance to finalize the sentence."

He was already walking away before he finished his last word.

Somehow, I made it the two blocks to the City Hall underground parking garage. In a daze, I stumbled around for fifteen minutes before finding my car. I slid into the driver's seat, started the engine, and stared at the dashboard. It was eleven o'clock. So much had happened in such a short period of time. But now patients were expecting me, and I needed to get to the hospital.

But what was the point? It might be better if I just started driving, stopping only after I went far enough, wherever that might be. Or perhaps I could take the

Pacific Coast Highway, and if I accidentally missed one of the sharp curves along the way, sending me over the steep cliffs, that might not be so bad. Death in the presence of beauty. A catastrophic failure.

But such self-indulgent thoughts had not been productive over the previous fourteen months, and they would serve no purpose now. I needed to pull myself together and get to the hospital, for although the judge had made me feel worthless, I was still a doctor, and I was determined to remain one.

I don't remember the drive; I just remember maneuvering my car into the doctor's parking lot. I grabbed my ID badge and made my way into the hospital and to the closest restroom. There, I wiped my nose and washed my face. Then, I went to my office to retrieve my white coat before walking over to the medical wards. I was greeted warmly by the charge nurse.

"Good morning, Dr. Kepler. Late start on rounds, eh?"

"I was a little tied up," I said.

She smiled, oblivious to my double entendre. I turned away and took out the patient list from my coat pocket; I had ten people to see. I tried focusing intently on the job as I made my way through rounds. It wasn't until I was in the middle of seeing the fifth patient that I started to feel alive again. By then, time had slowed down and I found myself lost once again in patient care, as though I was experiencing the purity of doctoring all over again.

Just as I was getting settled into that comfortable space, I was jolted out of it by an overhead announcement of, "Code Blue, emergency room!" Since I was responsible for taking care of all emergencies that afternoon, I quickly made my way down to the ER where I found a patient being whipped down the hall by paramedics. I rounded the corner just in time to see her flowing, black hair hanging over edge of the rapidly moving gurney.

"Sixty-eight-year-old woman with no medical problems, status post cardiac arrest at home," I heard one of the paramedics announce.

I followed the commotion into a cardiac room. A respiratory therapist quickly took over administering air to the unconscious patient by squeezing a stiff, rubber bag connected to the endotracheal tube in her windpipe. A blanket covered her body and when I removed it, I could see that her dress had been cut away to enable the placement of the defibrillator pads. Telemetry leads were placed on her chest and the monitor showed her to be in normal sinus rhythm. An automated blood pressure cuff attached to her arm showed that the blood pressure was excellent. From a cardiovascular perspective, she was stable, which was reassuring.

But her neurologic examination was far from it. She was displaying odd movements of the arms, called decerebrate posturing, which consisted of fully extending and inwardly rotating both arms. Furthermore, her pupils did not respond when I shined a light upon them. Both of these were evidence of serious brain injury due to oxygen deprivation from the cardiac arrest. After several minutes of assessing her and ordering various medications, I pulled away so I could speak with family that had just arrived.

As I made the fifty-foot walk to the family conference room, I prepared mentally for the job before me, and thoughts of prison were completely absent. On arrival, I found eight of the patient's family members seated around a long table, their faces etched with desperation and horror. After quick introductions, I asked for information on how the patient had been doing recently.

"She seemed to be fine," said the oldest daughter, a woman with a patrician nose and beautiful black hair, who told me her mother's name was Azka. "She was feeling a little tired today, so she took a long nap in the late morning."

"Did she eat breakfast?" I asked.

"She got up before dawn and ate and drank plenty," her daughter told me, her voice shaky.

The daughter then told me how Azka had sat down at the kitchen table, flanked by her two oldest daughters, to prepare the evening meal. They were cutting vegetables and Azka asked one of the daughters to pass her a knife. As her daughter placed it in her mother's right, upturned hand, Azka suddenly let her hand fall, as though the knife was too heavy to hold. She simultaneously slumped to the right with her head lowered. Her face was expressionless and she didn't appear to be breathing. Her daughter had reached over and shaken her mother's shoulder but there was no response. Remarkably, and with great calm and presence despite the circumstances, the daughter checked for a pulse at her mother's wrist and upon finding none, quickly instructed her sister to call 911.

The two sisters then placed their mother on the floor, speaking to her in Farsi, saying anything they hoped would bring her back. The paramedics arrived in less than ten minutes and upon discovering that Azka was not breathing and did not have a pulse, immediately began trying to save her life. Within several minutes, they had placed a breathing tube in her trachea, an IV in her arm, and defibrillator pads on her chest. When the heart rhythm was noted to be ventricular fibrillation, they shocked her three times, each shock causing the characteristic heaving of the chest into the air as the electricity arced through her.

By the third shock, the paramedics could feel a pulse. They rapidly bundled Azka into a collapsible gurney, carried her downstairs and into the back of a waiting ambulance whose siren began wailing as soon as the driver accelerated out of the driveway and into the night.

At this point in her narrative, the daughter began trembling, and so I put my hand on hers and thanked her for the information. The family sat staring at me, hoping for some positive news.

"How's she doing, doctor?" the daughter asked.

"She's stable. We'll be taking her to the ICU shortly, but I am concerned about the amount of time her brain was without oxygen. I think she might have suffered serious brain injury as a result."

The women started weeping while the men simply stared down at the floor. Through their obvious shock and sadness, I sensed resoluteness, as though they had placed their trust in a higher power. I waited for questions, but none came and so I excused myself so that I could return to caring for Azka.

After I checked on her and wrote admission orders to the ICU, I stepped outside to unwind from the intensity of the experience. I had about fifteen minutes before I needed to resume my rounds, and so I went for a short walk.

Soon, I started thinking about the federal courtroom again and called Ted to ask him about the solution he'd mentioned.   He told me he had already faxed a letter to the judge, which he emailed to me.   It read:

Dear Judge Natas,

I am writing to you following the hearing this morning in the above-referenced matter and out of concern that a miscarriage of justice has occurred.  I believe that the procedures this morning were fundamentally flawed and unfair and that, as a result, relevant information was not before the court that would have assisted its evaluation of all of the circumstances in determining whether to follow the recommendations of the parties and of probation and in imposing an appropriate sentence.  As a result, for example, the court was not fully informed of the extreme hardship that a custodial sentence would create for Dr. Kepler or of the full extent of Dr. Kepler's cooperation and assistance with law enforcement.

Accordingly, I object to the entry of judgment in light of these circumstances and urge the court to convene further proceedings at the court's earliest convenience.  In this regard, I am available this afternoon and have spoken to attorney Ann Moon, who would be available to appear before the court in Eureka next week.

Thank you for your attention to this matter.

Very truly yours,

Ted W. Cassman

I had never heard Ann Moon's name mentioned but Ted explained that she was an attorney at Ted's firm and, more importantly, a friend of the judge.   She apparently had helped him in his bid to become a federal magistrate judge several years previously. The reference to her was intended to embarrass the judge just enough so he would grant a continuation of the sentencing hearing.

After receiving a copy of Ted's letter to the judge, the AUSA sent her own letter a short while later.

Dear Judge Natas:

The government does not believe that a further hearing is necessary as there was no disagreement concerning the factual allegations, Dr. Kepler's partial custody of his young child was in the pre-sentence report and discussed at the sentencing, and Dr. Kepler's cooperation—including his trip to Charlotte--was also discussed at the sentencing. However, should a hearing be scheduled, the government will of course endeavor to provide any and all additional information requested. If a hearing is scheduled in Eureka, I respectfully request the ability to appear telephonically.

Very truly yours,

Valerie Richards

Assistant US Attorney

The judge had forty-eight hours to consider the two statements.

That night, sleep was nearly impossible. I had found out that the judge's wife was a physician, which made his behavior more understandable. Although there was no way to confirm it, I was sure he had discussed the case with her, even though judges are specifically forbidden to discuss pending cases with their spouses. I wondered if his ego, which had appeared substantial in the courtroom, would allow him to reverse his position.

Judge Natas was a magistrate judge. While district judges are nominated by the President and confirmed by the United States Senate for lifetime tenure, magistrate judges are appointed by a majority vote of the federal district judges of a particular district to help with lower level cases, such as misdemeanors. Only a little over two years prior to my sentencing, Natas had been appointed a part-time magistrate judge in a rural area of northern California where the courthouse offered minimal services, generally handling a calendar of sporadic infractions and misdemeanors. But to assist with the backlog of cases in the Northern District of California Federal Court, the judge would occasionally come to San Francisco to hear misdemeanor cases, such as mine. He had been assigned to my case only because he happened to be the magistrate available at the time of sentencing.

After having experienced a series of incredibly fortunate occurrences, my fate was now being determined by the judicial equivalent of "the help."

While I awaited word from the judge, Azka was fighting for her life at the hospital. Her heart repeatedly developed life-threatening arrhythmias which required various medications and multiple rounds of electrical shocks to the chest. The neurologist agreed she likely had severe brain injury with little chance for recovery. Informed of her prognosis, the family held a continuous vigil in her room, speaking to her, praying, and reading the Quran out loud. They remained convinced she was going to get better, but I knew her chances were exceedingly slim.

For whatever reason, perhaps it was because I felt I was facing similarly long odds, I felt a special bond with Azka. And so, I took considerable time to talk with various family members about her life. I learned she was the first of four children born to Persian parents in a small town thirty miles outside of Tehran, Iran. Because they were devout Muslims, her father chose the name Azka in part because it meant "pious". Father and daughter had the same playful personality and good humor, their distinctive big, brown eyes their most obviously shared trait.

By the time she was twenty-one, Azka was married to a man who was a member of the Artesh, the name for the Persian Army. After his conscription period had expired, her husband had decided to stay in the military. During their twenties, the young couple produced four children. Then came the Islamic Revolution of 1979, and in a violent street battle, Azka's husband was killed. Suddenly, at the age of twenty-nine, Azka was a widowed mother of four. Within a year, accompanied by her children and seven other family members including her mother and father, she immigrated to the United States. She never returned to Iran.

With the help of extended family and a network of Iranian friends, Azka raised her four children without a partner. She never remarried and, in fact, never even considered it. Her husband was her true love and she honored him by remaining alone. She filled her life with family and Allah-that was more than enough for her.

346

I listened to these stories with both sorrow and a sense of awe. And I became even more determined to do whatever I could to help Azka recover, even if my doctor's mind knew that was unlikely. I had personalized my care of the patient, just as I had done many times before, but never when I was so emotionally vulnerable.

Meanwhile, I continued to wait for Judge Natas to change his decision, convincing myself that his original verdict simply could not stand. I didn't take the MCAT or pre-med courses, but still I was a doctor and planned on being one for a long time. One man could not take that away. What did Judge Natas know about me? What did he know about my life, family, friends, history? Did thirty-five years of many good deeds and accomplishments in my life mean absolutely nothing? Was I to be defined only by a single fifteen-month period?

In the middle of my self-righteous rantings, something remarkable happened. At almost exactly the forty-eighth hour, Judge Natas granted a sentencing continuation. His ruling meant we would simply pretend the first hearing had never ended, that we had decided instead to take a very long recess. The news came to me by phone call from Ted as I was having lunch in the hospital cafeteria. I stepped away to take the call and was so caught up in the decision that I forgot to return to my food.

Later that afternoon, while still emotionally depleted, I encountered an even more remarkable event when I walked into Azka's room and called out her name. She opened her eyes! I nearly dropped my stethoscope. I stood there staring at her through watery eyes, trying to compose myself. When I performed a full neurologic exam, I noted that she was able to move her arms and legs and follow commands. Completely dumbfounded, I first called the neurologist, who was speechless. Only then did I inform her ecstatic family. There was much crying and hugging and thanking of Allah. By the next day, Azka was fully awake. We removed her from the ventilator and found she was able to communicate normally.

She remained in the hospital for another week. During that time, she underwent a coronary angiogram which revealed a partial blockage in the left anterior descending artery, which is one of the main arteries supplying the heart. This blockage, although incomplete, had caused a heart attack, which lead to the arrest. A stent was placed into the artery to keep it open. She also had a full recovery of her cognitive functioning.

On the day she was discharged, Azka was clutching a copy of the Quran, her faith deepened by her experience. I wished her well, and she thanked me profusely, ending with "Allah is good, and he will guide you." I nodded in affirmation, realizing what I had witnessed required at least that.

Buoyed temporarily by the good news, my mood soon shifted when I realized I had not yet told my parents what had happened in the courtroom. I couldn't fathom how I would be able to make the call. How would my mother, who had never even received a speeding ticket, react to the news that her all-star son had been sentenced to a federal penitentiary? I considered not telling them, but knew it'd be too hard to keep it from them.

I thought a lot about the sacrifices Mom and Dad had made for my brother and me over the years, and although our family life could at times be tumultuous, I also knew they had tried their best.   There was certainly never a shortage of love in our house, and I was never made to feel inadequate or unworthy.   For that, I had chosen to repay them by causing tremendous grief.

I decided to make the call before work, when I knew both of them would be home.   Mom answered.

"I need to tell you and Dad something.   Can you put him on the phone?" I asked her.

"Is there something wrong?" she asked.

"Just tell Dad to pick up the phone, please."

He came on quickly.

"What's going on, buddy?" he asked.

"I guess you guys forgot that sentencing was on January 5th?"

"Oh, that's right," Dad said.   "Did it go okay?"

"Not really."   My throat seized, and I was unable to continue.

"Oh no," Mom said.   "What happened?"

I swallowed and steadied myself.   "You're not going to believe this, but the judge sentenced me to six months in prison."

"What the hell!" Dad shouted.

"How could that be?" Mom asked.

"He just lost his mind and sentenced me to prison.   He was so angry with me."

"Why?   How could this happen?   I don't understand," Mom said.

I explained it to them.

"But Ted said there would be no prison," Dad said.

"I know, I know.   It's crazy what happened."

I told them about the continuation and that we still hoped to avoid prison.   That seemed to settle them a bit, but then they became progressively more upset.

"This is completely ridiculous," Mom said.   "I mean, come on.   Prison for a misdemeanor?"

"What's wrong with this guy?" Dad asked.

One thing about the Keplers, when it came to crunch time, they had each others' backs.

"We'll come out there," Dad said.

"No, that's okay, you'll need to come later for the second hearing."

"Are you sure?" Mom asked.

"Yes."   Although I appreciated their support, I didn't want to burden them further.   I really wanted to deal with the whole thing on my own, if only because I didn't want to experience the overwhelming guilt their presence would bring up in me.   I never told them the judge sent the hearing transcripts to the Medical Board.   I would share that with them later, I figured, if the Board changed their mind and decided to open an inquiry.   I doubted that would happen, anyway.

# CHAPTER TWENTY-SIX

The judge would make me wait six weeks for the continuation. Depending on context, six weeks can pass like a blink of the eye or last an eternity. My experience was the latter.

My anxiety ramped up to previously unknown levels. I was besieged with a longing to escape. I didn't know where I wanted to go or how to get there, I just knew I needed to escape, anywhere, anytime, anyhow. Escape from anxiety, escape from reality, escape from guilt, escape from everything. The feeling overpowered me and rendered me nearly non-functioning at times.

It was my daughter who saved me. She was such a magical presence, a true miracle of my life, sprung from a seed left eighteen years earlier. She needed a daddy and didn't care if I was a criminal or a doctor or whatever other label society wanted to drop on me. I was Daddy and that was all that mattered. I focused on being the best father possible, which not only grounded me, but also deepened my bond with her.

In the middle of my wait, I was scheduled to take a Lake Tahoe ski trip with Mark, my best friend from Boon. By this time, I had been working long overtime hours for the last six months and had set aside some money for the trip.   Although I had no interest in going, I went anyway because Mark was important to me and I didn't want to disappoint him.   He was also the person who had sat with me in high school while the Princeton football coach gave his recruiting pitch.   Since that day, our lives had taken divergent paths.   He had gotten a degree in electrical engineering at Purdue University and, upon returning home, he had taken a job as an engineer at a large steel-producing factory nearby.   But he grew bored with it and decided to open his own mortgage refinancing business.   This allowed him to create his own schedule, and he filled his free time with basketball, hunting and fishing.

On a cold February weekend twenty-two years after we graduated from high school, I found myself riding up a chair lift at Heavenly Ski Resort with him.   As Mark talked, completely unaware of anything regarding my legal issues, I was distracted by the surreal possibility that my liberty was at stake.   I could very well be in prison within several months, but for now I was on a ski lift in Lake Tahoe with a long-time friend who didn't have an inkling of the pandemonium going on inside my head.   I tried focusing on the parabolic movements of the skiers, the mini storms of snow dust kicked up behind them with every turn glinting the sun like a million tiny sparklers. So distracted was I that when we reached the top, I went left while he skied right, causing me to make my way down the mountain alone, until I found him waiting at the bottom, the familiar grin welcoming me back.

As I looked at him, I began having disturbing thoughts. I had previously considered myself special, perhaps better than Mark, because I had taken risks and gone away to an Ivy League school far away from home. Afterwards, while I spent the next fourteen years in a mad pursuit of degrees, awards, and advanced medical training, he had settled into a comfortable, secure (and to me, boring) life back in Boon. But after making the decision to engage in illicit and immoral behavior, I thought to myself, "Who's special now?"

Ski trip or not, I tried hard to cope with reality, but every day was a struggle. I met regularly with Dr. Steele to help me manage. He suggested prescription medications, but I refused. I wanted to process what was happening with full awareness; I hoped by doing so, I would move closer to my goal of wholeness, regardless of what happened legally.

On good days, I was able to draw inspiration from the movie *Apollo 13*, especially the part when Flight Director Gene Kranz, after being told, "This could be the worst disaster NASA's ever faced," replies, "With all due respect, sir, I believe this is gonna be our finest hour."

I did not want to blow this opportunity to invoke a significant change in my life, but the hard reality was that I still wasn't quite ready for true personal growth. Instead, I framed my pursuit of self-improvement into my usual life construct of: identify challenge, conquer challenge, move on to next challenge. Although this could be a particularly effective strategy in achieving goals, it was not necessarily helpful for personal evolution. That would hopefully come later. For now, I was simply trying to survive and manage my emotions.

Unfortunately, my strategy wasn't always effective. One late night, I worked myself into a frenzy thinking that it was Ted's fault the judge had sentenced me to prison. I decided Ted was not as good as everyone said, that I needed the help of his partner Cristina, and so I sent him an angry email.

Can I meet with you and Cristina on Wednesday afternoon?
I would like a fairly detailed outline of your strategy.
I don't want to hear on the court date that there is no recourse for whatever the judge decides (as you told me on January 5th and which prompted me to call my ex-wife and partners and tell them that I was going to prison). In medicine, absolute vigilance is necessary at all times. Otherwise mistakes are made and things are missed. Vigilance was not observed in anticipation of January 5th. I expect that will not happen again. There is a reason that people hire attorneys like you.
I want my plea bargain back, and I expect that is exactly what you're going to get. The other night I stayed up all night, working 14 hours, taking care of the sickest of sick, admitting patients to the hospital and watching over 45 patients already in the hospital. For that effort, I made enough to pay for 1 and 1/2 hours of your time.
I expect a whole hell of lot from you on February 8. I don't want to spend the next day contemplating anything less than what we agreed on with the government in July

2006. You should have known that if I didn't like the pre-sentence report prepared by Earles, the judge certainly was not going to like it.

I hope you're taking advantage of all the resources and connections available to you.

Ted responded immediately with, "I know you're stressing, but your tone is less than helpful."

Instead of checking my emotions, as indeed it should have, that only made me angrier.

My tone is of someone who doesn't want to go to jail and is expecting a whole lot of his high-priced attorney. It is also the tone of someone who should not be in this position after a plea bargain was reached 7 months ago. If you could read my thoughts and feelings and knew how I suffered and how badly I felt about what I did for the past 15 months, expecting that I was finally going to be able to reach some resolution on January 5 and continue to repair my life, perhaps I would have received more of a response than a couple of sentences commenting on my state of mind. I AM PISSED.

I still haven't heard a peep from you regarding how you're going to approach the hearing. I guarantee we won't be unprepared next time.

Ted did not respond and by the next day, I had calmed down. In fact, I couldn't believe I had completely lost control and was thankful Ted had not dropped me as a client. Instead, he asked me to write a biographical sketch of my life so that he could personalize my case for the judge.

A week later I sent him a thirty-page document, including many personal details of my life, some of which were clearly too intimate, as Ted pointed out.

"Your bio is very well-written," he said. "Way too long though. He definitely will not be interested in hearing about your loss of virginity." His comment made me chuckle.

Meanwhile, Ted was busy working on his legal strategy for the continuation hearing. He decided we needed to demonstrate to the judge that both Jessica and my patients needed me and thus a prison sentence would cause undue hardship. In order for this to work, we needed more letters of support, both from people at work but especially from Alice.

"I'll do it right away," was Alice's immediate answer, and then she delivered a letter to the judge that was emotionally difficult for me to read. Excerpts included:

I speak to you not only as Jessica's mother but also from the perspective of one who knows Max extremely well and is all too familiar with the strengths and weaknesses of his character, the genesis of his actions and the misperceptions that led to his more recent wrongdoings.

I would like the court to know that I have witnessed Max's continuous suffering and remorse about his past actions. We have had countless conversations since October 12, 2005, where I have had the opportunity to witness his thoughts and feelings related to the incident. He has attended therapy sessions consistently over the past four years. And I have seen him suffer, evolve and grow from this experience. He is eager and willing to repay society for his past actions through volunteer work and is open to cooperating with other recommendations from the court.

Since our divorce, Max has been intimately involved with raising Jessica. In spite of the difficulties with being a single father, working a full-time job and raising a toddler, he has always been an eager and active father, taking her fifty percent of the time, doing all her daily routines by himself, participating in school activities and play dates and carpooling to all her after school events. I have been amazed at his dedication and devotion.

When Jessica is at my house, she often misses her father and will call him at night. She sleeps with his blanket every night and often proudly shares stories about something that happened while she was with him. She undoubtedly has a strong attachment to Max that began in her infancy and continues to the present. To interrupt this bond by incarcerating Max for six months would be devastating to her. Our daughter has already had to experience the trauma of divorce, and she has had to continually deal with the frequent changes in her routine as a result of having two households. Additional disruptions would be quite difficult for her.

In writing this letter, I do not wish to convey any sense of a lack of appreciation for the seriousness of Max's wrongdoing and certainly do not want to absolve him of his responsibility to suffer appropriate consequences for his actions. But I would like to respectfully appeal to the court to find a punishment that will not take Max away from his daughter.

I also asked Sang to write a letter, which would be his second on my behalf. He prepared it within an hour but delayed releasing it until he was able to speak with Cade County's general counsel. I discovered the next day that counsel had balked on the letter.

"What's the problem?" I asked Sang.

"In writing the letter on county letterhead, I am a spokesman for the county. And this is a matter that could conceivably make it into the press," he replied.

"But what possible risk could there be to the medical center?"

"If I send the letter without the legal department's consent, and the press chooses to spin our support in adverse fashion, I would be vulnerable to criticism and potential disciplinary action for drawing negative press to the county."

"That seems ridiculous."

"If I could dictate how authority chooses to exercise its prerogatives, your situation would be very different. But I don't, and it isn't."

"This is making an already stressful situation worse," I complained.

Sang jerked his head around and gave me a steely stare, one that lasted for an uncomfortably long time. Then he said slowly, and with emphasis, "I realize you don't like the barriers people are placing in your way, but I am doing my best for you." Then he turned his back to me and began organizing his desk.

"Sorry. I'm just a little frustrated and stressed."

"I know you are, Max," he said, without turning around.

Realizing how self-pitying I must have sounded, I said, "I don't want to put you at risk. Forget about it."

"Let's just see what they say," he said.   It was clear the conversation was over, and I tiptoed out of his office.

By that afternoon, the legal department had given their approval, and Sang immediately sent off the letter.

After that, I went to another five people for letters, all of whom agreed to write them.   It was difficult to ask people for their help, not only because I prided myself on being self-sufficient, but because it was humiliating. Their rally to my defense, however, reminded me just how wonderful people could be during times of crisis.

Although all agreed to write letters, one person did not actually do it.   He was the ex-Chief of Staff and a kidney specialist, well-known for a number of improvements in patient care he had brought to the medical center.

"No problem," he said when I asked him for a letter. Several days later, I asked him again, to which he replied, "Working on it."   Similar reminders over the next week were met with similar responses, often accompanied by lack of eye contact and quickly breaking away.   By the fourth attempt, it was clear he was not comfortable with the request, and I never asked again.   He was the only person who did not provide help when asked.

If asking for letters stressed me out, Ted's next request nearly overwhelmed me with dread.

"I need you to invite friends, colleagues, and family to the hearing," he told by phone one day.

"For what reason?" I asked.

"Visual show of support.  It's important.  The judge has to look at them."

"There's no way I'm humiliating myself in front of everyone important to me. I'd rather face it alone."

"I'm sure you would. But you really have no choice. You have to invite them."

I had kept hidden the darkest details from everyone, and in doing so, I still had not fully accepted responsibility for my behavior. In the courtroom, everything would be exposed, and I was terrified people would think even less of me.

"Ten to fifteen people would be good," he added.

After a week, I still hadn't asked anyone.

"I want the list by the end of day," Ted demanded.

Forced into a corner, I started making the emotionally draining calls. Once I got started, I ended up asking twenty people to come, and every one of them agreed, which was thoroughly humbling. I thanked every person profusely, but my words always seemed inadequate.

One person I did not ask to come was Mom, and she did not offer. It was better for both of us that way. The courtroom would be too painful for her. She wouldn't be able to handle listening to all the bad things her son had done, and in turn, I didn't want to experience the shame associated with that. Instead, Dad would be there. Danny would not be coming, which wasn't surprising, given that he hadn't even called me once since the arrest. But that was part of the oddness of our relationship. It seemed we had never been more than acquaintances, even when we were children, and he wasn't really a source of support when I got sick with Wegener's Granulomatosis. Given the circumstances, it would have been disingenuous to say he disappointed me.

360

As I gathered commitments from friends, Ted worked on the Sentencing Memorandum, a document whose purpose was to persuade the judge to be more lenient. In the Memorandum, Ted included all relevant information that might impact the judge, such as a summary of my life, the bad things that had happened to me as a consequence of my behavior, and my potential to help society. Ted also described my relationship with my daughter, my full acceptance of responsibility, and my cooperation with the Government. Included in the memorandum were the letters of support I had asked for earlier.

Ted was also able to convince the AUSA to write a letter, titled, "The United States' Supplemental Sentencing Memorandum." This document summarized my cooperation with investigators, including my acceptance of responsibility. It also detailed my assistance in the investigation of Lance. It concluded with: "Therefore, the United States continues to recommend two years of probation with special conditions to include 500 hours of volunteer work in the medical field."

The letter was a remarkable accomplishment by Ted. He was able to convince an AUSA who was not very sympathetic towards me, one who had unabashedly joined in on the judge's carnage during the first hearing, to write an important letter endorsing the original plea agreement. This was an unusual action by the AUSA, and one that was directly attributable to Ted's lawyering skills and personal likability. And it was a reminder of why I was paying five hundred and fifty dollars per hour for his services. And why I had been so wrong to berate him for not doing enough for me.

With the submission of the letter, I headed into the continuation hearing fairly confident of my chances.

# CHAPTER TWENTY-SEVEN

Judgment Day, Part Deux, arrived, and I was ready.

Dad, however, did not share my enthusiasm. When I went downstairs to see if he was awake, I found him already dressed and sitting on the couch, looking like he had just eaten a bucket of bad fish.

Kris, a close friend whom I had met freshman year on the football practice field at Harvard, was sitting next to him, exchanging texts with one of his countless girlfriends. With a model's looks and a well-paying job in golf course management, he had plenty of options back home in LA. For now, however, he was here to support me, just like all the other friends who would be in the court room.

One of those friends was Mike, a man whom I knew well in college but had fallen out of touch with since. In fact, we hadn't spoken in nearly five years. Kris also knew Mike, and the two had run into each at San Francisco International Airport the day before the hearing. Mike asked Kris where he was going, and Kris proceeded to tell him about what I had done and that I had been sentenced to prison, causing Mike to drop his bag to the floor in astonishment.

"You're talking about the same Max Kepler I know, right?" Mike asked.

"Yes," Kris said.    "But they're giving him another chance tomorrow in court.    He asked me to be there with him."

Without hesitation, Mike said, "Well, I'm coming too." He then called his wife who, along with their five children, were waiting back in L.A. for his return from a five-day business trip, to tell her he'd be back the following day. Then he booked a hotel and changed his flight.

These were the kind of people that would be in the courtroom with me, and I couldn't believe the extent of their support.

The hearing was scheduled for eleven in the morning, and by a stroke of good fortune, my Harvard roommate Tom would be arriving from Ft. Lauderdale at San Francisco International Airport at nine-thirty, which meant we could pick him up along the way.    Tom had grown up the last of four children in a middle-class family in Plantation, Florida, and we had become instant friends during freshman year.    We had also played football together, although he was the third string safety behind me, which created a slightly uncomfortable dynamic. However, I got injured during the seventh game of our senior season, and then my back-up was injured in the final game for the Ivy League championship against Yale, so Tom was put into the game, the first time this had happened during his college career.    Despite his inexperience, he had a spectacular game, making the game-winning play with just two minutes remaining and etching himself into the Harvard football history books. I had always admired his commitment to the team, despite sitting on the bench each year.

When we pulled up to the airport, we found Tom standing curbside holding only a briefcase, as he planned to return home as soon as the hearing was over. He jumped into the back seat and after exchanging brief, subdued pleasantries, we were off. A jocular sort, he tried to lighten up the mood.

"I can't wait to see the assistant US attorney. Is she hot?"

"In a prosecutorial kind of way, I guess," I replied.

Dad loved Tom but nonetheless turned up the volume on the radio. The same Fleetwood Mac song that I had heard prior to my first interview with the Government fifteen months earlier was playing. I chose to consider the words a good harbinger.

Why not think about times to come?
And not about the things that you've done?
If your life was bad to you,
Just think what tomorrow will do.

There was no substantive conversation for the remainder of the trip. As we drove, I had a sense of time accelerating out of control, and before I knew it, I was parking again in that dreary underground garage. Although I was accompanied by my father and two friends and knew that soon many others would be joining me in the courtroom, I found myself feeling disconnected from everyone, particularly as I remembered something I had written soon after the arrest.

"Born alone and die alone, and we spend much of the time in between fooling ourselves that we are not."

On our walk to the federal building, I reached into my pocket and was reassured I had remembered the small vial of benzoin oil a friend had given me. Saying it would give me strength and calm my mind, she told me to dab a little behind each ear just before the hearing. In the security bin of a Federal Building, the vial looked suspicious. "What's this?" a guard asked as he peered at the small glass container.

"Aromatherapy oil," I said quietly.

Dad gave me a strange look. The guard frowned, thought for a moment, and then put the vial back in the bin.

"Move on through," he instructed.

In the cafeteria, we found Ted, who was energized as usual but seemed disconcertingly serious. He pulled me aside.

"Let's go over the names of all the people who will be in the courtroom today."

I handed him the list, which included both friends and co-workers, Dr. Steele, and Alice and her brother. Some people had come from as far away as Maryland. Ted quickly reviewed the names, shaking his head.

"It's amazing all these people came here to back you. I'm quite impressed. It says a lot about you."

"Seems like it says a lot more about them," I replied.

"I'll introduce all of them," he said. "Then I'll make my presentation. After that, we'll leave it up to the judge."

Ted started scribbling notes. I moved away from him and began to walk in slow circles around the cafeteria tables. My team of twenty was socializing. Dad sat at a table alone, watching me. Margarita, one of my staunchest supporters and confidantes during the whole ordeal, was on the phone. I had always admired Margarita, a short, fiery Nicaraguan woman five years older than me. Married with three children before she was twenty-five, she had gone to nursing school after her divorce at age thirty, despite having full-time responsibility for her three young boys. Subsequently, she had worked her way up to head nurse in the clinic, where I had met her three years prior. We had immediately become friends. Since my arrest, I had had many conversations with her, and she was someone I could always count on for emotional assistance and positive energy.

As I reflected on the cocoon of support surrounding me, I realized Alice wasn't there, and I started to panic. Maybe she had changed her mind, or forgot, or got lost. But then I realized it was Alice; there was no way she wouldn't be there, and so I calmed down a little.

Suddenly, it occurred to me that that I had forgotten the aromatherapy oil, and so I hurried to the restroom and found an empty stall. As I was unscrewing the cap, I dropped the glass vial, and it landed with a clatter but didn't break. I quickly dabbed the tincture behind my ears.

When I returned to the cafeteria, I went to where Dad was seated and pulled up a chair. His eyes widened, his nostrils flared and he reared his head back.

"What the hell is that?"

"Just something to bring me luck. Is it that noticeable?"

"You smell like a dozen fresh-baked vanilla cookies."

"Oh shit," I said before grabbing a napkin off the table and rubbing the oiled spots.

"Better?"

"Barely."

"Time to go," Ted announced.

All twenty-two of us piled into two elevators. I ended up in the one carrying my football buddies and my partner, Steve, a cardiologist who had been with our hospital partnership for ten years and who had guarded my position like a bulldog since I'd been suspended. I had heard through multiple channels that he had met repeatedly with hospital administration to convince them not to let me go. And he had been successful, a fact that was not lost on me in the slightest as I looked at him in the cramped space.

"I feel so small in here with you guys," he said as he looked at my friends, trying to add some levity. His words drew only some polite smiles. As I watched him, I wondered what it must be like for such a respectable person—he was also Chief of Medicine at the hospital—to be going into a federal courtroom to hear unsavory evidence regarding his partner. Would being confronted with all the details make him change his mind about me?

Having waited in vain for Alice to arrive, we were behind schedule when my team walked into the courtroom, and it was clear the AUSA was not happy. The judge was already seated. He watched carefully as we filed in, also seeming annoyed about something. It

368

occurred to me that it was February 8, 2007, one day before my forty-first birthday, as the clerk stood up to begin the proceedings.

I walked to the front with Ted. Every cell in my body was activated as the judge began to speak.

"First of all, I would like to say that the reason I asked to have a continued sentencing hearing is that Mr. Cassman felt he was taken by surprise at the last hearing because the Court did not follow the sentence recommendation of both the government and defense. I felt it was only fair to Mr. Cassman, as a professional, and also fair to his client, that they get an opportunity to respond."

The judge nodded at Ted, who returned the gesture with a smile. The judge then continued.

"I have had an opportunity to review the pre-sentence report again. In fact, I reviewed it on several occasions. I don't want to reiterate what we discussed last time. We pretty much went into great detail over the court's position and also the court's interpretation of the facts and the gravity of these facts."

The judge then proceeded to discuss minor legal details with both Ted and the assistant US attorney for several minutes before he announced that Ted could speak.

I had been looking forward to this part. Previously and with no script, Ted's oratory skills had been impressive. I expected a repeat performance on this day, especially since Ted had had time to prepare.

But Ted started off shaky. His voice cracked and his speech was halting, revealing that he had become emotionally invested in my case. I felt pleased that he cared so much, but his delivery created the impression that he was making an excuse for my criminal behavior.

About halfway through, however, he found his rhythm and returned to his usual eloquent, persuasive form. When he was finished, he asked the court's permission to introduce "some folks."

Permission was granted. I looked back as Ted introduced them and was greatly relieved to see that Alice was now sitting in the front row. I later learned that the babysitter had arrived late, causing her delayed appearance. Her brother Jarrett was right next her, and both were dressed in black. *Funereal black.*

"These people came here today to demonstrate to this court, not only their support for Dr. Kepler and their unwavering commitment to him, but also that in their esteemed opinion, these people that know him best, that it would be a mistake to incarcerate Dr. Kepler, to take him away from his patients again."

"One of the things I don't think the court may have understood at the previous hearing, is that Dr. Kepler was taken away from his patients and the practice for ten months. It was a terrible time for him and for his patients and for the hospital."

"Your honor, Max obviously made terrible mistakes, terrible lapses in judgment, terrible decisions. He was self-righteous and deluded. He betrayed his patients at his clinic and the commitment that this society placed in him. He has accepted full responsibility for that."

"Your honor indicated he had read everything. Did you have an opportunity to see his statement that he wrote?"

"Yes," the judge replied, his tone neutral.

"When he lost his job at the hospital, it was a devastating blow to the hospital. The court should know at this time, aside from his daughter, his commitment to his patients in the hospital is the most important thing to him. He is an empathic and caring doctor."

"That brings us to the question of how he could have so egregiously acted as he did. Max would tell you it was a combination of arrogance, anti-authoritarianism gone wrong; and I would add, a lack of humility, and reliance on twisted information from a person he thought was worthy of respect and obviously was not."

"So how should the court sentence Dr. Kepler today? He has suffered deeply and profoundly and is very remorseful. He understands the gravity of his misconduct, but he has also provided marvelous healing for his patients. He is a great healer. So, we ask the court to impose a sentence that does not take him away from his hospital and from his patients and from his daughter. Thank you."

"Would you like to say anything?" the judge asked the assistant US attorney.

She replied "no" and the judge hesitated, gathering himself before he spoke again, first to review his duty as a federal judge, then to address my particular case. To my surprise, I found that I was neither scared nor angry. Somehow, I had reached an internal serenity for the first time in fifteen months.

"Seeing the parties that are here for Dr. Kepler, hearing Mr. Cassman's presentation to the court, you are very, very lucky Dr. Kepler. You have an excellent attorney, probably one of the best defense attorneys in the Bay Area, if not the nation."

My heart jumped in anticipation of receiving mercy.

"However, good people do bad things."

And immediately I was in the gallows again, awaiting punishment. I looked back at the sea of familiar faces in the gallery. They were focused intently on the judge, but I already knew what was coming.

"When I read Mr. Cassman's detailed sentencing memorandum, specifically something that jumped out at me was the following part":

It was a mistake that did not arise from greed or avarice or other ill intent. With each of these substances Max's intentions were to provide wellness care at reasonable prices. From Max's misguided perspective, he ordered hGH from overseas, was that he could provide the substances to his patients very inexpensively.

"This is in complete and total odds with what is noted in the pre-sentence investigation report which read, "On September 8, 2005, inspector placed an undercover telephone call to Kepler. He stated he would like to sell the inspector additional hGH, but that his current supply was low due to the large number of customers he had."

"May I respond?" Ted asked.

"Let me finish," the judge barked.

Going back to the document, he began quoting my assurances that the hGH did not come from China, looking up to state, "It should be noted now that the FDA has only two approved indications for the use of human growth hormone. Not only did Dr. Kepler not use hGH for either of these indications, but from the pre-sentence

372

investigative report, prepared his own cocktail, including hCG, and used that and injected it into patients."

The judge had confused the facts once again, despite having an additional six weeks to review the pre-sentencing report and the memorandum submitted by Ted. And now once again I was going to receive a sentence based on these misunderstandings and mistakes.

Ted began to fidget noticeably.

"Could I please respond right now?" he implored.

The judge nodded.

"This is not correct. He didn't put it in any cocktail. That is not correct. He had a mesotherapy treatment that is completely separate from the hCG. The two were not part of the same problem."

At that point, the assistant US attorney confirmed Ted's statement. But then she continued in her own erroneous ways.

"There was not a drug application made to the FDA to use the so-called mesotherapy cocktail."

A drug application to the FDA or formal FDA approval was not necessary to use the cocktail. Mesotherapy clinics are still operating to this day all over the country using a cocktail very similar to the one I used. Once again, the assistant US attorney, although trying to help, was providing the judge incorrect information.

The judge acknowledged these statements and signaled Ted that he could resume speaking.

"The court has cited information regarding statements that Max made to the undercover agent. Many of them were false statements. He didn't have a lot of patients. He was apparently getting another shipment. He never sent it to her or any of her friends. Never did any of the things he talked about in that conversation. His behavior as indicated and represented by that conversation is completely egregious; but he didn't do those things that are reflected in there. And what he did do is bad enough. He injected himself and offered it to her and he did show her how to inject herself. That is bad enough. But he didn't do any of these things; and he only had five patients that got hGH."

When Ted finished, the judge sat quietly for about thirty seconds, scowling in concentration. Then he gathered himself to make one last judicial rationalization.

"However, as I indicated before, one of the things the court must do is engage in a balancing act to determine the collateral consequences of that sentence on innocent people. Children, for instance, is something that obviously comes to mind. We're lucky that even though Dr. Kepler is divorced, he apparently, from what I understand from the report, has a relatively appropriate working relationship with his ex-wife regarding his child, so that the child will have and does have the opportunity to have a family member available. Plus, a stepfather is in the home."

The judge didn't think it would be a problem for my daughter to be away from me. After all, there was always her stepfather. As I listened to his words, I knew that I was going to prison.

I tuned out, waiting for the inevitable, until I heard him saying to Ted, "I am going to order that your client be remanded to the custody of the Bureau of Prisons for a period of three months. I am going to place your client on a one-year term of supervised release. The first three months of that term of supervised release will be what is commonly called house arrest or home detention."

Immediately, I heard a loud, "Jeesus!" that I knew came from Dad.

In the background, I could hear the assistant US attorney talking. She was asking the judge whether he still wanted the court transcripts to be sent to the Medical Board.

Ted dived in to try to save me.

"Your honor, I was going to request the court not send the transcripts to the Medical Board. They have done their investigation. This matter is before them and in their jurisdiction and this matter is here before this court. So, we request it not go."

"That motion will be denied. Obviously, I will not engage in any decision on whether or not Dr. Kepler remains fit to practice medicine. That will be up to the California State Medical Board to make that decision."

I was done fighting. I was going to prison and I would have to deal with it. Then I was going to lose my medical license.

"Dr. Kepler, you have made each and every one of your appearances. Obviously, I am not going to remand you into custody today. You do need to be able to take care of some issues regarding family."

I stared at him blankly.

"How much time does you client need to prepare to surrender?"

Ted had not given up, however.

"Could I ask the court to reconsider and impose a sentence with electronic monitoring?"

"No, I have given..."

"I know the court has."

"This has troubled me for over a month now and I have thought about this almost every day and considered what's appropriate. Mr. Cassman, I do not take this lightly; but I feel this court has an absolute obligation to the community as a whole, considering what I have in front of me, that your client does require a period of time of incarceration. I have decided to split that sentence after your pre-sentencing report, given all of the balancing factors, in order to reduce that by half, to three months and three months of home detention so he may remain employable and therefore can take care of his daughter at that time."

The judge sounded almost like he was trying to convince Ted of the wisdom of his decision. But Ted would not yield.

"I'm just concerned that that's not going to accomplish the court's goal. I am very concerned he is going to lose his ability to practice at the hospital and serve the patients that are there. If the court would consider a nine-month electronic home monitoring instead. The court knows that under the guidelines and under the law that's equivalent of an incarceration—a sentence of incarceration. We're asking the court to impose that; and I would ask for nine months instead of this split of three and three."

Remarkably, the judge was allowing Ted to negotiate with him.

"As I indicated before, you're an excellent counsel. I have thought about this. I have thought about doing that, Mr. Cassman. That was not something that comes for the first time to the court this morning. I have tried to fashion a sentence that I think is appropriate, and every time I go through the paperwork, read what has taken place, the court feels that this is an appropriate sentence. I assure you I take absolutely no pleasure in doing this, but as I said before, it's my position that I believe that I have a responsibility to the community, and responsibility in this particular instance, that includes a period of incarceration."

Ted was silent.

"That will be all for this morning. How much time does you client need to surrender?"

Ted smiled at the judge, and then continued speaking in apologetic tones.

"I have to take one last shot. The recommendation is five hundred hours of community service though the hospital. That is a quarter of a year of his time donated to the hospital; and if the court imposed a nine-month home detention with that, I would think that would further the court's goals better than anything else."

"I understand your position. I will deny that."

Sensing an opportunity, I blurted out, "I don't know how I'm going to provide financially."

The judge ignored me and moved to schedule the time when I would report to prison.

"Today is February 8th."

"Can he have sixty days?" Ted asks

"I order him to report to the twentieth floor of this building on April 6, 2007, for service of sentence. Or he should report to his assigned facility as instructed by the United States Marshal Service."

"Would the court make a recommendation it be in halfway house?" Ted blurted out.

I was astonished by his persistence. Without hesitation, the judge replied,

"The court would not have any objection."

"I ask you to recommend," Ted pushed.

"Given everything that I have heard, the court at this time will make that recommendation."

At the very last moment, Ted had gotten me a get-out-of-jail-free card. The judge never realized what hit him.

"Good luck, Dr. Kepler. I hope you take the time to reflect..."

"I already have, your honor," I interjected.

"...And that you consider very strongly, as I mentioned before, every opportunity that this country has offered you and given you, and that you owe citizens of this country your true and correct services as a physician if you're allowed to practice again after this over with. Court stands adjourned."

# CHAPTER TWENTY-EIGHT

As soon as the gavel came down, I looked to Alice. She was still weeping quietly, and in that moment, everything in the courtroom washed away, and all I cared about was her suffering. I needed to get to her, seated there in the middle of the second row. My knees bumped the legs of friends and family as I pushed past them. When I reached her, she was still seated, so I bent down to her.

"I'm so sorry," I said repeatedly as I hugged her awkwardly, certain there had been no time in my life when I had meant those words more.

"It's okay," she reassured me. This went on for several minutes until I felt a hand on my shoulder. I turned to see Ted.

"Let's go out to the lobby," he said.

By that time, people were streaming out of the courtroom, clogging the doorway. The AUSA, head down, weaved between us to escape.

Once outside, a loose circle formed around Ted and me. The rumble of confusion filled the space.

"I'm not going to prison, right?" I asked above the din, still a little confused about the rapid sequence of events at the end of the hearing.

Suddenly, it became perfectly quiet. Ted shook his head.

"I convinced him at the last second to send you to a halfway house instead."

Feeling numb and still unable to fully comprehend all that had just happened, I simply shook my head in amazement and said, "How in the hell did you do that, Ted?"

"We just got lucky, Max. He let me keep talking and so I kept trying to convince him."

I stood silently for a moment, trying to understand how my life's trajectory had suddenly changed so dramatically in a thirty-second span at the end of the hearing, simply because of the spectacular efforts of my attorney. I looked up at Ted, and I wanted to say, "thank you," but it felt too shallow and inadequate. Ted must have sensed this because he reached over and patted me on the shoulder, which caused me to reflexively hug him.

Still finding the situation too inordinate, I quickly let go of him and turned to the practical.

"Where's the halfway house?" I asked.

"There's one in San Francisco, I believe. And you can still work at the hospital while you're there."

"So, I just sleep there at night? And I can keep my job?"

"That's right."

"That's great news," my partner Steve interjected.

At that point, several people came up to me, offering congratulations and encouragement. Elsewhere, small groups of three to four people broke off into conversation. I heard people criticizing the judge. Some people stood staring into space, too stunned to engage. My psychiatrist remained by himself. One of the hospital administrators was patting Dad's back as he stared at the floor. On the other side, I saw several people reassuring Alice, who was no longer crying. She saw me look at her and smiled ever so slightly.

Just then, Adita, my Indian partner, came over and put her hand gently on my arm.

"Are you okay?" she asked solicitously.

I nodded and smiled at her, but I was tired and wanted to go home. I turned to face the others, and said, "Thanks to everyone for coming. It meant more than you can imagine." I didn't know what else I could possibly add to what I'd already told them, repeatedly, so I stopped there.

People starting heading for the elevators. By the time we left the building, only the three people I had come with remained. As we walked back to the garage, Tom and Kris began discussing their respective careers. Dad and I slowed our pace to put some distance between us and them. Dad put his arm around my shoulders, and we walked that way, silently, until we reached the car.

We dropped off Tom at the airport, and then drove back to Redwood City. Along the way, we picked up food at my favorite Mexican restaurant. Once home, we collapsed onto the couch and turned on the television, content to sit there and mindlessly watch as we ate. Almost immediately, Ted called. His voice was serious.

"We need to discuss something."

381

I stood up and walked a few steps away.

"I just go off the phone with a couple of people in the Bureau of Prisons. Turns out, since the judge sentenced you to prison, you'll have to go there after all."

"What in the hell are you talking about, Ted? Didn't he tell you I could go to a halfway house."

"He said he would *recommend* a halfway house. But he didn't sentence you to a halfway house. He sentenced you to prison."

By this time, Dad and Kris had put down their burritos and were looking at me intently. I shook my head as I listened to Ted.

"That doesn't make sense."

"The Bureau of Prisons doesn't follow recommendations; they follow sentences."

"And there's nothing we can do?"

"We need to get the judge to modify his sentence."

"There's no way in hell he's going to do that. He already granted us a continuation, and he wasn't happy about it."

"Too bad. He said you could go to a halfway house, and we're going to hold him to his word."

"So, what's the plan now?"

"He has seventy-two hours to sign off on the sentence. We need to get him to modify the sentence before that, and so I'll start working on it. I'll call you later."

After I hung up, I gave Dad and Kris the news. Without a word, Dad picked up his burrito, walked into the kitchen, and dumped it into the trash. Then he came over and hugged me briefly, before going into the bedroom and closing the door behind him.

At 5:50 that evening, Ted faxed his letter to the judge stating that, "In order for the Court's recommendation of a halfway house to be effectuated, the judgment must be corrected pursuant to Rule 35 (a)." Now, it was just of matter of waiting to see what the judge would do.

I decided to call Ted late that evening. Dad and Kris had already gone to bed, and I sat on the couch dazed by the glare of the television. I was feeling very lonely and needed someone to talk to. I knew Ted would listen, even though he was getting ready for bed when I called.

"First it was six months' prison, then three months' prison, then three months' halfway house, and now three months' prison again," I said.

"An odyssey, no doubt. Haven't seen anything quite like it," Ted replied.

"I don't have the heart to tell Alice right now. I'll wait until the judge makes his decision probably."

"It was really touching to see you go to her after the hearing."

Images of the courtroom and words from the judge filled my head. Twenty people were there for me, but now I was alone again.

Ted was still on the phone.

"My God, we have to figure out a way to keep me out of prison. It would be too tough on Jessica."

"I've faxed the letter already. And I'm going to call the judge's clerk first thing in the morning and see if I can nudge him to act on our request."

"I appreciate it. By the way, I listened and watched you very carefully in court today, and I could see that you really cared. That made me feel good, and I wanted to thank you for it."

383

"You're welcome. Nice of you to say so, especially under the circumstances. And yes, I do care. It means a lot that it helped you, if only a little."

"This just doesn't make sense."

"But you make sense, and now we'll see if the judge does. Get some rest, Max."

To help persuade the judge, Ted felt I needed to get more letters of support. For some people, it would be the third time I asked. Each subsequent request was harder to make, but I was in survival mode.

Naturally, I went to Sang first. He was just getting ready to leave for a scheduled meeting.

"Would it be possible for you to write one more letter?"

He leaned back in his chair, rested his head, and sighed.

"What do you need now?" he asked, sounding irritated.

"Another letter. Please."

"I have a meeting right now. Can I do it later?"

"The problem is that the judge could sign off at any time. So, this is a time-sensitive issue."

Sang nodded and then picked up his phone.

"Please cancel my meeting that started five minutes ago," he said to his secretary.

He motioned for me to sit down.

"What exactly do you need?"

As I told him, he swung around to his computer and began typing.

"Who should I address it to?"

"The Honorable Judge Vandor Natas," I said derisively.

"Tell me how many patients you see typically."

"About one hundred and ten patients per week, seventy in the inpatient setting and forty outpatients."

As Sang typed, I sat there feeling like a child waiting for a permission slip. The wait seemed interminable, and when he finally finished, he read the letter aloud, and then signed it. After thanking him, I scurried out as quickly as possible.

After that, I went to the Chief of Staff, Chief of Medicine, an administrator in the medical clinic and Margarita. All prepared and faxed a letter within hours. Once again, I was amazed how people just kept coming through for me, however draining it was to keep asking for help.

Later that night, I called Alice to talk about what had happened in the courtroom.

"I felt so bad as I stood there and watched you cry," I said.

"I didn't mean to, but I just lost control. Actually, I was embarrassed. I was a nervous wreck and felt so many emotions, even now. I can't even describe it. I've had weird dreams."

"I'm so sorry for causing you more pain."

"Seeing you up there, thinking about our little girl, seeing all your closest friends and family ....me sitting up front eye to eye with the judge who had control over your fate and Jessica's fate, it just hit me to the core. I don't know why it felt so raw and surreal at the same time. It seemed like you, me, Jessica and the judge were in that courtroom alone."

In the background, I could hear the soothing music of Miles Davis. I remembered all the times we had listened to jazz together.

"I know exactly what you mean. I kept looking back at you.  Ted had to keep reminding me to look at the judge."

"Can you believe after the whole thing I was so disoriented and disconnected that I couldn't find my way home? I had no clue which direction to go."

"I know that feeling of dissociation all too well, unfortunately."

"Jerry told me to give you his best.  He's sorry he couldn't be there."

"I understand.  Tell him thanks."

"Regarding my tears, at least they weren't futile. The judge looked at me twice while your attorney was negotiating in the last minute and I think it might have had some impact on him. It's so ridiculous how the judicial system works, but at least you're not going to prison."

I needed to tell her. I cleared my throat and as I was about to speak when suddenly I heard Jessica in the background calling for her. Alice got up and went to the bedroom, and I heard their muffled voices.  Jessica settled down quickly, and Alice came back, resuming our conversation in a whisper.

"When do we know more? I am carefully considering how we are going to deal with Jessica."

"Within a couple of days. One more thing," I said, before hearing Jessica call out to her again.

"Let's talk some other time," she interrupted.

I breathed a sigh of relief. It was probably better for her not to know anyway.

The decision came just before the seventy-two-hour mark.

"He's modified the judgment," Ted told me by phone. "No prison for you."

I wanted to jump up and down and scream as loud as I could, but I was in the hallway of the hospital. Instead, I told him, "Thank you," as I sighed deeply.

"You're welcome. You'll have to report in sixty days."

"You'll give me more details later?"

"I'll fax you a copy of the Amended Judgment. And I'll call you in a couple of days. Congratulations."

I hung up and sat quietly. There were no tears, no laughter, no smiles; just relief. I didn't feel like jumping up and down anymore. I simply wanted to get back to my patients, because of the respite they provided from the realities of life. I had even come to the point that I longed for the boredom I formerly abhorred.

I waited until that evening to call my parents. They were both on the line when I announced the news.

"That's great," Dad said immediately. "Sounds like the asshole finally came to his senses."

"I can't tell you how relieved I am, Max," Mom said.

"I know, Mom," I said, feeling a building pressure in my chest.

"I was worried sick about the possibility of you going to prison. I haven't been able to sleep for the last few days."

"I'm really sorry, Mom," was all I could manage. I didn't want to start relieving the guilt again.

When do you have to start?" she asked.

"Sixty days."

"Where is it?" she asked.

"Somewhere in San Francisco."

"Who else is going to be there? Is it dangerous?"

"I don't know, but I doubt it," I said gently, trying to reassure her.

"You'll be fine," Dad said. "Try to…"

"What a mess," Mom interrupted.

"Yes, it is," I said apologetically.

"What a mess," she repeated, seemingly to herself this time.

My final sentence was three months in a halfway house ("community confinement," in the parlance), three months' home detention, and six months of probation. Equally punishing was the fact that the transcripts from the two sentencing hearings had been sent to the Medical Board of California. I called to tell Gordon, as he would not hear about it from the Board for a week or more.

"A Board analyst will review the transcripts and then forward them to the San Jose investigational unit," he said.

"But they've already closed the case."

"With the sentence you've received, they might re-open it. Should anyone from the Board attempt to contact you, do not talk to them. Please refer them directly to me."

"If we're lucky, maybe they'll see I've already received significant punishment and not pursue the issue further."

"To be honest with you, Max, I don't think they really care."

# CHAPTER TWENTY-NINE

The halfway house was located in the epicenter of the Tenderloin section of San Francisco, only four blocks away from the federal building where I had been prosecuted. Fortunately, there was a parking lot close by, on Ellis Street. Cornell Corrections, a private company that contracted with the United States Bureau of Prisons, ran the House. I was to discover that all the other residents were ex-convicts who had served anywhere from one to over thirty years in a federal penitentiary, most often in maximum security. The age range was wide, with the average being somewhere in the mid-thirties. The ethnic mix was equal parts black, white and Hispanic, with a sprinkling of Asians.

An informational packet I received in the mail informed me that residents could leave the halfway house only through sign-out procedures for approved activities, such as seeking employment, working, counseling, visiting, or recreation. While at work, residents could expect staff to visit or call to check up on them. There would also be random drug and alcohol tests, along with frequent head counts throughout the day. Furthermore, residents were required to pay a subsistence fee to help defray the cost of their confinement. My subsistence fee turned out to be $72.43 per month. For three hots and a cot. Those checks would prove to be the most painful I had ever written.

I called the facility for more information and discovered I would be permitted to spend a maximum of ten hours each day outside of the House, and that time could only be used for work. The maximum number of hours per week outside the House would be fifty, and one day a week I would not be able to leave the House at all. No laptops were permitted in the House, but since I was a doctor, I could have my cell phone with me. I had hoped to arrange my schedule ahead of time so there would be no interruptions in patient care, but the facility director informed me that, "We'll work things out once you're here."

I tried to impress upon her the need for advance planning, but she cut me off, stating, "I'm sorry, but I can't do anything else."

"I understand," I replied, mindful of Ted's earlier admonition to "kiss their asses." Before she hung up, I said, "One more thing. I have a five-year-old daughter. Will I be able to arrange time with her?"

"She can visit you in the facility one day each week," the director said.

"Are there any other options for seeing her?"

"Not for at least three weeks. After that, privileges such as family visits depend on a number of factors."

"Such as?"

"Participation in chores, adherence to schedule, class attendance, and other behavioral factors."

The vagueness bothered me, and I worried how Jessica would react to my absence. It would be the first time we were away from each other for an extended period of time. There was not a chance I would allow her to come to the House.

"I guess we'll discuss the details after I'm there?"

"That's right. Is there anything else Mr. Kepler?"

"No ma'am. Thank you. See you on April 6."

She hung up without a reply.

As I prepared to enter the House, I continued working long overtime hours to help pay off my legal debt. My social life was non-existent, which was perfectly fine with me. I couldn't imagine dating under the circumstances.

*"I know we've been seeing each other for a month or so, but I can't see you for the next three months," I would have to tell any theoretical girlfriend.*

*"Really? Why's that?" she'd ask.*

*"I've been sentenced to three months in a halfway house."*

*She would look at me quizzically and ask, "Are you going to be doing some medical work there?"*

*"No, actually I'll be a prisoner. I was convicted of illegally importing human growth hormone from China."*

*"I see," she would say, keeping her tone neutral.*

*"And then for ninety days after that, I'll be on home arrest and have to wear an electronic ankle bracelet, so I won't be able to leave the house except for work."*

*There would be prolonged silence, and then the inevitable would be delivered.*

*"Um, I don't think this is going to work out," she would say as she prepared to leave, and I would not protest. How could I?*

So, I decided not to date. It wasn't a big deal anyway; I hadn't been on a date for over a year. What was another six months?

Alice, in the meantime, was about to have her second child with Jerry, who continued to be a wonderful stepfather for Jessica. I was so relieved Alice had made such an excellent choice of a partner.

In the hospital, rumors were swirling regarding the reasons for my ten-month leave of absence. Since the case was under seal, it was not in the public domain, and only my partners knew the real story. That didn't prevent others from speculating, and I heard a number of theories, including:

*He's a drug dealer.*

*He's a drug addict.*

*He had a sexual relationship with a patient.*

*He stole drugs from the hospital.*

*He had a mental breakdown.*

Mom worried mightily about my reputation.

"What are people saying at the hospital?" she kept asking. "Does anyone know what happened?

"It doesn't matter, Mom," I told her, but I don't think she believed me. It was true. By now the trauma had virtually obliterated my ego. People were free to interpret and contextualize me, as I knew in the end those perceptions would be imprecise and inconsequential. I wanted only for people to consider me a good-hearted person, and, those at the hospital, a good doctor. To that degree, I was still invested in their thoughts.

392

I tried to let Mom know that my challenge was not to worry about my reputation, but rather to be unflinchingly honest with myself but her response was always the same: "I hope no one finds out what happened."

While Mom was stressing about my reputation, I turned my attention to trying to reconcile living in a halfway house with a bunch of convicted felons while still working as a doctor.   In some ways, I would have to disassociate, or perhaps compartmentalize, to make the two vastly different roles mesh.   Sometimes I would simply remind myself that the House was like a rest stop on my journey towards a new evolution.   Various other mind tricks were helpful.   But I could not deny one absolute certainty:   I had seen and been in places over the previous two years that I could never, even in the most imaginative recesses of my mind, have anticipated, and I still had a way to go.

But there was an unexpected and gratifying consequence of the turmoil:   Jessica and I had become closer than ever over the previous year.   I viewed every moment I spent with her as a privilege, and used our time together meaningfully.   Sometimes we would go on walks or visit the playground.   Other times we did art projects together or I would read her a book.   Regardless of the activity, we spent a lot of time talking, and I became very familiar with her developing personality.

But now, with reporting time rapidly approaching, I needed to speak with her about the halfway house.   I decided to do it two weeks in advance.   We had just finished dinner, and I pushed away my half-eaten meal. Her favorite stuffed animal, a little white rabbit with pink ears, sat on her lap. I rested my elbows on the table, chin in hands, and stared at her. I did this frequently, and it always made her shy. She playfully pushed one of my arms, causing my chin to drop.

"Daddyyyy…"

"I'm sorry. I was just thinking how lucky I am to have you."

She smiled widely and started flapping the rabbit's ears back and forth, giggling.

"Jessica, I need to talk to you about something. Okay?"

She nodded her head and quieted her hands.

"Daddy needs to go away for a little while. I'm not going far, just to San Francisco."

"When?"

"In two weeks."

"Where are you going?"

"I'm going to live in a big house with some other men."

"But why, Daddy?"

"Because I'm gonna to try to help these men. They have a lot of problems."

"Kinda like how you help patients at the hospital?"

"Kinda."

"That sounds like a good idea, Daddy. But where will you sleep?"

"I'll sleep in the house."

"But where will I sleep?"

I cleared my throat and looked away briefly.

"You'll be staying with Mama, but I'll call you on the phone every day."

"So, I won't see you?" She started to look worried.

"Not for a little while. But I'll see you as soon as I can."

394

"But Daddy, I'll miss you." She started to whimper.

"I'll miss you too, but I'll still be able to see you after a couple of weeks. We just won't be able to spend the night together. And the whole thing will be over before you know it."

"A couple of weeks is a long time."

"I know, but I'll call you every day."

She sat quietly at the dinner table, her five-year-old brain trying to make sense of my words. I stayed with her, holding her hand and looking into her brown eyes as she wiped away tears.

"I don't want you to go."

"I don't want to go, either. But I have to."

I pulled her into my lap and held her. After a while, she stopped crying.

"Come on, let's play Zingo," I told her.

She lifted her head off my shoulder and smiled at me.

"Only if I get to be the dealer," she said.

She was quiet while we played, and when we were finished, she asked if she could sleep in my bed that night. I told her that was fine and after she bathed and put on her pajamas, we crawled into bed and snuggled while I read her a story. Soon, she fell asleep, and I lay there with her for a long time, holding her warm foot. When sleep finally came for me, the nightmares of her witnessing the raid returned, awakening me, and I spent the rest of the night once again berating myself for my profound irresponsibility.

# CHAPTER THIRTY

The day of reckoning arrived.    But first I had to pack.
Told I could bring enough clothes to fit into two drawers,
I gathered seven dress shirts, five pairs of slacks, one pair
of sweatpants, underwear, socks, three pairs of shorts,
three tee shirts, two pairs of dress shoes and one pair of
sneakers.  I brought *Crime and Punishment* to read, smiling
to myself as I stuffed it into my shoulder bag.  I grabbed
my cell phone and wallet off the counter.  Before I left, I
wrote "Welcome Home" in big letters on a blank piece of
paper and left it on my bed.

Although I didn't have to be there until two, I left before
noon so I could familiarize myself with the area.  I turned
off the radio and drove the forty minutes to San Francisco
in silence.  Along the way, a thought popped into my head
with such abruptness and force that I almost pulled over
to the side of the road.

*I deserve this.*

Although it had come about through judicial bumbling,
the judge got it right.  My egoism had told me I was
different from the rest of the herd, special, and as such, I
could make my own set of rules.  I had held onto blaming

the judge—even, at one point, Ted—for my having to serve any time. But as I drove to the House, I finally realized that I, and I alone, was to blame for my predicament. My failure to do this before was partly due to the fact I was distracted by my battle with the legal system, but, more importantly, it was my unwillingness to accept that I was human and had made terrible mistakes that prevented full recognition of culpability. But now I realized I needn't protect myself any longer, and it was the simple acquiescence to that reality, my acknowledgement of being completely responsible, that gave me a relief and solitude that I hadn't experienced in a long time. Even as I was about to start my confinement, I was shedding the shackles.

When I reached the city, I drove just past the House at 111 Taylor Street, and stopped the car. The House proved to be a nondescript, fairly modern apartment building with front glass windows that were darkened, preventing anyone from seeing inside. I drove another half block and found the parking lot on Ellis Street surrounded by a high chain link fence, layered on top with barb wire. The attendant there was an Indian man with a warm smile.

"How long will you be?" he asked as I pulled in.

"Three months." I replied, causing him to laugh.

"I'm serious," I reassured him.

"In that case, you'll want to buy a monthly pass."

Once that was taken care of, I parked my car, but then realized I still had forty-five minutes. I sat there for fifteen of them, gathering my thoughts. Sixty days of anticipation and worry were over, and I found myself actually eager for the challenge. I decided to go in early.

Shirts on hangers slung over my right shoulder, duffle bag hanging from the left, I walked out of the wired confines of the parking lot. As I hit the street, I found myself immersed in a colorful blend of humanity and illegality, and I could only imagine how out of place I looked. Milling around were odd-looking people with far-off looks on their faces, young men selling drugs, prostitutes, homeless people, drunks holding up walls, and ordinary people. I was relieved when I reached the front of the House.

Although the all-glass exterior was tinted, at this close range I could see men and, to my surprise women, walking up and down a staircase located about twenty-five feet away. Some of them paused long enough to stare wide-eyed out at the street. I pulled at the door several times, but found it locked. The noise attracted the attention of a man inside. I motioned to him, but he remained expressionless and stationary, pointing down at a painted yellow line he was apparently not to cross.

I pushed the buzzer, which still brought no assistance, despite the increasing attention. So, I pushed it again, waited a minute, and did it again, this time holding the buzzer down. A small crowd had now formed. Suddenly, a scrawny white man wearing an irritated expression and a polo shirt with "Cornell Corrections" on the pocket, came to the door.

"What do you want?"

"I'm checking in."

He looked at me curiously, before scanning my clothes and the shirts slung over my back.

"Name?"

"Max Kepler."

He looked down at a clipboard in his hands and nodded. "Come in and have a seat over there," he said, pointing. "Someone will be with you shortly."

He left me and walked behind a counter that served as the reception desk. Standing there was an impatient black man with an oversized white tee shirt barely obscuring equally large arms. He did not acknowledge me.

I took a seat on a hard-plastic chair, one of those single-pieced scooped-out objects, slippery and uncomfortable, and I sat there feeling like a fool in a barren lobby as the dispersing residents walked past me, shooting occasional fleeting glances. No one stared, however, and I would later learn there was an unwritten rule against that, a carryover from prison.

The sunlight filtered through the front windows, creating a dream-like atmosphere. The outside world suddenly seemed very far away. A buzzing at the front door startled me. Soon, a young man escorted by a parole officer entered.

"Jeremy Baird," the officer told the man with the clipboard, "From Folsom State Prison."

A real live convict. I tried not to stare.

The parole officer shook Jeremy's hand, telling him, "I'll stop by in a week or two to check up on you."

"No problem," he replied, beaming. As the parole officer headed for the door, Jeremy sat down directly across from me, making eye contact as he did.

"Hi," he said cheerfully. I noticed his young face and wide smile, which revealed crooked front teeth.

"Hello," I managed, before averting my gaze.

"Are you coming or going?"

"Coming."

"Cool. Where'd you come from?"

His presence and energy outsized his five foot ten, one hundred sixty-pound frame. His close-cropped brown hair and chiseled, white face combined to give him the appearance of a Marine. I noticed he had brand-new clothes, as I could see the fold wrinkles on the shirt and shorts. His tee shirt was cut off at the sleeves, revealing well-muscled arms.

"I'm originally from Ohio."

"No, I mean what joint did you come from?"

"Prison, you mean?"

He nodded his head.

"None. I came straight from home."

He gave me a puzzled look. He started rummaging through his duffel bag. I looked out the front windows, relieved the conversation was over.

"Have you been waiting long?" he asked.

"About a half hour."

And then he was back into his bag.

"Incredible day. Absolutely beautiful. Very little traffic, too," he commented as he pulled out a pair of socks.

He was well-spoken, even charismatic. I wondered what had sent him to prison. Perhaps he had been a stockbroker, caught in insider trading. An attorney who got mixed up in drugs?

Whoever or whatever he was, I could see he was completely unaffected by the House.

Fortunately, we didn't have to wait long before a short Latino man who fit the medical definition of "morbidly obese" came panting into the lobby, holding a clipboard. He rotated around to face us.

"Baird and Kepler?" he asked.

We nodded in unison.

"Both of you come with me."

Belongings in hand, we walked up two flights of stairs to a small office on the second floor. By the time we got there, the man was wheezing loudly. Several uncomfortable minutes passed during which I was worried that he would have a respiratory arrest, and I'd have to save him. If that happened, I figured it would at least gain me favor in the House. However, his labored breathing eased after he sat down, even as beads of sweat formed on his forehead.

"Gonna do both of you at the same time," he said, motioning to chairs on the other side of the small desk. Once we settled in, he opened up a manila folder and looked at Jeremy.

"You first, Max," he said.

Jeremy's peculiar smile caused the man to take a second look at the mug shot in the manila folder. His eyes bounced back and forth between the picture and Jeremy several times while he tapped the picture with his index finger. Suddenly, he pivoted towards me.

"You're Max," he said, pointing.

I acknowledged that I was and then looked over at the mug shot, which had been taken in the federal building on the day of my arrest. The picture flooded my brain with memories: the handcuffed walk past alarmed passersby on a midday San Francisco sidewalk, the elevator ride with well-groomed, suited men, the fingerprinting, the suffocating silence of the holding room. The courtroom. The emotions of that day began to return, and I was glad when the man started talking.

"Let's go over a few things," he said, flipping through the pages.

"You were arrested on October 12, 2005. Plead guilty to a misdemeanor. Sentenced on February 8th, 2007..."

It was clear this interview would be vastly different than the others I'd had in my life, such as those for college, graduate school, medical school, residency, fellowship or my first job as a physician at Cade County Hospital. For those interviews, my files held gleaming records of achievement, growing in thickness and impressiveness with each succeeding year. But in a short eighteen months, I had flipped that dynamic upside down and created a new and darker history.

"Max?"

"I'm sorry. What did you say?"

The intake session lasted twenty minutes. Once finished, the man announced Jeremy and I would be roommates.

Jeremy smiled, but I was still focused on just trying to keep myself together.

Our room was on the second floor, down a long hallway lined with numbered doors. The man opened the door to #202 to reveal a room approximately six by ten feet in size, with stained dark carpeting on the floor. Two bunk beds were at one end of the room, so closely situated that I could stand between them and place an elbow on each. A window that looked down on Taylor Street separated the bunks at their head. Two bureaus, one containing four drawers and the other two, took the remaining space at the other end. Beyond that was a bathroom and small shower. A slightly foul odor permeated the air.

Jeremy jumped on the top bunk to the left, and I began unpacking my clothes, placing them into the top two drawers of the larger dresser, as I had twice as many clothes as Jeremy. Out of the corner of my eye, I noticed Jeremy staring into space, grinning. I meticulously folded and refolded my clothes, trying to take up as much time as possible. Nevertheless, I was finished in about ten minutes. By then, Jeremy was looking at me and so I turned towards him.

"It's a great day, Max," he said immediately.

"Why's that?" I asked, feigning interest.

"Because I hugged my daughter for the first time."

"That's great. How old is she?" I asked.

"Fourteen."

The answer rattled around in my brain for a few seconds.

"And this is the first time you've hugged her?"

"Yes. I was sent to prison when my wife was pregnant. I just got released today. And they never allowed me any physical contact with her when she visited."

Life serves up moments that are not adequately touched by words, so I said nothing.

"The most amazing experience of my life," he continued.

I thought that was most definitely true. And I wanted to hug this man I didn't even know. But then I thought of all the lost time, and I didn't know whether to be happy or terribly sad for him. I decided happy because he was so happy. And then I sat down on the dirty floor of my new home, leaned against the wall, and listened as Jeremy told me his story with very little prompting from me.

Jeremy's parents had divorced when he was five, and his father subsequently moved out of state and mostly out of his life. Without a male influence at home, Jeremy got into trouble, so his mom shipped him off when he was ten to live with her father in a log cabin in a rural area of California, where he spent his free time learning to hunt and fish. Under the steadying influence of his grandfather, his behavior improved.

"But then those woods started closing in on me, and I got restless." Jeremy said. "I knew I had to get out of there, so I moved back in with my mom."

"Was that a good thing?" I asked.

"It was alright, but unfortunately she lived in kind of a rough suburb of Sacramento. Before long, I was running with some of the neighborhood boys, getting caught up in shit I shouldn't have."

The surrounding area was divided along ethnic and geographic lines, providing fertile grounds for distrust between different groups. Jeremy embraced the developing social structure so vigorously that he began espousing the virtues of "whiteness" to the malleable young, middle-class boys who looked up to him.

"We talked about white pride, about taking care and protecting our brothers," he told me. "We didn't dislike other groups because they were black or yellow or whatever. We disliked them because they were from a different group. We spent most of our time talking about how we could improve ourselves and our race, not how we could destroy others. We tried to foster ethnic pride."

"What was your role in the gang?"

"I was the leader, brother," he said, smiling as though that should be obvious. In fact, it had run through my mind, given the charisma I'd noticed even in the short time I'd known him. "I've always had good leadership skills. I'm smart, and I know how to organize people. I don't know why that's so, especially since I grew up without a father."

Unfortunately, some of the group's activities included criminal forays, consisting mostly of petty theft. A string of arrests eventually landed Jeremy in juvenile hall, where he spent close to six months.

"Judy scars you, brother. I was angry when I came out of there. That's when things really started to unravel."

The first stay was followed by multiple other arrests, causing Jeremy to spend most of his teenage years in various forms of custody.

"How'd you end up going to prison?" I asked him at one point.

Jeremy looked at his watch. "Doesn't dinner start at five?"

I shrugged my shoulders. It was five-thirty.

"Let's go see," I suggested, realizing I had another fifty-nine days to get the rest of his story.

We made our way down to the cafeteria on the first floor in the rear of the building. At one end was a doorway with a split door, the bottom part of which was kept closed. Food was served through the doorway, the efficiency of the process being a direct consequence of which staff was working and how the residents behaved. If the employees were feeling particularly passive-aggressive or lazy, the food delivery could take some time, and griping would resonate down the line of waiting residents, followed by sarcastic remarks to the staff. But things never got out of hand, as the ex-cons were practiced at knowing precisely how far they could push it.

As Jeremy and I stood in line, I had the sense I was being watched, without noticing anyone really looking at me. We were new blood in the House and our arrival had disrupted order in the House. I would learn that convicts don't like that. Disorder represents chaos, and in prison, chaos leads to injury or death. Still carrying the institutionalized mindset ingrained in them over the years, they valued the inherent safety of order. They would need to know who we were and what we were about so that we could be characterized and cataloged, thus restoring House harmony.

I was also to learn that the residents were very adept at reading body language. In prison, the anticipation of danger—and sometimes even survival—requires good instincts. They paid close attention to the smallest details, such as how a man held his shoulders, or cast his eyes, or where he kept his hands.

After the unidentifiable meat, mashed potatoes and canned green beans were dumped on my plate, I took a seat next to Jeremy at one of the tables. Almost immediately, a pale white man, probably about fifty years in age, introduced himself as Bob. He was a short, slight man with light brown hair that hung straight down to just above his eyebrows, giving him the look of an over-the-hill skateboarder. Although he initiated the conversation, he appeared timid, making only fleeting, intermittent eye contact. He spoke quietly and earnestly and seemed surprised that we were listening to him. Sometimes, in fact, my mind did wander off while he was still talking.

Bob's story did intrigue me, however. When he was twenty-one and unmotivated ("work never agreed with me," he would later tell me), he decided to become a bank robber after watching the movie *Bonnie and Clyde*. To prepare himself, he read books about bank robbing in the local public library, the only books he had read in his entire life.

His first robbery was in his hometown, in a rural area of Kansas. Dressed in a face mask and holding a fake gun, he walked into a bank on a rainy, Saturday morning, pointed the gun at a teller and tossed a pillow case at her, demanding she fill it with cash. Several minutes later, he walked out the front door and into a nearby alley where he removed his mask and jacket and tucked them and the booty into a duffel bag. In some woods nearby, he counted the ten thousand free dollars, and from that point forward, he was hooked. He spent the next several years robbing banks across the country, eventually deciding to use a real gun after a security guard took a shot at him. Inevitably, the FBI caught up with him, and he was convicted of multiple armed robberies and sent to prison for twenty years.

By the time Bob was finished with his tales of pillage, dinner was over, so Jeremy and I started to make our way back to our room. Before we got far, we were stopped by one of the staff supervisors.

"You're the new guys here, right?"

"Yep," Jeremy answered.

"You fellas got cafeteria clean-up duty. Tom over there will show you boys what to do."

"What's this bullshit, dude?" Jeremy asked.

I took a small step backwards. The supervisor stood strong, pointing at Jeremy as he spoke.

"Every new guy has to pull House duties for the first two weeks he's here, and you ain't no exception."

"I didn't know nothing about this," Jeremy said.

"You do now," the supervisor replied, and then walked away.

I followed a cursing Jeremy over to Tom, who described our duties to us. First, we were to wipe down all the tables and benches. Then we had to push the tables back against the walls to create a common area where people could watch television and play cards (no betting, of course) and board games, read, socialize, or just hang out. This was to be followed by a sweep and mop of the floor. Finally, we were responsible for cleaning up the food prep area. Soon, we would learn this was a coveted job, as we were permitted to take left-over food and drink.

During the middle of our first clean-up, I heard Jeremy exclaim, "Cool! A microwave!" I walked over to find him playing with the buttons and opening and closing the door. Fourteen years is a long time to spend away from civilization.

By the time we completed our chores, it was past the eight o'clock curfew and the cafeteria was empty. We returned to the room and hopped into our bunks. Within ten minutes, a tall and skinny Hispanic man, baseball cap pulled down low above his eyes, walked in and introduced himself as our new roommate. Javier had a pretty face with refined facial features and a calm, quiet demeanor. He took a quick look around the room.

"Fo' sho'," he said.

I heard that phrase every day for two weeks until I finally asked him what it meant. He laughed.

"For sure," he explained.

He unpacked his bag and took up space in the bed below Jeremy.

"Where you coming from, bro?" Jeremy asked him.

"Taft."

"What'd you get sent up for?"

"Pirating Direct TV signals."

"Cool. How'd you do that?"

"Found a way to bypass the decoder card."

"And they sent you to prison for that?" Jeremy asked. "Dude."

"There was some other stuff too."

"Like what?" Jeremy persisted.

"Meth."

"Ah, man, that shit's wrong," Jeremy said.

Jeremy considered methamphetamine, freely available in the Sacramento area, to be the white man's scourge, having witnessed many a friend succumb to addiction.

Conversation continued until a House counselor swung open the door and announced, "lights out," at eleven o'clock. Although I was completely exhausted, I couldn't sleep. The mattress was too thin, the bed too short, and the room too loud, with the continuous cacophony of shouts, tire squeals, scuffles, arguments, and various unidentified sounds drifting up from Taylor Street through the open window. The smallness of the room made me claustrophobic. Every several hours, the door would suddenly burst open, filling the room with light while a staff member performed a quick bed check. I nearly jumped out of bed the first few times it happened.

To pass the time, I stared at the ceiling and wondered whether this was the bottoming-out I had heard of. But then I thought of my daughter's beautiful face, which comforted me and eventually brought sleep.

# CHAPTER THIRTY-ONE

I awoke early the next morning, took a quick shower in the tiny bathroom, and dressed. Jeremy and Javier were still sleeping when I left. I didn't bother stopping by the cafeteria for breakfast and instead went directly to the reception area to check out. After waiting in line with other residents, I signed a log where my exact departure time was recorded. Then I was handed a box lunch and informed I needed to be back by five-thirty. Being even a minute late would cause the loss of privileges.

On my way to the car, I passed a homeless man asking for money. I gave him the lunch instead, and over the next three months, we would repeat the same routine each day at the corner of Taylor and Ellis.

I struggled to make it through work that day. My partners wanted to hear about the House, but I lacked the energy to describe it. Plus, I was a little too shell-shocked by my new surroundings to adequately put it into words. Worried about making it back in time, I left an hour early and spent the extra time getting pretzels and chips from a convenience store. Upon my return, I blew into a

Breathalyzer and signed the log. Staff searched my bag, finding the snacks.

"You can't have any food in the room. You'll have to eat that in the cafeteria," a staff member grumbled.

I ate some of the food and tossed the rest in the trash. Returning home, I found Jeremy and Javier lying in bed, looking out the window. I got into my bunk and joined them in watching the activity below. The crack addicts were easy to pick out, with their nervous habits, busy hands, and random movements back and forth on the sidewalk. Every twenty to thirty minutes, they would pull out a glass pipe, take a hit, and then resume their erratic behavior. They repeated this pattern incessantly, creating a real-life scientific demonstration of crack cocaine pharmacology. I marveled at the rapidity and ease with which they used the drug, and recoiled at the terrible self-destruction they were inflicting. Not able to watch the idiocy anymore, I rolled over on my back, picked up *Crime and Punishment* and began reading Chapter Five, having read the first four chapters in the week before I arrived at the House.

Soon, I came across a fascinating conversation regarding an article about crime written by a man named Raskolnikov that another character named Porfiry wanted to discuss with him. Porfiry summarizes the article by saying, "There is, if you recollect, a suggestion that there are certain persons who can ... that is, not precisely are able to, but have a perfect right to commit breaches of morality and crimes, and that the law is not for them."

Raskolnikov points out that this is a bit of an exaggeration, but Porfiry presses on, saying, "...all men are divided into 'ordinary' and 'extraordinary.' Ordinary

412

men have to live in submission, have no right to transgress the law, because, don't you see, they are ordinary. But extraordinary men have a right to commit any crime and to transgress the law in any way, just because they are extraordinary."

Raskolnikov, still feeling this is a distorted version of his thoughts, counters by presenting a modified version of a similar concept, in which he states, "I simply hinted that an 'extraordinary' man has the right ... that is not an official right, but an inner right, to decide in his own conscience to overstep ... certain obstacles, and only in case it is essential for the practical fulfillment of his idea (sometimes, perhaps, of benefit to the whole of humanity)."

The shock of recognition evoked by the words caused me to put the book down and stare at the ceiling until it was dinner time. This concept, so precisely stated by Raskolnikov, had played a central role in my illegal actions. I had been so driven by the pursuit of a cure for hair loss, something that countless others had tried and failed to accomplish, that I was willing to readily break the law. In my mind, our research was so important to so many people, and so potentially lucrative, that any means used to successfully bring our hair peptide to market were justified. My full acceptance of the wrongness of my actions, which first took place on my initial drive to the House two days earlier and which now recurred as I considered Raskolnikov's words, not only gave me comforting clarity, but also made it impossible for me to ever do such things again.

413

By the third day, the three of us roommates had settled into a routine. Then, in the middle of the night, a man carrying with him both a duffle bag and a bad smell burst into the room.

"Hey there, fellas," he greeted us.

I sat up in bed for a glimpse. The man was looking around.

"Looks like that empty bunk down there is mine."

By now Jeremy was awake. "Hold on, dude. What's going on?"

"Just got out of Lompoc, bro.    Did a four-year deal there."

"Alright, brother!" Jeremy jumped out of the top bunk, flipped on the switch, and vigorously shook the man's hand.

"I'm Barr," the man said.

He was a forty-year-old white man with a receding hairline and a friendly face. Standing about five foot ten with a medium build, he was not physically intimidating, particularly given his pleasant, affable demeanor. He acted like he already knew us, and he beamed with excitement over being out of prison.

He also smelled progressively worse as he peeled off clothes until he was completely nude.

"You fellas mind if I jump in the shower real quick?"

"Feel free," I urged.

After Barr had showered and climbed into the bed below me, he and Jeremy stayed up late talking. What I overheard was that Barr was a methamphetamine addict turned dealer and that was the reason for his downfall. He came from a family of addicts and dealers and could not remember a time when his parents were clean. The

414

drug business in his house had become so routine that even at the tender age of twelve, in the middle of a raid by the cops he had the sense to grab drugs hidden under the bathroom sink and flush them down the toilet. His parents rewarded him for his resourcefulness with a new twelve-speed bicycle.

By the age of fourteen, Barr was smoking pot regularly. But meth was king in the white suburbs of Sacramento, so by eighteen, Barr was using the drug almost daily. Dealing was a natural progression in his family's evolution, and Barr began selling as he entered his twenties. A series of busts, however, had led to him spending eleven of the last fifteen years in prison. It was in prison that Barr developed his talent as an artist, producing a series of remarkable paintings depicting the anguish caused by drug addiction.

Like the arrival of Jeremy and Javier before him, Barr's appearance was a happy event for him because he was on his way out of the system. My entry in the House, on the other hand, marked the beginning of my formal punishment, and so my emotional experience of it was the polar opposite of theirs. And those emotions had exhausted me, causing me to fall asleep as my three roommates continued in excited conversation.

The next week in the House allowed me to develop some level of comfort with my surroundings. I had begun to accept my new newest challenge and was determined to make the best of it. Intermittently, residents would seek me out for advice or to confide certain things to me. I was one part priest, one part doctor, one part sounding board. This dynamic created a situation where people

415

seemed to be comfortable sharing personal details with me, for which I was grateful. It made my time there more meaningful, as I felt that I was helping the residents in some small way. It also meant that I was well-liked, or at least valued, by the residents. I had even picked up the nickname of "Doc."

I did notice, however, that some residents were bothered that I hadn't come from prison. The joint was like an identifying feature, similar to your hometown. It gave people a sense of context. But it was never a big problem, and I was generally well-received by most of the residents I had met thus far. Because of my profession and perhaps because I hadn't been in prison before and thus hadn't been exposed to the social stratification that occurs there, racial lines apparently did not apply to me, so I moved freely among the different groups.

Although people segregated themselves along racial lines, invariably there was mixing, due to the confined space, causing lots of commotion. But it usually remained orderly, respectful and civilized. No one wanted to be sent back to prison for bad behavior, even though with a house full of ex-cons, some deviance was inevitable. And one time, a resident named Harold made me the object of that deviance.

I had met Harold in the House's fitness center, a small room with outdated and often broken equipment. He was a tall, soft-spoken black man in his fifties who approached me during the middle of my daily workout, asking if I was Doc. When I nodded, he stuck out his hand and introduced himself, telling me in a deep baritone voice that he had been released from prison several days earlier, had spotted me in the cafeteria and, after asking a couple of the fellas, found out my story. Calling himself a loner, he said he was interested in meeting me because, as a doctor, my socioeconomic background was similar to his. He had been an executive in a large financial services firm but was sent to prison for eight years for income tax evasion. That seemed like a particularly harsh penalty to me.

After about five minutes of conversation, he asked if we could be friends.

"I guess so," I replied as I got off the stationary bike, now finished with my workout.

"That's great. I'll see you around," he said, and then walked out.

After that, Harold always managed to find me during mealtime, plopping himself down next to me. He talked a lot, building a sympathetic picture of himself. Jeremy eyed him suspiciously and often ignored him, but it never occurred to me to ask why. At dinner one night, Harold told me he had just put a television and DVD player in his room and had plans to catch up on a bunch of movies while in the House. I returned to my room after dinner, and soon there was a knock at the door. It was Harold, and he motioned for me to step into the hallway.

"Do you want to come over to my room and watch a movie?" he asked.

This was an odd request, as it was well-known that no one was permitted to have other residents in their room at any time. As I looked at him, I suddenly realized what he was asking. Embarrassed, I blushed and stammered something like, "Thanks for the offer but I can't," and quickly went back in the room.

"What did he want?" Jeremy demanded.

"He asked if I wanted to watch a movie with him," I replied sheepishly.

Jeremy's expression grew so dark and cold it gave me goosebumps. He jumped down from the top bunk and headed for the door.

"Where are you going?" I asked him.

"Don't worry about it."

In prison, Jeremy had become highly skilled in martial arts. Although only five foot ten and one hundred sixty pounds, he was known as a fierce fighter and it was this characteristic, along with his intellect, that had brought him status in prison, earning him the title of "shot caller." In prison, every ethnic group has a shot caller, the leader who has the power to negotiate with other shot callers, direct members of his racial group, and dole out punishment for misbehaving inmates of the same race. Jeremy's influence as a shot caller carried over into the House, and I noticed how other residents showed him deference.

Ten minutes later, he returned to the room, and hopped back into the top bunk.

"What happened?" I asked.

"Business," he replied.

For the rest of my time in the House, Harold never so much as glanced at me. Fortunately, my roommate had protected me, and I was even more grateful when I later found out that it was a predilection for little boys that had extended Harold's years behind bars.

By the second week, our rooming group had become very comfortable with each other. Not Harold-comfortable, just men-hanging-out comfortable. One of our favorite ways to pass time was to watch the activity down on Taylor Street through the large window at the end of our room. Soon, we began to recognize the regulars. One particularly interesting character was a homeless man who had lost both of his legs. Rumors filtered through the House regarding the cause, the most glorified being that he had stepped on a mine while saving a comrade in Vietnam. The most inglorious story was that, being a junkie, he had passed out on a curb, half-lying in the street, and his legs were run over by a truck.

He was nicknamed Skateboard Pete for the ingenious way in which he moved about by strapping his torso to a skateboard and using his knuckles, protected with thick leather gloves, to propel himself. Over the years, he had developed remarkable grace and agility, and we would marvel at his ability to dart effortlessly between pedestrians or shoot across intersections, just ahead of oncoming traffic.

Pete was well-loved on the street because of his big personality and constant smile. People looked out for him, often giving him food, water and clothing. Within the House, he had developed an almost cult-like following, and I could often hear inmates calling out to him from the open windows of the House. He always returned the salutations with a raised fist, while continuing to paddle away at the asphalt with his other hand. He had an on-again, off-again girlfriend, a homeless crack addict who could sometimes be seen walking along next to him, an odd couple if there ever was one.

I met Pete one day, sans girlfriend, while walking down Taylor Street. He was coasting on his skateboard, and I extended my arm towards him, asking him to stop. He

419

had crisscrossed a rubber car trunk strap across his waist and then under his skateboard, which secured his body in place. He had a brown, tangly beard and where there was less dirt, I could see his face was ruddy. He was missing his left front tooth, his nose was bulbous, his ears big, and his hair, which he kept in place with a yellow bandana, long. He wore a twill sports jacket with sleeves two inches too short.

"My Sunday finest," he remarked as he smoothed down a lapel.

"Very nice," I replied.

"How can I do you?" he asked.

"I just wanted to introduce myself. I live in the halfway house over there and I see you all the time and wanted to say hi. I'm Max."

"Right on, dude," he replied, shaking my hand vigorously. "So, you're in the joint, huh? Rob a bank or something?" he asked, laughing.

The way he laughed made me laugh and so there I stood in the middle of the Tenderloin cracking up with a homeless man with no legs strapped to a skateboard. Our laughter finally died down, and we spoke briefly before I realized I needed to get back. He slapped me a low five as I left. From that point forward, I called out to him every time I saw him on the street below. He always had a humorous reply, such as:

"Living the dream."

"The day is rolling."

"Going boarding today."

"Putting my feet up."

"Getting new shoes."

"Going out for a spin."

One quiet Sunday morning, I looked out the window to find a dismounted Pete perched on the sidewalk next to his girlfriend, both their backs against the wall. Every so often, she would stand up, walk a few steps away and take a puff from a crack pipe. This inevitably led to a shouting match between the two of them.

In between hits, she set up a small camping stove on the sidewalk and started cooking meat. For the next hour, she alternated smoking crack with tending to her pot. At some point, Pete fell asleep so his girlfriend decided to smoke while sitting next to him. He awoke just as she was lighting up, and he immediately swatted the pipe out of her hands. It shattered as it landed on the sidewalk, and she went into a rage and attacked him. Suddenly, they were brawling on the sidewalk, and in the midst of the struggle, they knocked over the pot. Outraged, Pete's girlfriend picked up his skateboard and started beating him with it until a bystander pulled her away.

Poor Pete gathered himself, strapped his body back in, and took off. It was the last time we saw him, for a week later, an article appeared in the *San Francisco Chronicle* about Pete's death. He had been struck by a U.S. Postal Service trunk at the corner of Townsend and Third Street, just as he was crossing the intersection.

Someone tacked the article to the bulletin board, and residents wrote kind messages around it. It was our memorial to Pete.

# CHAPTER THIRTY-TWO

After two weeks in the House, I still had not seen Jessica. I decided to address the issue with my parole officer during our first meeting in the federal building. On my way there, I ran into the assistant US Attorney who replaced Marissa Long right after my plea agreement was reached, the one who felt I had gotten away with a sweet deal and tried to stick it to me in the courtroom during sentencing and with her letter to Judge Natas.

"Hi," she said as we passed each other. I nodded, wanting to say, "Fuck off," or something equally impertinent. Instead, I smiled and kept walking. But I was shaken by the encounter, and it took me a few minutes to gather myself before I proceeded to the Probation Department on the fifteenth floor. Once there, I was met and escorted into a back office by my newest parole officer, a young, attractive brunette with a great body. I watched the lovely curves of her hips, accentuated by her tight-fitting skirt, as she walked ahead. When we reached her office, she asked me to take a seat.

"Nice view," I said, looking out the window.

She nodded, unaware of my true meaning. As she settled into a chair, she opened my file and began shuffling its contents.

"How's it going in the halfway house?" she asked.

"It wouldn't be my first choice in lodging," I quipped.

There was no reaction as she began reading from the file.

"Your sentence is three months of community confinement, three months of home detention, and one year of probation."

I sat still.

"Well," she said impatiently.

"Oh sorry, that's correct," I responded.

"Looks like you've been adhering to all the rules. And I see you're working at the hospital," she said with just a hint of interest.

"I'm doing my best."

"Here's the counselor's report," she mumbled to herself as she picked it up.

As she read it, I thought about the counselor who had been assigned to me. All residents had one. Mine was in his twenties and studying to be a social worker. His job was to make sure I obeyed the rules, attended all classes, engaged in meaningful employment, etc. He was also supposed to be my resource person should I experience difficulty in the House. I hadn't bothered to ask him about seeing Jessica; he was too low on the totem pole to have any influence so I figured it would be a waste of time.

"There don't seem to be any problems," she said after reading the report.

"Can I make a request?" I asked.

She took a deep breath and looked at her watch. I didn't wait for a response.

"I'd like to be able to spend some time with my daughter."

"After three weeks, you'll be granted limited visiting privileges," she said.

"Is there any way I could see her sooner? It's been hard on her."

At that, she gave me an annoyed look.

"Listen, the halfway house is not vacation. It's meant to be punitive. It's meant to be hard. You'll have to work it out with the director."

"What a heartless bitch," I thought to myself, looking away so that she would not see my rising anger. When I did, I noticed in her bookshelf a framed picture of her in a wetsuit hugging a dolphin. I felt like flinging it against the wall. But then I reminded myself that my anger was misguided, for I was the one responsible for my inability to see Jessica, not her, and with that realization, I was able to release the tension in my body and simply nod.

"Okay, then," she said, standing up. "I'll walk you out."

On the way back to the House, I called Alice. The noise of the city street made hearing impossible, and so I ducked into the lobby of a large office building.

"I met with the parole officer today but she couldn't give me an exact date when I could see Jessica," I told her.

"Not even an estimate?" she asked.

"She just said sometime after three weeks, but I have to figure it out with the halfway house people."

"Try to do that right away, please. Jessica told me today her heart is always hurting and she feels like she needs a hug all the time, even when she's in school."

I put my hand to my forehead and looked down. This was what I had been dreading since the judge sentenced me.

"She also said she sometimes feels like crying at school," Alice continued. "I keep telling her it's just for a short period of time but she seems depressed. So, I just let her stay in my bed at night and talk about why 'nothing is right' and 'everything is not good'"

I looked outside at the cars racing down Turk Street.

"I can't believe she's saying all that," I said, shaking my head.

"I thought of getting her a pet but that's probably just to relieve my own worries."

There was nothing I could say or do to make things better.

"I'm so sorry, Alice," was all I could manage.

That night the terrible dreams returned, but worse.

This time, Jessica stood at the top of the stairs as Jurgenson handcuffed me. When he spun me around to face the apartment, I looked up to see her standing there, confused. As they started marching me up the stairs and past her, she cried out, "Daddy, what's wrong?"

"Get her out of here," Jurgenson yelled to one of his minions. The man picked her up, and she started kicking.

"Daddy! Daddy!" reverberated against the walls as they carried her away. Eventually her screams faded.

"Where'd they take her?" I demanded.

"Somewhere where you'll never see her again," Jurgenson snarled. "You don't deserve to be her father anyway."

His words woke me up and I sat bolt upright, profusely sweating. My roommates were still sleeping and since the noise of Taylor Street had settled, the only sound in the room came from my heavy breathing. Eventually, I calmed myself enough to lie back down, but I was afraid to fall asleep again. Feeling the need to do something— anything—I typed out an email to Jessica on my Blackberry. I had been writing her emails every day I'd been in the House, but this one was more to settle myself down.

Hi Jessica,

It's Daddy. I'm here at the house where I am staying in San Francisco. There is a lot of fog here so it is a lot colder than the suburbs. I met some other men here who have daughters too. They miss their daughters very much, just like your daddy. I can't wait to give you a big hug again. Well I'm going to go to sleep now. I sent mommy a picture of me to show you. Tell your sisters I said "hi."

xoxox

Daddy

Three weeks in the House passed without any scheduled visiting time with Jessica, so Alice started bringing her to the hospital twice a week for lunch with me, which Jessica seemed to enjoy. But I struggled with the deflated, empty feelings that overcame me each time I watched her ride away.

Then, at four weeks, the director granted me permission to spend three hours weekly with Jessica. I told her this just as she was ploughing through her peanut butter and jelly sandwich in the hospital cafeteria.

"Daddy is going to take you to a park next week."

Her eyes opened wide.

"Do I get to sleep at your house?"

"No, but we'll spend three hours together!"

"That's a long time, daddy. What park are we going to?"

"Let's go to the one in San Mateo. The one with the big play structure."

"Yes!" she said, giving me a big hug.

By the second month, the director granted me two three-hour slots per week to see Jessica. Despite the increased time, she still struggled with our separation, which Alice told me about on the phone.

"Jessica gets tearful about you every night at bedtime," she said. "I told her you and I are very proud of her for handling this so well. Her eyes lit up when I mentioned this to her. You might want to talk to her about that."

"I'll do it when I see her tomorrow."

In addition to our visits, e-mails seemed to provide some reassurance and a sense of stability for Jessica, so I continued sending lots of them to her throughout my stay in the House.

Hi Sugarplum,

Daddy just got home from work and I'm tired. But I'm also really, REALLY excited. Do you know why? Because I get to see my little girl tomorrow. Yeahhhhhhhh.

Max Kepler

Today as I was driving home, I saw the Bay to Breakers race in San Francisco. Many of the runners were dressed in very funny clothes. One man in a gorilla costume was chasing a group of people dressed like bananas.
Sweet dreams my little girl.
Daddy

Alice religiously replied to each of my emails, typing out Jessica's response.

Dear Daddy,
You just said that you saw those Bay to Breakers...Hey! you know what's cool, I went with Sally and watched a show and on our way back, I think I saw the gorilla. I also saw a girl with pink hair, Spiderman, Superman and I think we even saw people with no clothes. But I am not sure. And I think Sally saw a banana. I am not sure but I think so. Well Daddy, didn't you see a banana? I think I saw 2 bananas but I am not sure. And I love you daddy. I think I need some "x"'s and kisses to go with this
xoxoxoxoxoxoxoxoxoxoxoxoxoxxoxoxoxoxoxoxoxoxoxoxoxoxo
xoxoxoxoxoxo
Love you daddy...kiss and hug!! Bye Bye!!

Sundays were the hardest in the House, as I had to remain there all day, except for a single one hour break to run errands. I spent much of that time thinking about and missing Jessica. I tried passing the time by working out, washing clothes, and reading, mostly Dostoevsky. Sometimes I sat in the cafeteria and talked with residents or watched them visit with friends and family. Just as I would never allow Jessica to visit me in the House, I didn't want any friends coming either.

Safety was never a concern during my time in the House, except when I was around Manase, a twenty-two-year-old Tongan man with a face that looked like it had just wrapped up puberty. He was short, perhaps five foot eight inches in height, and seemed as wide as he was tall. I was in the fitness room when he first spotted me.

"You Doc?" he asked.

I nodded.

"How ya' doing, dude? I'm Manase," he said with a smile, extending his hand.

"Nice to meet you."

"Hey Doc, do you think you could take a look at my elbow? It hurts right here," he said as he pointed with a stubby index finger.

"Sure," I said hesitantly. "Let me see." I picked up his elbow and performed several different maneuvers, and then I pressed on certain spots around the joint. I stopped when he winced with pain.

"You have something called lateral epicondylitis, otherwise known as tennis elbow. It's a type of tendinitis that you probably got from working out."

"Well, what can I do about it?"

"You can take ibuprofen and put ice on it. Some people benefit from a tennis elbow brace. And, of course, you should avoid exercises that make the pain worse."

"Hey, thanks, Doc. I'll try the ibuprofen." He shook my hand, and looked at me closely. "Doc, why you in here? Is it true you were some kind of big steroid dealer or something?"

Now I realized why several residents had asked me about anabolic steroids.

"Naw, nothing like that. I got into trouble for importing certain medications into the country."

"Fucking government. Have to get their nose in everybody's business."

"Yeah."

"What joint were you in?"

"I never went to prison. My sentence was this halfway house."

"Are you kidding me? This is like vacation."

"Yeah," I said, trying to act nonchalant. "Why are you here?"

"Gun possession."

"What kind of gun?"

"AK 47."

"Oh," I said.

"That's one bad-ass gun. One night I was cruising with one of my homeboys, and we pulled up to this red light. Just then, this nigga from another gang pulled up next to us. So, I got out of the car with my AK, and then I was like *pa, pa, pa, pa, pa* on the muthafucker. And you know what?"

"What?" I asked, struggling to keep my voice calm.

"After I was done, I walked around to the other side of the car and saw bullet holes. They had done gone clean through that muthafucker."

I wasn't sure if he meant the car, or the human being, but I wasn't about to ask. Instead, I felt like sitting down.

"Can you believe that shit?" he asked.

"Wow," was all I could manage.

He shook his head and made a clucking noise with his tongue. And then he started doing pull-ups again.

"Well, see you around," I said, making a move for the door.

I didn't see Manase until a week later when the fire alarm went off in the middle of the night, causing a full evacuation of the House. When the confusion died down, I discovered I was standing on the sidewalk next to him. He had taken a peculiar stance, with his legs wide apart and knees slightly bent.

"Ain't this a bitch, Doc?" he asked.

I nodded at him and then stared out at Taylor Street, waiting for House employees to tell us to return inside. Within minutes, I saw a white van slowly approaching the corner where we were standing. The driver, a young black male, appeared to be staring at Manase. I turned towards him, and was alarmed to see him return the black man's menacing look. I looked back at the van and suddenly the front passenger leaned towards the driver's side, lifted a large rifle, and pointed it at Manase. Instinctively, I dropped to my knees, put my arms over my head, and closed my eyes. When I opened them, the van had passed, and Manase was still standing next to me, grinning widely and nodding his head with big, exaggerated movements.

I was amazed I hadn't wet myself.

"Those pussies think they're so tough," he said.

"Who was it?" I asked in a shaky voice.

"Doc, stand up, would ya'?" He pulled me to my feet. "It was another gang. But they ain't gonna do nothing. Just a bunch of pussies."

I was unable to speak. Sensing this, Manase put his arm around me. One of the House staff started announcing it was safe to return.

"Let's go back in. It looks like you're gonna have a heart attack, Doc."

Then he walked behind me, placed his hands on my shoulders, and directed me back to the House.

There were half a dozen more fire alarms during my time in the House. Each time, I made a point of searching out Manase, and then taking up a position as far away from him as possible.

In a House full of ex-cons, I felt that violence was lurking around every corner. This was graphically demonstrated one day in the cafeteria.

The flare-up involved Malcolm, a tall, athletic, well-muscled black man whom I first met while he was coaxing a Dr. Pepper out of an obstinate vending machine. With a bit of teamwork, we were able to extract the soda, and afterwards we walked together to class on the third floor. All House residents attended mandatory classes every Tuesday and Wednesday night. The topics included drug education, basic criminal theory, and approaches to rehabilitation. A frequent topic was recidivism, and counselors spent significant time going over strategies to prevent convicts from returning to prison. The statistics were alarming: over seventy-five percent of inmates released from prison committed crimes again.

In the classroom, Malcolm spoke up frequently, expressing strong opinions on a variety of subjects. Although not always eloquently expressed—a failing likely attributable to his limited formal education—his contributions were insightful, and I suspected criminality had stolen his considerable potential.

However, there was an edge to Malcolm that made me nervous. He told me he had grown up in a rough area of San Francisco, the third of four sons in a single-mother household. In his teenage years, he became involved in petty crimes that grew increasingly serious, so that by the age of eighteen, he had spent a significant amount of time in various juvenile halls. Finally, at the age of twenty, he was sentenced to prison for armed robbery of a liquor store when he was high on cocaine, netting a mere one hundred dollars.

After serving three years, he returned to his previous lifestyle and soon was busted for gun possession while on parole, which led to another two years in prison. Just before he was arrested, he had a major disagreement with an associate who reneged on an agreement to share in proceeds from a hold-up the two had pulled off days before. Malcolm had not forgotten this betrayal, and his anger had hardened with each passing year in prison.

Set free at the age of twenty-seven, he was able to secure a job as a short-order cook in a small fast food restaurant. While flipping hamburgers one day, Malcolm spotted the man who had shortchanged him years before, eating with a female companion. Without hesitating, Malcolm grabbed a pot off the stove, scooped out hot grease from the deep fryer, and walked calmly into the dining area and over to the man's table. As soon as the man looked up, Malcolm tossed the hot grease into his face. Then he simply walked out of the restaurant and kept going. He could still hear the blood-curdling screams half a block away. The police arrested him several hours later while he was hiding out at his girlfriend's house.

He was sentenced to eleven years in prison, later extended to almost fifteen years due to poor behavior, spending much of that time in a special confinement for problem inmates and coming to the realization that he needed to turn his life around if he were to avoid prison in the future. Finally, at the age of forty-two, he was released to the House.

I was surprised by how forthcoming Malcolm had been with me, and after he finished the story, as we sat together in the cafeteria, I told him, "I hope everything works out for you, Malcolm."

He shook my hand and said, "Thanks, Doc," just as a female visitor arrived for him.

I moved to a different table and was reading a magazine a few minutes later when Malcolm's loud voice suddenly broke my concentration. People began clearing out of the area, but I remained there, pretending to read while watching the scene out of the corner of my eye. The woman was upset about text messages on Malcolm's phone from another lady. Malcolm didn't want to hear her complaints, and his booming voice was reverberating against the bare, concrete walls. I couldn't believe that no staff came into the room. Then suddenly it happened. Bam! Bam! Just like that, Malcolm hit the woman twice across the face with an open hand, the force of his blows rocking her head.

Instinctively, I yelled out, "Whoa, Malcolm!" which caused him to whip his head around to face me. The fury in his glare took my breath away, and I realized I was in danger, so I quickly said to him, "Hey man, I don't want you to go back to prison." His face quickly registered recognition, and he gave me a slight nod before turning back to the woman and telling her, "Get the fuck out of here." Just then, a staff member came into the room, looked around, saw nothing amiss and walked out.

After the woman left, Malcolm fished into his pocket for some change, walked over to the vending machine, and bought a Dr. Pepper. He sat there sipping it for several minutes while I didn't dare move. Finally, after waiting for what seemed like an eternity, he looked at me and said with a smile, "Thanks, Doc." I smiled back, and then left the room as discreetly as possible. Thereafter, I was the equivalent of the Chosen One for Malcolm.

# CHAPTER THIRTY-THREE

Time in a halfway house often goes very slowly, and that allowed me plenty of opportunity to think. I spent a lot of those hours considering whether my criminal behavior represented a fundamental moral flaw in my character. Despite multiple sessions with my psychiatrist, I still had not fully resolved the question for myself. I wondered whether I was any different from the other residents in the House. Given the opportunities afforded me, I thought it possible I might even be more defective. The only reason I hadn't spent time in prison like the rest of them was that I was able to afford a top attorney.

And since most residents came from violent, criminal, and/or socioeconomically-depressed families, criminality was a more plausible choice for them. In some cases, it even seemed inevitable. I, on the other hand, had come from a much different background, yet still succumbed to criminality. What did that say about my character? Was it possible that I was worse than the men with whom I was now living?

But then I thought about men like Malcolm or Manase. Surely, I was different from them. Or how about Terry, an overweight man in his twenties who had set up a makeshift meth lab in his room next to ours, seemingly convinced he could proceed undetected?

One common attribute shared by these three men and many others in the House was the contempt for all authority and rules. The intensity of this contempt caught my attention, most notably because it was a clear departure from my own feelings on the subject. Granted, I, too, tended to dislike authority, but not nearly with such vehemence, and I limited my disdain to authority I considered arbitrary. And unlike other residents, I didn't feel that society had somehow cheated me or that the government was filled with inherently bad people who were the enemy.

Instead, my perspective was subtler and more heavily rationalized. My transgressions were born out of a strength—the ability to maneuver around convention—which I turned into a weakness by using it to circumvent laws and ethics. Unlike other residents of the House, I was not at war with the existing power structure; rather, I was trying to manipulate that structure for self-gain. Furthermore, I didn't presume that society owed me anything, but I did think that I could pick which of society's rules I needed to adhere to on my path to fame and fortune. And it was this blatant disregard for convention that had put me into a place with other miscreants, right where I belonged, and, I believe, needed to be.

Besides examining issues of criminality, I had time to consider other issues, such as labeling. Whereas before I had too often embraced titles and awards, I now knew that they were incomplete and often misleading. For example, House staff treated me as just another convicted criminal, but in the hospital, I was still accorded the highest level of respect, even by those who knew my story. Simply donning a white coat created an entirely different dynamic, even though I was the same Max Kepler. I hadn't magically changed in a thirty-minute drive.

Occasionally a tour group, usually consisting of younger people affiliated with various charitable organizations or social programs offered by the city, would come through the House. As they walked around, I felt like an animal in a zoo. I could only imagine what they would tell their friends later that night about their brush with hardened criminals.

"If only they knew I had an M.D. and Ph.D.," I would sometimes think.

But what difference would that really make? I was learning that labels and what others thought of me truly didn't matter; what mattered was coming to a better understanding of myself and my weaknesses. As I developed a keener awareness of how my strengths could be turned upside down and lead to illegality and self-destruction, I came to realize that although I was a most definitely flawed human being, I wasn't a morally flawed criminal.

Despite this new-found awareness, I still needed to deal with serving my sentence, and to do so, I reverted to my comfort zone by reformulating the crisis into a challenge, and then going about conquering it. I still wasn't finished playing the game; it was all I knew. Even as I sat in the House, I planned for my return to glory. I was going to be the amazing come-from-behind success story. This thinking may have gotten me through, but it prevented me from coming to a true understanding of the core reasons for my behavior.

# CHAPTER THIRTY-FOUR

Departure day eventually arrived. Although I had barely slept the night before, I was completely filled with energy when I awoke. I packed my things quickly and went down to have one last mystery breakfast sandwich with Jeremy. He still had three months left and was sad to see me go. I felt good about our time together because he had calmed down significantly, found a job, and applied for college, all of which I had repeatedly encouraged.

As we sat together sharing that last breakfast, Jeremy finally told me the reason for his incarceration. He said he had been busted because of a string of increasingly bad decisions, the last of which occurred when he was twenty-two, on a night when he took several friends cruising in his van. At some point, they decided to stop at a convenience store for a drink. As they pulled up, they saw a black man from a rival gang walk into the store. The man had been involved in an altercation with one of their gang brothers several weeks earlier, and now was on their turf. They waited until he emerged from the store before jumping him. Jeremy had remained in the van, watching the assault, and saw the man's buddy pull up in a truck. Getting out, Jeremy picked up a brick and broke the truck's front windshield, enabling his friends to finish their beat-down and follow him back into the van, after which they drove off.

All three were later arrested, but the DA was unable to prosecute Jeremy since he hadn't participated in the actual assault. However, the case was reported to the assistant U.S. Attorney at the time, a black man looking to not only send a racist white man to prison but also to advance his own career. He filed a federal civil rights suit against Jeremy but lost the case. An appeal was lodged, however, and this time the jury found Jeremy guilty. The government argued that although he hadn't participated in the assault, Jeremy was the ad hoc leader of a white supremacist group, and as such, he exerted considerable influence. Because of that influence, the men felt obligated to beat up the black man, the government reasoned. Once he was convicted, the judge considered Jeremy's extensive criminal record and sentenced him to fifteen years in a federal penitentiary. His wife was seven months pregnant at the time. Soon after the baby was born, his wife divorced him.

Jeremy never considered himself a white supremacist, and he certainly didn't appear to be one while I lived with him. In fact, one month into our stay in the House he began corresponding with a black woman he met at the restaurant where he was working. Furthermore, I never heard him use racist language. Society, however, had labeled him a racist, and sent him to prison for a long time based on that misperception. When he entered the halfway house with me, he was full of bitterness from those fourteen years behind bars. But over time, and after many long conversations I had with him, I could see that he had started letting go of those feelings. That pleased me and made me more than a little sad to be leaving him.

Only temporarily sad, of course, as I was on my way home.

At five minutes to nine, Jeremy walked me over to the front desk. Several residents had gathered around to see me off. I shook hands and exchanged hugs. Some staff members whom I had gotten to know over the three months also came up to wish me farewell. Then I signed the log a final time, slung my bag over my shoulder and walked over the yellow line and into the San Francisco sunshine. I looked back to see my reflection in the darkened windows and smiled. I felt incomparably elated, and I practically skipped to the parking lot.

"I won't be seeing you anymore," I told the attendant as he handed over my keys.

"Good luck to you, Doc," he said.

As I pulled out, I looked back to the House and saw Jeremy hanging out the window, waving. I waved back, and punched the accelerator. I still had three months of home arrest, but at that moment, I couldn't have cared less.

I arrived home just before ten in the morning. My roommate was at work and so the house seemed exceptionally quiet. It also felt a little unfamiliar, as though I had spent way more than ninety days away. I walked upstairs and found my bedroom door closed. Inside, the air was stale and my banana plant was dead; Jeff clearly had forgotten to water it. I picked up the

"Welcome Home" note I had left on the bed and smiled. I remembered how frightened I had been when I wrote the message for myself three months earlier. A wave of relief coursed through me as I stared at the message for a minute or so before wadding the paper into a ball and throwing it away. Then I lay down, luxuriating in the softness of my bed, and stared into space.

Later that afternoon, a man from a private security company came to the house to install the home monitoring unit and to fit me with an electronic ankle bracelet. The bracelet consisted of a black box half the size of a pack of cigarettes attached to a rubber strap about an inch in width. I asked him to leave the bracelet loose enough so that I could slide it back and forth. Although weighing less than a pound, it felt like a cannonball strapped to my leg.

I would only be permitted to travel to and from work, with an additional hour allotted for errands. I was forced to take one day off per week, which was disappointing since I wanted to work as many overtime hours as possible to pay down my debt. On that off day, I could spend five hours outside my house, as long as I filed the necessary paperwork describing exactly where I'd be and with whom. I would never be permitted to travel outside the northern district of California, and I could never be outside my house after dark.

I wasn't permitted to drink alcohol during my home confinement and the parole office would show up at random times to check on me. At eight in the evening, I might hear a knock at the front door. I'd invite him in, he would ask how I was doing, glance around the house and leave. Usually, his visits lasted no longer than five minutes, but they were disconcerting nonetheless, especially when my daughter was with me. Fortunately, he was always very discreet and nonchalant around her.

One of the first things I did after having the bracelet placed was test the range of the base unit. There was a red light on the unit that lit up whenever the bracelet was too far away. Anywhere in the house was fine, but I wanted to see if the pool and the Jacuzzi were within range. When Jeff got home that night, I asked him to watch the base unit carefully as I established an outside perimeter for the bracelet. I was relieved to discover that perimeter included the pool and Jacuzzi, even though I had to keep the bracelet above water to prevent it from going off. My ability to enjoy the water even with my right foot resting on the pavement above greatly eased the pain of home detention.

The bracelet was impossible to hide from Jessica and within the first several days, she noticed it. I was lying in bed reading and had absentmindedly kicked off the covers. Before I could do anything, she was in my bed pulling at it.

"What's this, Daddy?"

I looked down at her. She was staring at me with her wide-open, inquisitive eyes. Older now, and more aware, she had both hands cupped around the bracelet. The juxtaposition of her innocence with the criminality the bracelet represented was heartbreaking to me.

"It's so the hospital can keep track of me," was the first thing that came to mind.

It was a half-truth, and she seemed satisfied by the explanation.

"Does it hurt?"

"No," I responded, before quickly adding, "Hey, do you want to play Chutes and Ladders?"

"Yes!"

I moved out of bed to grab the game from the closet, a sick feeling in my stomach.

After that, I made sure to wear only my longest pants to work every day. I found that even when sitting, if I pulled the pants down and pushed the bracelet up as high as possible, it could not be seen by others. When I had on shorts, I wore bulky socks to try to disguise it. The device drove me crazy after a while, and I wanted to rip it off many times, especially at night in bed when it made me feel anxious, like I was being corralled by some unseen force. Other times, I felt like a tagged animal in the wild.

But on occasion I forgot about it entirely, like the time I cared for a forty-two-year-old man with pneumonia. I had sat down in a chair next to his bed, admiring a colorful tattoo on his right leg of a hibiscus flower growing out of someone's anus.

"Beauty can be found anywhere," he explained.

"No shit," I replied, smiling.

He chuckled, and then went on to tell me he had grown up in a rough area of San Francisco and started using heroin at the age of seventeen, which eventually led to a string of serious health problems. Along the way, he had been incarcerated over ten years for drug dealing. It was in prison that he collected the impressive array of tattoos that adorned much of his body.

But it was the calf tattoo that I found most interesting, and after studying it for a time, I sat back in the chair and crossed my legs. In doing so, I unwittingly exposed the electronic bracelet.   Suddenly, the man's eyes widened, and he sat upright in bed.

"Whatcha got there, Doc?" he asked with a smile.

I looked down and, to my horror, saw the bracelet.

"I…uh…it's a…" I stammered.

"I know what it is.   I wore one for six months."

"I don't know what to say," was all I could manage.

"No worries, Doc.   But I have to admit, I never thought I'd see a doctor wearing one of those."

"Neither did I."

I felt more relaxed at work after my release from the halfway house, probably because the end of my ordeal was in sight.   I didn't really mind that I was still under house arrest, as I had little interest in going out at night anyway.   Instead, I wanted to focus on being the best doctor and father that I could be.   And even though I had become less judgmental about the addicts I cared for at the hospital, they could still annoy me with their ongoing self-injurious behavior.   But now when I looked at the prisoners in their bright orange jumpsuits, I had nothing but compassion for them.   I realized how close I had come to being one of them.

Other than my usual daily interactions with colorful and sad characters, home arrest was relatively uneventful. Things were winding down and the nightmare was fading. By doing as many extra shifts as permitted, I was slowly working my way out of the debt I had accumulated.   And before I knew it, October 7, 2007, the last day of home arrest, arrived.

My probation officer told me I could cut off the bracelet on my own and mail it in. I left work that day at eleven so I could be at home when I removed the godforsaken thing. I didn't call anyone to announce the event. It was a beautiful, sunny day, and as the last minutes ticked away, I sat in the backyard thinking about everything I had been through. I felt an overwhelming sense of relief that there was nothing more to worry about, no more timelines, no more restrictions. I realized it was the first time in my life where the conquering of a challenge was not tinged with a bit of regret that the process was over. Time had moved at a glacial pace for the previous few years, but now as I watched the seconds tick off on my watch, it was all coming to an end.

At exactly twelve, I cut through the rubber strap and the monitoring device fell from my leg. I took off all my clothes, dove in the pool, and swam for a little. I felt cleansed, startlingly alive, and entirely unburdened. But all too soon, awareness came back over me: I had to get back to work. Disappointed that the euphoria had left so quickly, I climbed out of the pool, dried off and got dressed. Then I tossed the monitoring bracelet into a pre-addressed, padded envelope left by my probation officer and dropped the package off at the Post Office.

"Have an amazing day," I remarked to the postal worker as I left. I don't remember ever saying that to someone, but the worker smiled widely in response.

That night, I went to celebrate alone at a Mexican restaurant nearby in Burlingame. It was the first time I had been outdoors after dark in six months. I sat at the end of the bar near the window and stared at the swath of light laid down on the street and sidewalk by the streetlight. Behind me, a group of six women dressed in work clothes chattered around a heaping plate of nachos.

They appeared two-dimensional to me, as if I were watching a movie of them. Their voices seemed tinny, reminding me of the sounds from our first television, a Zenith Chromacolor that sat in a wooden console on our living room floor in Boon for many years. I was always on the couch next to Dad, wearing those oppressively hot, one-piece pajamas with the built-in footies and watching "The Lawrence Welk Show" every Sunday night on that old TV.

I took out my cellphone and started going through my contact list. Alice, Dad, Greg, Laurie, Margarita and Mom went by as I scrolled alphabetically. But I never dialed a number. What would I say to them if I called?

*I'm free, and I'm sitting here in a Mexican restaurant drinking alone.*

*Can you believe it's over?*

*Wow, what a relief, huh?*

I put my cellphone back in my pocket. They had heard enough from me over the past three years. I needed to leave them alone. And anyway, they would never be able to understand how I felt in that moment. How could they? It is really true that one can never know how sweet freedom is until it's taken away.

Instead, I told the bartender, who was hand-drying glasses, that I had just gotten released from home detention. He stopped and tossed the towel on his shoulder.

"Next one's on me," he said, and then proceeded to the other end to take a drink order. That was the end of our conversation on the topic, which was probably good. I wouldn't know where to start or end the story. Afterwards I ordered food. Then I began strategizing on how to get my life back to a semblance of normalcy. I thought it best to focus first on continuing to pay back the one hundred and fifty-thousand dollars I had accrued in legal costs by working overtime, then try to recoup the nearly two hundred thousand dollars I had lost in salary. I grabbed a napkin and began jotting down the numbers, soon coming up with a five-year repayment plan based on adding twenty hours per week of overtime to my schedule.

Not only would I pay back the debt, but I would also regain the respect of people at the hospital. The comeback would be impressive. By the time I finished my burrito and second beer, I was excited about the challenge ahead. Without realizing it, I was still immersed in my comfort zone, the place where I thought I was at my best. Not only would I achieve financial and reputation goals, I would also shed the guilt and feelings of inadequacy that continued to weigh me down. External factors would compensate for internal deficiencies—or so I still believed.

# CHAPTER THIRTY-FIVE

A week after home arrest ended, it occurred to me that I hadn't renewed my Drug Enforcement Agency narcotics license. This license was essential, as I frequently prescribed narcotics to my rheumatology patients. Although I had received the renewal notice several months previously, I had postponed responding after seeing the question: "Have you ever been convicted of a crime involving a controlled substance?"

Emotionally, I still didn't feel like dealing with the issue. My past conduct seemed a lifetime ago, and I preferred to ignore my misdeeds rather than own up to them on a DEA application. Furthermore, I worried the Government would come after me again, even though I realized that was illogical. However, regardless of my concerns, the deadline was approaching, and I had no choice but to complete the renewal form.

As I understood it, hGH, as defined by the Controlled Substance Act, was not a controlled substance and thus the correct answer was "no." Still, I wasn't completely sure of this interpretation, so I decided to once again turn to my Medical Board attorney, Gordon. But then I remembered he was always slow to respond, and by this time I needed to get the application done within a day. I figured that the only answer that could get me in real trouble was "no." If I guessed wrong in checking it, I could be accused of lying on an application for a controlled substance license and that would surely bring me additional grief.

Second-guessing myself had become a problem since I was arrested. I couldn't seem to trust my instincts about judgment calls anymore. I was paranoid about making wrong decisions, especially if they could be construed somehow as unethical. In the case of my DEA renewal, I figured that since I had already pled guilty and served a sentence, I couldn't be punished any further and so the best answer would be "yes." So that's what I clicked on before sending the application electronically. Problem solved.

Within minutes, however, I began to panic, wondering whether a "yes" answer might actually get me into more trouble. I cursed myself and banged on my desk before trying to calm down by talking to myself. "You're being irrational, Max. Everything is fine. There is nothing left for them to do to you."

That made me feel a little better, so I put on my doctor's coat and walked to the wards to see patients. An hour later, as I was leaving a patient's room, the panic returned, but this time it was worse. I was convinced the feds would be coming for me, probably right away. It would be better if I took off my white coat so that I wouldn't be arrested while wearing it. I made my way back to my office, took off the coat, and tried to call the

DEA office, but by that time it was after five o'clock and the office was closed. I tried calling Gordon, but he had left for the day. Needing something to occupy me, I wrote him an email describing my predicament.

Afterwards, I stumbled to my car and sat there for about ten minutes before driving home. I did not have Jessica that night, which was a good thing. I kept the house dark, pacing from one room to another, intermittently checking outside for the agents that I was convinced were about to arrive. It wasn't until early morning that I lay down in bed, and I spent most of the remaining hours of darkness conjuring up the image of the question on the DEA application and replaying the sound of the mouse as I clicked "yes."

The local DEA office didn't open until nine. Fortunately, someone answered when I called at 9:01. I was nearly hyperventilating when I began talking.

"This is Dr. Max Kepler. I renewed my DEA registration online yesterday and made a mistake. I'm just calling to correct it."

"What kind of mistake are you talking about?"

"I answered one of the questions incorrectly."

I tried to focus on my breathing, slow and steady, in and out.

"Which one?"

"The one that asks, 'Have you ever been convicted of a crime involving a controlled substance?'"

"So, you haven't been convicted of a crime involving a drug?"

"I have, but it's not a controlled substance," I said, trying to sound firm and confident without being pushy.

"Which drug is that?"

"Human growth hormone."

"I see," she said with newfound curiosity. "Sir, can you give me your DEA license number?"

*Fuck.*

After I provided it, she put me on hold for several minutes, leaving me to listen to Kenny G through the earpiece. My heart felt as if it were about to burst out of my chest. And I like Kenny G.

"I'm sorry, but you've already submitted the application and it can't be retracted. We are going to have to look into this and speak with the Medical Board."

I realized I needed to stay calm; otherwise I might arouse more suspicion.

"I don't think that's necessary. They've already looked into it."

"That might be, but we'll still have to check with them."

"Can't I just rescind the application and send in a new one?"

"It's too late for that."

I tried pleading with her for several more minutes before I realized it was futile.

I hung up and then sat down in my office chair, now completely paralyzed with fear. I simply couldn't believe what I had done. Was I still being reckless? Or was it something deeper? Perhaps, I felt that I got away with something when the Board had decided to close the case, and now my guilty conscience needed punishment, so that there might be absolution. Or maybe I was still looking for challenges. Perhaps this was self-sabotage. Maybe there was something fundamentally wrong with me.

The timing for this issue to have come up could not have been worse. It was 2006 and human growth hormone was still front and center in public consciousness, mostly because of the ongoing BALCO scandal involving professional athletes and performance-enhancing drugs. The public was fed up with doping in sports, and the federal government had embarked on a crusade against hGH. That no doubt explained the excitement I had heard in the woman's voice.

I didn't have the energy to tell my parents. I didn't think they could handle it.

The news came two weeks later, about a week before Thanksgiving. It was a Tuesday, and I picked up Jessica after work. When I arrived home, I found a notice in my mailbox that there was a certified package from the Medical Board of California waiting at the Post Office. I calmly set the notice down, went into the bathroom, and tried to collect myself. After a few minutes, I splashed water on my face and then went to the kitchen to make dinner. Jessica was sitting at the table drawing pictures with crayons.

"Daddy, look," she said as I walked in. "This is our house."

"Jessica, that's really good."

She smiled and looked up at me through her long eyelashes. Her brown skin color was radiant in the late afternoon sunlight filtering through the window. I looked at her small hand holding the crayon and felt a rush of adrenaline. Just then, I knew that whatever was to come, I would fight all over again, for both of us. The

Feds had let me off easy, that was true, but the Medical Board was unlikely to be so kind. I had to be ready.

I was unable to go directly to the Post Office in the morning, as I had to drop off Jessica at school and then see patients in the hospital. My first chance to go was at lunchtime. My heart pounded as I handed the worker the notice. He disappeared into the back and returned several minutes later carrying a large, manila envelope stamped "Medical Board of California." I could barely manage to sign the release form.

Once outside, I found the nearest bench and sat there for several minutes, holding the unopened envelope in my lap. I so didn't want to go through it all over again. I *couldn't* go through it all over again. But I knew that's what I'd might have to do, so I ripped open the envelope.

I flipped quickly through the packet, which contained a summary of my criminal case. On the last page, I discovered what the Medical Board was seeking: a hearing to determine whether to revoke or suspend my license. Upon reading that, I scooped up the papers, walked to the car, and tossed the packet into the passenger seat. As I drove back to the hospital, I realized this time around could be more difficult, for although my liberty was not at stake, my livelihood was. Ten years invested in learning a highly-specialized skill was now at risk due to nine months of illegal behavior. Again, I was wallowing in the unfairness of it all.

There was no way I could fight this battle alone. Facing that reality was painful, as I had once prided myself on being self-sufficient. But I had no choice: I would have to ask a lot of good people for help all over again.

I called Gordon later that afternoon with the news, including how I had answered the DEA application.

"Should have called me," he said, stating the obvious. "Maybe you could have answered the application differently. Still, it's surprising."

"I would say so, especially since they closed the case a year ago," I replied.

"Quite unusual."

"They didn't even open an investigation when they received the sentencing transcripts from the federal case," I said.

"Very odd."

"It must have been pressure from the DEA."

"Maybe."

"I'm freaking out a little bit here, Gordon."

"That's not going to help. You need to settle down and try to relax."

"What do we do now?"

"I'll need to contact the Board attorney right away to see if we can settle this quickly and avoid a very expensive, prolonged case. Remind me again of your sentence."

I gave him the information.

"I will file a Notice of Defense along with a Request for Discovery with the Medical Board of California. Whose name is on the paperwork?"

"Lester Arnold."

"Alright. He's a Deputy Attorney General. Let me initiate discussions with him. I have had several cases with Mr. Arnold and have always found him to be a fairly objective, reasonable attorney to work with. I will keep you advised of any proposal that he makes."

"When will I hear back from you?"

"Within a week."

Two weeks later, I still hadn't heard from Gordon. Typical of him. Too anxious to wait any longer, I called him.

"I was hoping to hear back from you sooner," I chided him.

"I was preparing to contact you."

"I was preparing to hear from you," I couldn't resist replying

He let out a long sigh.

"I received from the Board the investigative file concerning the accusation issued against you, and I called Mr. Arnold and asked him exactly what the Medical Board of California has in mind regarding your license. He informed me that the Board is of the opinion that a permanent revocation of your license is appropriate."

I started pacing in circles in my office. "What are you talking about?" I nearly shouted. "That can't be."

"Settle down a bit. After a great deal of discussion with Mr. Arnold and my going through the documents that he forwarded, I was able to create some doubt in his mind about a license revocation."

"This doesn't make any sense. They closed the case! This doesn't seem fair."

"Max, you must keep in mind that the mission of the Board is to protect the public. Last month Kepler Jones became the new Executive Director of the Medical Board of California. Ms. Jones is on an agenda to show the politicians in Sacramento just how tough she is."

"So, she wants to make an example of me?"

457

"I think so. We need to recognize the political setting that we are confronted with. It's much different than it was a year ago."

"What are we going to do?"

"I would like you to prepare a document for my eyes only that would support the contention that you should be allowed to maintain your license and practice medicine. In short, prepare something that makes it difficult for someone making the decision about your license to take it away. Make them see that you are an asset to the medical community and, more importantly, to the public."

"I'll have it to you by the end of the week," I said as I hung up the phone.

But I was distraught. Not only about my license but about Gordon's response. In order to succeed in my fight, I needed more of a commitment to resist from my attorney. Gordon thought a penalty was inevitable, based on his four decades of dealing with the Medical Board. Patterns observed over the years had become hard-and-fast truths in Gordon's mind. But that wasn't good enough for me. I saw no reason to accept any outcome other than the best possible. I decided to give Gordon a pep talk, in the form of an email.

Hi Gordon,

I was dismayed to hear you tell me that my license is on the line and that in the least I would receive some kind of sanction. I suppose it's a difference of philosophy, but I choose to believe that nothing of significance will come of all this. Why should I approach this issue with the expectation of some negative outcome? If I had done that in the criminal case, I would probably be a convicted felon and would have spent time in prison.

I would like for you to obtain an outcome where I receive some kind of letter of rebuke that is NOT public record. Nothing else. That is why Ted found someone of your caliber to represent me. This does not come from a place of entitlement or a sense that I am beyond reproach. My misdeeds occurred in the setting of an aesthetic medicine practice only, and I have subsequently (in a written statement to a federal judge) affirmed that I will never again practice aesthetic medicine. My record in my chosen specialty, both before and after the offense, has been exemplary. As such, a punishment from the Medical Board would serve no purpose at this point.

The Medical Board previously chose not to open my case. They have done so now at the request of the DEA, and I'll bet they are looking for a relatively easy way to conclude the whole thing. I hope you have a plan for facilitating this.

As always, I'm grateful for your help, Gordon.
Max

The email did not have the desired effect on Gordon, as I learned in a letter I received several days later.

Dear Max,

I must state, in all candor, when I received your email late Monday evening, I sat down and dictated a letter to you terminating our attorney-client relationship. But, I have learned over the years to sit on termination letters for a least 12 hours and re-evaluate.

I have been representing healthcare providers for over 43 years. I have literally represented thousands of healthcare providers with the various California licensing boards, particularly with the Medical Board of California. I believe that I have a very realistic and objective evaluation process that allows my clients to make appropriate judgments on how their matter should be resolved. There are some lawyers who would have demanded a $25,000 retainer and before you were through, you would have paid out between $75,000 and $100,000 in a case such as yours. I do not subscribe to that type of legal representation. I can be tenacious and demanding at the appropriate time.

Insofar as your desire that I obtain an outcome wherein you receive some type of letter of rebuke that is not of public record, and "nothing else," that simply is not realistic. The Medical Board does issue letters of public reprimand. They do not issue letters of private reprimand. I can also assure you that the fact that you have gone through a criminal proceeding and have been punished in that form is essentially irrelevant to the Medical Board of California. I would strongly suggest that you give me a call, and that we have a meeting so that we can discuss these issues. If you wish to accept my offer regarding termination of my services, that is acceptable as well. Please give me a call after you have a chance to review the above.

Gordon

Gordon was a good man, and I really liked him. He was the cuddly grandfather every grandchild wants. Right at the beginning, he had given me his home phone number and had said I could call him anytime I wanted, even if it was the middle of the night. And he could have commanded twice the hourly rate he charged me. Nonetheless, if I had felt it was possible, at that moment I would have dropped him.

Unlike Ted, Gordon was not a visionary thinker. I wanted him to transcend his constrained thinking process and consider something he hadn't seen before. What meaning does "simply not realistic" carry? Who defines "realistic" or "unrealistic?" Wasn't he simply hypothesizing based on previous situations?

In addition, I felt that Gordon took way too long to respond to me and at times I wondered if he was on top of everything. This made me feel as if I had to monitor him closely, which greatly increased my anxiety. But he did have contacts at the Medical Board and also a good reputation there and, as I had seen in the criminal case, relationships could be very important in the practice of law. Furthermore, I was afraid that if I terminated our relationship, it would be viewed unfavorably by the Board. Given these factors, I decided not to end our relationship, but I would need to repair the damage my email had caused.

I drove down to San Jose to meet Gordon in his office. His assistant was on the phone when I arrived and gave me a dismissive point and wave in the direction of the conference room. Twenty minutes later, Gordon walked into the room, breathing heavily. He settled into a chair across from me, at the other end of the table.

"Thanks for agreeing to meet with me," I said.

461

He grumbled something under his breath and nodded, looking like he needed a hug.

"I want to apologize for upsetting you with my previous e-mail. I really think there was a significant miscommunication, as it was not my intent whatsoever to criticize you."

"I didn't see the point of it all," he muttered.

"It was meant to be a rallying cry to overcome my current predicament with the Board."

He looked puzzled.

"When you get to know me better," I said, "I think you'll understand."

"Perhaps."

"I'm sorry for the email. I hope that you'll continue to represent me."

"Apology accepted," he said, his face relaxing. "I'll stay with you to the end."

I got up and walked around the table.

"Can I give you a hug?"

He pushed back his chair and gave me a stiff, half-standing, one-armed hug. Then he sat back down.

I started back for my seat, nonchalantly addressing him as I did so. "Hey, let me ask you something, Gordon. Have you ever seen the Board close a case and then re-open it a year later?"

"No."

"Never in over forty years of practicing law?"

"Never."

"That's kind of my point. Anything is possible. Including an outcome where I receive no sanction."

"I see where you're coming from. But it's not going to happen."

"I don't think this is unrealistic, Gordon, I really don't."
From the other end of the table, he shook his head at
me. It seemed he always chose to sit far away from me.
I leaned forward on the conference table.

"I don't think the Board is interested in being heavy-
handed with me. I think they were forced into opening
this investigation by the DEA."

He didn't respond. Instead, he scribbled something in
the folder in front of him. I knew further attempts to
persuade him to my way of thinking would be futile. I
would simply have to manage him from that point
forward, watching him closely to make sure he didn't miss
anything. And so, for the remainder of our relationship, I
would always be wary of him. Unlike Ted, he never had
my implicit trust.

Frustrated with Gordon, I emailed Ted to ask him
whether the FDA agent who had investigated would be
able to speak on my behalf.

He responded:" I'm sorry to hear about the Medical
Board, but I know you will weather that storm too. You
have the energy, commitment and zeal to overcome, as
you have shown again and again. You may remember
that the female FDA agent left the agency, retired and
went into private practice. I'll try to find her. Truth be
told, I expect that your case with the Board will not be a
big deal."

I fervently hoped he was right.


As Gordon prepared my defense, I continued to work at
the hospital, but I was finding it difficult to sustain my
rheumatology clinic because of my inability to prescribe
controlled substances. The DEA had refused to renew

my license until the Medical Board finished its inquiry, which Gordon informed me could take up to a year. But many patients in rheumatology have chronic pain and require narcotics for relief. Without a DEA license, I could not effectively practice my specialty, and so I would be forced to find someone to take over my clinic. Since rheumatology was half of my practice at the hospital, my salary would be reduced significantly. I hadn't come close to paying off my debt from the criminal case, and now I was accumulating more debt because of the legal costs of the civil case. The reduction of salary would be devastating, and there was no way I could do enough overtime to make up the difference.

Desperate for a solution, I met with my partners. Steve, the leader of our group and the man who had nearly single-handedly saved my job, was irate about the DEA's decision. He suggested we ask Administration to petition the DEA for an exemption, but I knew that had no chance. There was no negotiating with the DEA.

Another partner named Gion, a lung specialist whom I had recruited from Stanford four years earlier, suggested I simply stop prescribing narcotics and allow the pain clinic to do this. Gion had held a soft spot in my heart ever since he had extended me the interest-free, twelve-thousand-dollar loan several months earlier. Born and raised in Hong Kong, he and his family later moved to the U.S. where he ended up attending one of the finest universities in the world. But his English was still spotty at times, and his word choices could be sub-optimal, particularly when he was excited.

"The DEA, yeah, they need one big kick up the ass," he exclaimed.

Despite the seriousness of the issue, I couldn't help but laugh. Although I appreciated his suggestion, I knew there were simply too many patients for the pain clinic to handle.

More conversation followed before Adita, who had been sitting quietly for the entire meeting, spoke up.

"We'll use my DEA license for all narcotic prescriptions," she suggested.

Everyone stopped talking and looked at her.

"But I probably write two or three every day," I said. "And in order to legally write those prescriptions, you would need to hear about each one of those patients. That could take a fair amount of time out of your day."

"I know that, Max," she said firmly. "I'll make it work."

And she did just that for the next nine months, which was a huge hassle for her and made me feel like I was a medical student again. Regardless, she never complained once about it. It was one of the nicest things anyone has done for me. Her sacrifice made it possible for me to keep my job in the clinic, thus preventing a dramatic drop in my salary.

Approximately one month after my meeting with Gordon, Mr. Arnold sent a letter requesting "documents relating to the federal investigation of Dr. Kepler, including the following: Audiotapes and/or transcripts of interviews with Dr. Kepler and conversations between Dr. Kepler and the undercover officer, statements of any witnesses and/or victims, and Dr. Kepler's medical charts for each of the victims."

Gordon passed this request on to me but suggested we simply ignore it, as the information would be too inflammatory. It would be best to try to work out a settlement before this information was reviewed, and so we just waited it out. In the next two months, the only contact from the Board was a notification that an administrative hearing before a judge had been scheduled for July 28, 2008. That was still six months away. The slow torture would continue.

Meanwhile, I continued to keep Gordon aware of my goal of no sanction, careful to limit the frequency and intensity of my correspondences. Having to worry about my attorney only exacerbated my anxiety. There were many nights I stayed up going over everything in my mind, wondering whether he had missed something.

But Gordon, to his credit, had been discussing my case with Mr. Arnold at regular intervals, and eventually his efforts paid off. The Board finally agreed to a settlement conference on April 4, 2008. Its purpose was to achieve a final resolution of the matter without the need for a full administrative hearing. In short, a successful settlement conference would mean I could continue to practice medicine.

"So how do these things usually turn out?" I asked Gordon.

"They always result in a signed agreement."

"And then everything is over?"

"The Medical Board has to formally approve it first, but they always do."

The news gave me a great measure of relief, and true to Gordon's word, Mr. Arnold informed us he would come to the settlement conference with an agreement in hand.

The crux of the agreement was that I would be placed on five years of probation but would not lose my license. I probably should have been more grateful than I was but I pushed Gordon a bit, telling him I had been hoping for a better outcome. He insisted this was the best solution he could negotiate. Although I doubted he had worked hard enough to achieve my goal of no sanction, I wasn't about to ask him at that point, "Did you do your best for me, Gordon?" And, after all, perhaps he had, and the fact was that I would still have my license, regardless of the sanctions.

# CHAPTER THIRTY-SIX

The settlement conference would take place in Oakland at the California Office of Administrative Hearings (OAH), established by the Legislature in 1945 as a quasi-judicial court that hears administrative disputes between government agencies and individuals or businesses.

Gordon had instructed me to meet him there thirty minutes before the start of the hearing. When I arrived, he was already seated, on time for once. I joined him at the table and he immediately went over last-minute details regarding the sequencing of the conference. He was finished within five minutes, and then we sat in silence, waiting for Mr. Arnold, who arrived a short while later. He greeted both of us and sat down.

At the scheduled start time, the judge walked in unannounced. She was wearing street clothes—no robe—and smiled at us as she took a seat, which I hoped augured well for me. A court reporter was the only other person in the room.

"We are here for a settlement conference involving the Medical Board of California vs. Max Kepler, M.D.," she began. "As I understand it, Mr. Arnold has brought with him today a settlement agreement. Is that correct?"

"Yes, your Honor," he answered.

"And there are stipulations to the agreement?"

"Yes, there are. In order for the Medical Board to feel comfortable that Dr. Kepler's license should not be revoked, Dr. Kepler must demonstrate three things. After listing them, he turned to me and asked, "Dr. Kepler, do accept responsibilities for your actions that have led to this Medical Board inquiry?"

He caught me off guard, and I hesitated before answering.

"Yes. Definitely."

"Can you tell us what you have done to demonstrate rehabilitation?"

I was surprised I'd be answering questions from the table, unlike at the federal proceedings, but it certainly made me feel more comfortable.

"I have been seeing my psychiatrist, Dr. Rick Steele, at weekly intervals. I have worked hard during these sessions to understand the reasons I participated in such behavior, and to make sure I don't repeat the same mistakes in the future. I have also been taking care of patients at Cade County General Hospital without any problems whatsoever. I've worked hard to atone for my misdeeds."

"How can we be sure the public will be safe in the future?"

Gordon handed me the agreement I had signed with Sang when I returned to work ten months earlier, and I read it aloud for the court. It included such things as agreeing not to engage in unprofessional conduct, refraining from practicing cosmetic medicine, and limiting

469

my practice of medicine to rheumatology and general internal medicine. I also was required to meet quarterly with Sang for a period of two years so that he could review my clinical practice and prescribing patterns.

When I finished, the judge asked, "Does that satisfy the conditions set forth by the Medical Board, Mr. Arnold?"

"Yes, your Honor."

"Have you seen the agreement yet, Dr. Kepler?"

"No, your Honor."

"We'll give you a chance to review the agreement in a moment, Dr. Kepler. Mr. Arnold, does the Medical Board have any additional stipulation for this agreement?"

"Only that Dr. Kepler reads the agreement carefully and admits guilt for the charges listed therein. Once he accepts responsibility, he will be free to sign the agreement."

"Then I'll ask you to give it to him. Dr. Kepler, you can step outside the room with your attorney and review the agreement. I will meet individually with Mr. Arnold."

Gordon and I walked into an adjacent room, agreement in hand. The beginning of the document summarized my behavior that led to the criminal conviction.

At the end was the judgment. It called for a revocation of my license with a stay, which meant I actually kept my license. The five-year probation included a fifteen-day suspension of my license, completion of an ethics course within sixty days, monitoring of my practice by a designated Board employee, psychiatric evaluation within thirty days, ongoing psychotherapy with quarterly reports, quarterly declarations submitted by myself and monitoring costs of three thousand dollars per year.

I felt some of those terms were unreasonable and asked Gordon to get them changed. He agreed to try and with that, we returned to the courtroom.

"Are there any issues you would like to discuss?" the judge asked.

"Overall the agreement seems satisfactory, with two exceptions. We think the fifteen-day suspension is unnecessary since Dr. Kepler was already suspended from his job at the hospital for ten months. Secondly, we would like to request that probation be reduced from five to three years."

"Mr. Arnold?"

"I'll have to discuss those issues with the Board."

"Then I'll ask you to step out while you do that, and I'll talk with Dr. Kepler and his attorney privately."

Once Arnold was gone, the judge asked if we had any additional concerns. Gordon could not think of any and by that point, I just wanted to sign the amended agreement and get out.

"We can eliminate the fifteen-day suspension but the five years of probation has to stand," Mr. Arnold said when he returned.

"Is the agreement acceptable to your client?" the judge asked Gordon.

Gordon looked at me. Overcoming my instinct to fight, I nodded.

"Yes, your Honor."

"Then, Dr. Kepler, you'll need to sign the agreement."

I signed two copies and handed them to Mr. Arnold. Once he had signed them, he returned one to me.

"If there is nothing further, this settlement conference is concluded."

The entire session had taken twenty minutes. Mr. Arnold quickly gathered his things and stood up. He walked over to me and extended his hand.

"Good luck, Dr. Kepler," he said as he shook my hand. He seemed like a genuinely nice man.

Because of Gordon's arthritic knees, it took us awhile to make it to the parking garage. As usual, I felt uncomfortable around him and tried to fill the time it took with banter about the weather and the traffic on the San Mateo bridge. When we finally reached the garage, Gordon turned to me.

"Good luck to you, Max."

"Thank you for everything, Gordon," I said, shaking his hand.

"You're welcome. The agreement should be formalized at the next Board meeting. Probably within a month."

"And then it will be all over?"

"Yes."

"You're sure now? There's nothing else?"

"I'm sure, Max. It's just a formality now."

"That's great. I can't believe it's over."

He smiled warmly and then turned towards his car. I watched him limp along, holding his weathered brown briefcase in his right hand, and felt grateful, not only for his help but also because after he delivered the Board's verdict, I would no longer need him. Once he was gone, I got in my car, turned up the radio, and rejoiced in the successful completion of yet another goal.

As usual, it didn't take long for the euphoria to subside. Back to the grind of work, I called Gordon for an update.

"I had a telephone conversation with Mr. Arnold, and he said he's going to present your case to the full Board within the next four to five weeks," he told me.

"That long?" I asked.

"Apparently, they're very busy."

"Is it possible for us to attend the meeting?"

"Unfortunately, no. We don't have the right to appear before the Board as his client. It's not necessary anyway."

"I just want to cover all the bases."

"Don't worry. I'll keep you informed," he reassured me.

Weeks of waiting went by and life largely returned to normal, except for my persistent thoughts of the Board's impending decision. Despite my attorney's assurances that the decision was a mere formality, I still worried about it.

Then, five weeks after the settlement conference, I received a call from Gordon just as I arrived home from work. He seemed particularly uptight, and his voice was even more halting than usual. After brief pleasantries, he got right to the point.

"I had a lengthy telephone conversation with Deputy Attorney General Lester Arnold today."

"Great," I interrupted. "What'd he say?"

Gordon paused for a moment, causing my heart to drop. Then, he slowly said, " I'm sorry to inform you the Medical Board has rejected the settlement you signed."

I nearly stumbled on the stairs.

"You're telling me they reneged on the agreement?"

"Mr. Arnold informed me that he presented your matter to the full Medical Board yesterday. There were seven matters on the calendar, and the Board had set aside one hour to hear all seven matters. Your case was the first called, and the Board spent forty-five minutes discussing your matter. And they decided to reject the settlement."

"I'm just flabbergasted," was all I could manage.

"Mr. Arnold informed me that he presented the matter in a most favorable light for you. But he said Board members seemed to focus on the premeditation that it took to make all of the arrangements you had to make to get the drugs into California and then provide them to your patients. It was this premeditation that resulted in the Board directing Mr. Arnold to accept nothing short of a surrender of your license."

I stood dumbfounded for a moment. I hadn't even considered such an outcome.

"This is crazy, Gordon. The Board offered a written agreement at the settlement conference and were in real-time communication with its representative during that hearing. A full six weeks later, they renege on that agreement. How can that possibly happen?"

By the last sentence, I was shouting. Gordon, on the other hand, droned on.

"In discussing this matter with Mr. Arnold, he agrees that our only option is now to proceed to a full hearing before an Administrative Law Judge. We are probably looking at a hearing sometime in the middle of summer."

"That's four months away!" I shouted, but Gordon remained quiet, so I kept on venting. "The way the Board has handled my case is reprehensible. They close the case, then re-open it one full year later, agree to a settlement, then renege on it, then schedule another hearing four months later. What am I supposed to do in the meantime? Look for a new career? I have a daughter I have to support and I'm still paying off the huge debt accumulated through this whole process. This is wrong, Gordon, despite whatever I did in the past."

"I want you to know that I am still optimistic that we can present this matter in a convincing manner during the Administrative Hearing and convince the judge to write an opinion that is so strongly worded it has to be accepted by the Board eventually."

I wanted to believe him, but I kept remembering his confident reassurances after the settlement conference. For now, however, I needed to get out of my apartment and take a walk. It would be a week before I told anyone the news. I spent that time processing the information and gathering my strength for the fight ahead. As I did, I realized I was moving beyond the self-loathing and guilt. I was tired of it, along with all the drama. Gone too were the self-aggrandizing goals. I just wanted to end everything once and for all so that I could live my life instead of just trying to survive. I convinced myself that if I could get through this one final step, my life would be good.

# CHAPTER THIRTY-SEVEN

I didn't have the heart to tell my parents the Board settlement had been rejected. It would be like opening a wound that wasn't fully healed. I did inform my partners, hospital administration, Alice and Greg. I didn't want to bother any others with my continuing saga. I would try to handle this one last hurdle a little more on my own.

I returned to work the day after receiving the news from Gordon, and two days later, I worked an overnight shift. On that night, I was resting comfortably in the hospital sleep room, watching *Whose Line Is it Anyway?*, when I was called by a nurse who told me a patient had fallen down when getting out of bed.

"She's so overweight, we can't get her up," the nurse informed me.

"I'll be right there." When I got there, the woman was lying prone on the floor, moaning in pain. She had just undergone a hernia repair the day before, and the discomfort from the operation, along with her weight of three hundred and fifty pounds, meant she was helpless there on the floor. After a fair amount of strategizing,

476

we were able to slip a blanket under her body and lift her into bed, using six men. Once there, I examined her and found her stable.

"I just want to get out of here so I can go back to my daughter," she said.

"How old is she?" I asked.

"Six weeks."

"You'll be home soon," I said, touching her cheek. Then I went out to the nurses' station to scribble a quick note. I had only been there for about a minute before the nurse yelled out, "She's seizing, doctor!" I ran back into the room to find the patient's whole body shaking. I quickly ordered a medication, but before it could be given, the seizure stopped. I immediately went to her bedside to examine her.

"Hello, Mrs. Diaz?" I asked. "It's Doctor Kepler. Can you hear me?"

As I peered down at her, I noticed her breathing was becoming more labored until suddenly, she simply stopped breathing. I shook her twice, calling out her name, and then reached to check her carotid pulse. When I discovered none, I hit the Code Blue button on the wall behind her. Within minutes, the room filled with medical personnel. It took everything we could do to keep her alive. After reviewing the labs and EKG, I decided she most likely had suffered a pulmonary embolism, which is a blood clot to the lungs, usually caused by sluggish blood flow in the legs.

I continued ordering rounds of epinephrine every three to five minutes, as thoughts of the six-week-old baby swirled in my head. Meanwhile, I kept checking for her pulse, nearly pleading for it to be there, but it wasn't.

Just then, a nurse announced the patient's husband had just arrived with the couple's two children.

Two children?

The tension in the room immediately escalated. By then the resuscitation attempts were nearing twenty minutes, and the rhythm was still very abnormal. Her chance of survival was dropping dramatically. We continued the struggle against the inevitable for forty-five minutes. Slowly, the energy started to drain from the room with each passing moment, and I could sense people looking at me to make a decision I dreaded. Still, I pushed on another ten minutes until it was absolutely clear that further attempts were futile. I looked at the charge nurse, and she shook her head. I knew it was time.

"Let's call it," I said. "Time of death is 2300 hours."

People began filing out of the room, while I stood at her bedside, staring at her massive body, thinking about her two young children. Before I knew it, the patient's husband was in the room, pushing past me to get next to his wife.

"Gloria! My Gloria!" he kept shouting. A nurse rushed to his side, putting her hand on his back. He stopped yelling and put his head on his wife's chest and starting sobbing. Finding the scene gut-wrenching, I made my way out of the room. Fifteen minutes later, I would explain to him what had happened, and after that thankless task, I returned to the sleep room to grieve alone. Turns out, I'd grieve a lot that night, so much so that I began to wonder why my grief was so intense and prolonged. Of course, the death of a young woman with two children was incomparably sad, but I suspected I was also grieving for myself, for what I had done, how I had placed something so valuable and for which I worked so hard, at risk. And now I was on the verge of possibly losing that privilege.

Meanwhile, I plugged along at the hospital, constantly aware that the skill set developed over ten years of training could suddenly be rendered useless by a group of people in Sacramento. With this backdrop, even routine experiences in the hospital took on increased importance, as in my appointments with a sixty-five-year-old woman named Lucia with rheumatoid arthritis. Her disease was under control, so most of our time together was spent socializing. Per usual, she would show up with homemade tamales, a tradition she had started years previously. I had long given up on trying to convince her to stop, and, truth be told, I looked forward to the delicious Mexican comfort food she brought each time she came.

One month before the administrative hearing, she walked into my office and handed me the familiar package as she sat down.

"Five chicken and five pork," she said. "Just as you like."

I smiled broadly and set the bag aside.

"How are you doing?" I asked her.

"No pain at all," she said, holding up her hands and opening and closing her fingers.

"Excellent," I said. Then, I examined her, reviewed her labs and refilled her prescriptions.

"Thank you for helping me, doctor," she said, as I gave her the paper. "I don't know what I'd ever do without you."

I looked at Lucia, realizing I felt the same way about her. I couldn't believe I had ever been bored and frustrated with patient care. It occurred to me that day that I might never see Lucia again, as her next appointment would be scheduled for a date after the Administrative Hearing. "You're very sweet for saying that. Thank you," I answered.

"See you in four months?" she asked, her face bright.

All I could do was nod.

As I worked long overtime hours, both to pay down my debt and to distract myself, Gordon was preparing for the hearing. Near the end of the waiting period, he called to tell me I needed to ask Sang and Dr. Steele to speak on my behalf at the hearing, which I was reluctant to do yet again.

"It's very important," Gordon emphasized.

I went to see Sang first. As always, he was buried in work when I leaned into his office.

"Do you have a couple moments?" I asked.

"Please," he said, waving his hand at an empty chair.

I sat down and squirmed. I wondered how many times I had asked for his help in the previous three years.

"Do you need something?"

I cleared my throat and shifted again. The chair felt enormous around me, and I was surprised my feet touched the floor.

"As you know," I forced out the words, "I have to appear at an Administrative Hearing of the Medical

Board on July 25. Although I realize it's a significant request, would you be willing to speak on my behalf for ten to fifteen minutes there?"

"Where and when? I'll have to see if I can make it."

I wondered whether he was tired of it all. Or maybe he had lost faith in me.

"I'll have to get back to you about the time," I said. "But the location is Oakland."

He nodded.

"If you feel that you cannot do this, I understand. It becomes more and more embarrassing to ask for your help in these matters."

Sang gave me a long stare. He turned to his computer, absentmindedly typed a few words, and then pushed aside the keyboard to create room for his elbows, which he leaned upon. His expression suddenly became resolute.

"I've stuck by you through thick and thin, and I'm not quitting now."

I was taken aback by the forcefulness with which he stated this.

"I hope that I can somehow repay you for all your generosity over the last three years," I managed.

"You're a fine and caring doctor, and we need you."

His words lifted me, and I rode them like a wave as I left the office. Within minutes, I called Dr. Steele and left a voice message. He returned the call by the end of the day.

"Email me the directions and the time, and I'll be there," he said.

Several days later, I received a certified mail notice from Gordon. I picked up the heavy envelope from the Post

Office the next day, and I waited until I got home to open it. There was a cover letter from Mr. Arnold on the front of the packet. My hands began to shake with the first sentence:" Enclosed are transcripts of the FDA undercover telephone and meeting tapes."

*Transcripts?* I thought there was just one, taken from the time the undercover agent visited my office. But as I flipped through the packet, I could see there were transcripts of every phone conversation and email exchange I'd had with her, twenty-six pages of them. I tossed the packet on my bed. It had been three years since the conversations had taken place, and I had tried hard to forget the details, but now I would have to relive the experience, this time in a courtroom.

As I stood staring at the transcripts, I realized I was clutching the crumpled cover letter in my right hand. I released my grip, smoothed out the paper, and resumed reading. My heart rate seemed to be increasing by the minute as I did. I discovered the Board was going to bring an expert witness to "testify regarding the substantial relationship of respondent's conviction, including the conduct admitted in his plea, to the qualifications, duties and functions of a physician."

How could I possibly survive this onslaught?

I sat down and stared at the wall. Then I stood up again and paced for a time, before picking up the packet and forcing myself to read every single word of every transcript. I read the famous "trust relationship" phrase quoted by the federal judge when he had called me a drug dealer and had gone into a fit of rage. I read a part I'd been unaware of, caught by a hidden microphone after the agent left my office: "Okay, so let me undo my surveillance thing here so we're not being recorded any longer. Okay, the time is 1:03, and I am out of Dr. Kepler's office, having just purchased some human growth hormone. That was pretty easy."

If it was easy for a federal agent to have gotten me, it would be a cinch for an accomplished attorney. I would fall on the sword of my own words. The administrative hearing would be a mere formality in the Board's effort to take my license.    Nonetheless, the near intellectual certainty of that outcome was in direct contradistinction to what I still felt on a gut level.    I simply couldn't believe that I would lose my license.

In the end, I read the transcripts multiple times, until I no longer felt sick to my stomach. I don't know if it took thirty minutes or three hours, but I do remember reliving the whole experience again.    And as I went through it, I began to understand that that Max Kepler no longer existed.    The confused and reckless man who had done such unimaginable things just a few short years ago was gone.    And with that, I felt just a bit of hope that I could finally let go.

But later that evening, I was still obsessing about the transcripts, playing them in my mind like a looped recording.

"Failure of the qualifications, functions or duties of a physician."

I resorted to sleeping on the couch again, music playing in the background.    I was so pissed at myself for my mental weakness.

The following day, I took Jessica to Ocean Beach in San Francisco.    As we parked, I could see that the usual mid-summer fog had receded, revealing a brilliant day. I got out of the car and stood on the sidewalk, looking at the endless blue water. After several minutes, I realized Jessica wasn't next to me. Panicked, I looked over my shoulder and spotted her in the back of the car, trying to get my attention. The engine was still running.

"I'm so sorry, Jessica," I said as I pulled her out.

"Were you just going to leave me, Daddy?"

"I'd never do that, sweetie." I opened the driver's door, turned off the car, and took out the key.

"Let's go play," she said, sprinting for the sand.

I followed her numbly, unable to appreciate the warm sun or the gentle ocean breeze. Instead, I reverted back to thinking about whether I was as bad as they said, and if I was, it would follow that I must also be a bad father. Feeling nearly catatonic, I dropped down in the sand to watch Jessica. She was playing in the shallow water, which was foamy from the incoming waves. The longer I watched, the less I thought, and at some point, my mind must have been quieted, because I was overcome with a sense of calm.

The setting sun eventually jolted me back to consciousness, and a short while later we left the beach. On the drive home, it occurred to me that I had experienced the inner stillness I'd found at the beach before, but only under extreme circumstances, such as while engaged in an intense physical or mental activity, like playing in a college football game or taking standardized examinations during medical school. The focus required for those events quieted my mind, and the resulting tranquility was intensely pleasurable. But once the activity ended, my mind would start up again and the unrest would resume.

That night, after dropping off Jessica at her mom's house, I wrote a poem about the day's experience.

Whiteness washed over her tiny feet.
And all I could see were those feet,
And that sky, and that sunset, and that whiteness
Of that ocean cleansing those beautiful feet.
And all I could feel was love,
Free of clichés, expectations, obligations.
I felt love as pure as I could ever imagine it.
Her squeals of delight filling my soul,
And blurring all sense of time.

I sat at my desk staring at the poem, and then went to the kitchen to get a beer. Then I stood for the longest time in Jessica's room, sipping on the drink and looking into the darkness. I remembered the times as an adolescent when I would go into the woods behind my house, where I had constructed a rudimentary bench. I would sit there among the trees, in a spot near a little creek, and listen to the trickling sounds. My mind was clear during those moments, and I felt peace.

At some point, my life had been overtaken by goals serving the self-image I developed: the small-town boy who made it to Harvard and beyond. But in the process, I had forgotten about that twelve-year-old boy alone in the woods. But now I remembered him, and by reminding myself of that time, I realized I had a choice. I could continue to obsess about future events over which I had no control, or I could quiet my mind by focusing only on

485

the present.    I had spent the previous three years lamenting the loss of control in my life, but I had defined control solely in external, structured terms.    I had looked towards a future in which I could regain control, not realizing it existed within me the entire time.

Going through this process of developing self-awareness, I was helped by *The Power of Now*, a book by Eckhart Tolle given to me by a friend.    According to Tolle, unease, anxiety, tension, stress, worry — all forms of fear — are caused by too much future, and not enough of being present in the current moment. Guilt, regret, resentment, grievances, sadness, bitterness, and all forms of non-forgiveness are caused by too much past, and not enough present. And when I was successful in letting go, I felt empowered and free for the first time in my life.

It was only by ending the chasing that I would be free to experience life fully:    I could still have goals, but they would be structured around process, instead of end results.    In turn, life would be more experiential, instead of being played out in my mind as some projected future event.    I would accept the raw version of me, the twelve-year-old boy in the woods, and by doing so, my humanity and goodness would be revealed, and that would allow for a sense of connectedness to life and those around me. Then I could be the father and human being I had always wanted to be, and then I would have peace.    And self-acceptance.

The beer was finished.    I tossed the empty can into the trash.    The apartment felt so empty.    I called Greg.

"How about some golf this weekend?" I asked him. "You're about due for another trip to San Francisco, anyway."

"The beat-down I delivered last time wasn't enough for you?" he asked.

"It'll be different next time around."

I could never give up tackling challenges, I'd just let go of the self-destructive and self-aggrandizing behaviors that had characterized my past.

# CHAPTER THIRTY-EIGHT

I arrived thirty minutes early at the California Office of Administrative Hearings in Oakland. I parked in the multi-level, concrete garage directly across the street from the building, a modern structure with a facade made almost entirely of tinted glass, effectively serving as a one-way mirror. For someone about to hear evidence obtained surreptitiously, this seemed fitting.

My phone beeped with text messages.

"Good luck today." Alice wrote.

She had dealt admirably with three years of wondering not only whether her daughter's father would go to prison, but also whether he'd lose his job. I thought of how many sleepless nights she must have endured, when all I really wanted was to never cause her any more pain. I was humbled by her unwavering support in the face of my gargantuan fuck-up, and I wondered whether I would have done the same for her so unstintingly.

The second text was from Mom.

"Thinking about you, Max. Call me when it's over."

I could feel her presence. I was transported once again to my elementary school, about to confess my sins with her standing just outside in the hallway, making sure I was okay.

Although I appreciated her message, I was still not convinced Mom had truly forgiven me. And I could understand why. Not only had I embarrassed and disappointed her, I had been dishonest in the worst of ways. But I was determined to repair that lost trust; I would prove to Mom that I could once again be that man worthy of the title, "Doctor," if only given the chance.

I turned off my phone and walked into the lobby. I was alone again. There wouldn't be twenty people in the courtroom with me this time around. Despite that, I didn't feel the fear I had become accustomed to, perhaps because I had begun to detach myself from the outcome. I knew this day would bring an ending, good or bad, and that would lead to a new beginning. And so, despite the momentousness of the occasion, I felt a certain inner peace.

Gordon was waiting outside the door of the hearing room. I had never seen him in a suit, the ill-fitting navy blue clothing hanging awkwardly from his rotund frame.

"How you doing today?" he asked. His attempts at connecting were always devoid of any real intimacy.

"Fine," I answered. "Ready to get this thing over with."

He smiled, but I knew he cared only from a professional standpoint. He was there to fight because it was his job. I would not be hearing an impassioned plea in the courtroom, like the day Ted fought heroically for my freedom eighteen months earlier. I continued to believe that the constrained thinking of my attorney had been a real impediment.

"Now listen, they're going to make you look bad, but just try to remember that's their job. Don't get overly involved with what they say."

I always wondered how personal attacks could not be taken personally.

"Your role is to take your beating and accept full responsibility. My role is to show you've been rehabilitated. I will not try to argue with them in any substantive way."

I nodded.

"Got it," I said. "The public flagellation is coming."

There was no laugh, not even a smile. He merely checked his watch and said, "Let's go inside."

I nodded and followed him into the room. We made our way to the conference table on the left, about fifteen feet from the judge who was already seated at the bench, which, unlike in the federal courtroom, was not raised. It was a different judge from the settlement conference: a middle-aged woman with long brown hair and a friendly face. She looked at me without contempt, and for that I was thankful.

The room itself looked like a regular conference room. There were no pews for a gallery; just a few misaligned chairs behind the conference tables. The entire space was the size of a typical classroom, with most of it unused. A court reporter sat to the left of the judge. She glanced at me, and then checked a nail on her right hand.

Within minutes, Mr. Arnold came into the courtroom, accompanied by his expert witness, Dr. Albert Morgan, who shook hands with Gordon first and then, much to my surprise, me. I noted he was about my age and height, but had retained all of his hair. He gave me a forced smile and remained silent while we shook hands. As he sat down at the adjacent table, and things were about to get underway, I took a deep breath, reminding myself that although they were going to carve me up, there was nothing more they could do to me.

At nine-ten, the hearing started. After some initial proceedings, Mr. Arnold called the expert witness, Dr. Albert Morgan, to the stand. He stood up and straightened his tie, and then walked slowly to the witness stand, located to the right of the judge. As he turned around, the clerk came in front of him to administer the oath. Afterwards, Mr. Arnold stood up at the conference table.

"Doctor, would you please introduce yourself to the Court and state your current position?"

"My name is Dr. Albert Morgan. I am Associate Professor of Medicine in the Division of Cardiology at the University of California, San Francisco."

"And can you give us your training background?

The bona fides tumbled from the witness stand like the swollen mountain streams of early spring. Pure and cold. I considered momentarily the irony that we both had worked at UCSF.

Meanwhile, he was still going. They had brought a heavyweight into the ring.

"Have you had a chance to review the materials supplied to you and which are found in the documents supplied to Mr. Fanning and this Court?"

"I have."

"Dr. Morgan, are you familiar with human growth hormone, otherwise known as hGH?"

"I am."

"Dr. Morgan, what are the FDA-approved uses of human growth hormone?"

After listing them, Dr. Morgan looked at me with a look of contempt and added, "It should be noted that off-label use of hGH is not permitted by law."

I quickly looked away as Mr. Arnold continued his questioning.

"I would like to read to you the following conversation that took place between Dr. Kepler and the government agent."

Agent: That was the other thing 'cause I checked on the FDA website, and it says hGH cannot be used for anti-aging.

Dr. Kepler: Well, it's not an approved indication. But it can be used off-label. Every FDA-approved medication, essentially, can be used for off-label purposes. And that's legal.

Agent: So it's no problem even though it's for anti-aging?

Dr. Kepler: That's not a problem.

Mr. Arnold put down the transcript and paused before speaking.

"Dr. Morgan, since anti-aging or wellness is not an approved indication for the use of hGH, does this conversation demonstrate qualities consistent with the qualifications, functions or duties of a physician?"

492

"No, it does not."

"Dr. Morgan, are there known side-effects of hGH?"

"Yes, many. They include nerve, muscle, or joint pain, swelling due to fluid in the body's tissues, carpal tunnel syndrome, numbness and tingling of the skin, and high cholesterol levels. Human growth hormone can also increase the risk of diabetes and contribute the growth of cancerous tumors."

Although I disagreed with him, knowing that the side effects listed occurred only with doses much higher than I used, I remained quiet and expressionless, remembering what Gordon had told me: "Just take the beating."

Mr. Arnold continued. "In his discussion with the undercover agent, did Dr. Kepler disclose potential side effects of hGH?"

"No. Potential adverse effects of the drug were not disclosed. It is the responsibility of a physician, upon prescribing a new medication, to review not only the benefits of a drug, but also its potential side effects. Not doing so represents a failure of the qualifications, functions or duties of a physician."

"Dr. Kepler, in his conversation with the undercover agent, stated that the use of one to two units of hGH per day was without any risk. Are you aware of any data to support that contention?"

"There is no data suggesting that a low dose of hGH is safe, especially over a protracted period of time. This violates the principle of non-maleficence, embodied by the phrase, "First, do no harm," or the Latin, *primum non nocere*.

*Shit, now he's speaking Latin. I haven't got a chance.*

493

"Dr. Kepler described the benefits of hGH, including muscle growth, fat loss, improved sexual performance, increased skin thickness, decreased wrinkles, improved sleep, a sense of well-being, increased bone density, hair growth, fat loss, and faster recovery from injury and rigorous work-outs. Was this consistent with the qualifications, functions or duties of a physician?"

"No. The discussion of potential benefits was exaggerated, incomplete and misleading."

*Clearly, he's never used the drug.*

"In his conversation with the agent, Dr. Kepler reported that hGH could cause patients to lose thirty percent of body fat. Dr. Morgan, is this consistent with qualifications, functions or duties of a physician? If not, why?"

"No, it is not. Dr. Kepler exaggerated the potential benefits. This behavior violates the well-known medical ethics concept of beneficence. Specifically, a practitioner should act in the best interest of the patient. *Salus aegroti suprema lex.*"

*I didn't realize it was going to be this bad.*

"Regarding the use of prescription medications in the United States, is there a standard to which physicians must adhere?"

"Yes, drugs provided to patients in the United States must meet strict criteria set by the FDA in terms of the manufacturing of the drugs."

"Dr. Kepler has said that he visited the factory in China where the hGH had been manufactured. Does this meet the standard for assuring safety of a prescribed medication?"

494

"Dr. Kepler's statement that he visited the factory in China and thus felt the drug was safe is outrageous."

*I couldn't agree more.*

"Dr. Morgan, let's listen to another conversation between the FDA investigator and Dr. Kepler."

Mr. Arnold then proceeded to read the discussion I had with the "Jill Monroe" regarding the source of the hGH, including the part where she specifically asked whether the drug was from China and I replied, "No." When he was done reading, Mr. Arnold spun away from Dr. Morgan, transcripts raised above his head, and stared at me for a few moments before resuming his questioning.

"Dr. Morgan, is the conduct displayed by Dr. Kepler in this exchange consistent with the responsibilities of a physician?"

"No. This conduct is an outrageous break of the trust relationship between a patient and doctor. Dr. Kepler was dishonest with patients. Dr. Kepler was asked a direct question and lied. By doing so, he mislead the patient."

By this time, I had slipped back into my familiar place of self-loathing. Maybe they were right; I wasn't worthy of being a doctor. My very existence demeaned the whole medical profession. I sank into a progressively deeper and darker place as these feelings washed over me. I was nothing more than a common criminal. It didn't matter that the Medical Board attorney and his expert witness were telling everyone I was a bad doctor, because I already knew that. I remembered a Christmas party in San Francisco, attended almost entirely by doctors, where I had felt completely out of place after my arrest. As I looked around that night, I became convinced I didn't belong with those respectable members of society. If they had known my history, surely, they would have cast me out.

"Dr. Kepler violated multiple ethical and professional principals, including beneficence, do no harm, patient-doctor relationship, good faith examination, accurate assessment of benefits and risks of a treatment, adequate follow-up, and the use of a medication for non-approved purposes."

"Thank you, Dr. Morgan. I have no further questions, your Honor."

"Mr. Fanning, do you have any questions of Dr. Morgan?"

Gordon grabbed the legal pad and quickly scanned the few notes he had there. He leaned back and slid his thumbs up and down his suspenders for a few moments. Then he shook his head.

"No questions, your Honor," he said.

"In that case, the witness can step down."

Dr. Morgan looked like he had just dined at the best steakhouse in the area, complete with a cigar and a fine cognac. And well he should have; he had just finished obliterating me.

"Mr. Fanning, you may proceed with your arguments," the judge said.

" Thank you, your Honor." Gordon pushed back his chair and struggled a bit to stand. "I wish to review some of the background history in connection with this matter," he began.

My heart sank as I realized I'd have to listen to yet another summary of everything that had happened. I blocked out the words and instead focused on the judge's face as Gordon spoke. She was listening carefully, her head cocked slightly to the side. Occasionally, she jotted down a quick note. Soon, Gordon had finished with his summary and was on to the consequences I had suffered as a result of my arrest. The judge appeared impressed by this part, which I found reassuring, even if the description of the fall-out from my arrest brought back bad memories.

"As part of his arrangement to return to work at Cade County Hospital," Gordon continued, "Dr. Kepler agreed in writing to a number of restrictions and conditions. We understand that the Medical Board of California might feel that the above sanctions do not fully satisfy their need for punishment for the actions of Dr. Kepler. Nonetheless, we hope the Board will consider the sanctions and penalties Dr. Kepler has already suffered in determining their course of action."

Gordon then thanked the judge and sat down next to me, patting my back as he did. I just stared at him, afraid of making any gesture the judge might misinterpret. Overall, however, I had been impressed with Gordon's firm and confident delivery, and I found his arguments persuasive, but then again, he was on my side.

"Mr. Fanning, would you like to call a witness?" the judge asked.

"Your Honor, at this time I would like to call Dr. Chang."

Sang walked briskly to the witness stand, touching my shoulder as he passed by. Once he was finished with the oath, Gordon approached him slowly.

"Sir, would you be so kind to introduce yourself and give us your title?"

"My name is Sang-Ick Chang. I am the Chief Medical Officer of Cade County Hospital."

"Can you tell us how long you have known Dr. Kepler?"

"I have known Dr. Kepler for the six years he has been on the full-time medical staff of Cade County Hospital."

"Would you say that your doctors are committed to caring for the underserved?"

"Yes. Ours is not a typical hospital environment and doctors that choose to work here, and remain over time, are a rare group indeed."

"Can you comment on Dr. Kepler's work history at Cade County Hospital?"

"Dr. Kepler has been an exemplary physician in his work. He is highly respected by his colleagues as a compassionate and brilliant rheumatologist and internist. I regularly receive letters of appreciation by patients who praise Dr. Kepler for his kindness and his willingness to take the extra time to explain complex and frightening conditions to them. The sentiments are clear and consistent: Dr. Kepler is an outstanding human being and physician."

"I understand you are also a physician. Would you be comfortable referring your patients to Dr. Kepler?"

"As a practicing physician as well as a county health administrator, I regularly refer patients to Dr. Kepler, and have been grateful for his outstanding care."

"Other than patient care, has Dr. Kepler contributed to Cade County Hospital in other ways?"

"Dr. Kepler's participation on the Medical Staff has been very strong. He was in charge of reviewing research protocols for the Medical Executive Committee and he served as chairman of the pharmacy and therapeutics committee."

"Can you comment on what the loss of Dr. Kepler would mean to Cade County Hospital?"

"Dr. Kepler contributes daily to the lives of the underserved and the disadvantaged, as well as the safe and effective running of a county hospital, and is without question a critical part of our safety net system of care in Cade County. Were we to lose Dr. Kepler, our ability to replace his specialty expertise, much less his compassion and contribution, would be nearly impossible."

"Thank you, Dr. Chang."

"Would you like to question the witness, Mr. Arnold?" the judge asked.

Mr. Arnold walked right up to the witness stand.

"Dr. Chang, are you willing to stake your professional reputation on Dr. Kepler?"

"With my presence here, I already have."

"Are you aware of any documented or reported allegations of misconduct by Dr. Kepler, outside the scope of the current matter?"

"I am not, and we have examined that closely. Dr. Kepler's record, the current issue notwithstanding, is exemplary."

"Then, how do you explain his unethical behavior?"

"It would not be proper for me to speculate. I have found Dr. Kepler to be quite forthright in his discussions about the matter. I trust that you will find an honest response from him regarding this."

"Thank you, Dr. Chang."

Finished with his testimony, Sang ambled back to his seat behind me, shooting me a grin and a wink as he passed by.

"Mr. Fanning, would you like to call your next witness?"

"Thank you, your Honor. The defense calls Dr. Richard Steele."

Rick looked uncertain as he walked to the front. I suspected he felt uncomfortable with the surroundings.

"Please introduce yourself and tell us how you know Dr. Kepler," Gordon said.

"My name is Dr. Rick Steele, and I have been Max's psychiatrist for over five years."

"What has impressed you about Dr. Kepler in your sessions with him?"

"His complete willingness to confront the reality of what he had been doing. It amounted to an epiphany."

"Did Dr. Kepler ever blame others for what happened to him?"

"Max never scapegoated, rationalized or justified his misconduct. He looked deep within, applying candor and brutally honest self-assessment. At every step in this process of revelation, recognition and rebuilding, he has been a model human being."

"Did he accept responsibility for his actions?"

"I believe Max has been the harshest judge of his character and has been unstinting in this."

"Have you treated other physicians in your practice? And if so, how does Dr. Kepler compare with them?"

"Max stands out among physicians. His augmented capacity for accountability only builds on this. He's been able to see his way clear to a life of conscious and thorough ethical conduct."

"Do you think he should lose his medical license?"

"How all this should affect the court is beyond my experience. But I did want to make explicit my unwavering conviction in Max, his moral intent and his capacity to make that intent actual. All of my sixty-five years of life and the nearly forty years I have spent working with people as a psychiatrist tell me that Max has recognized, metabolized and internalized the heretofore missing pieces of his moral equipment. We are left not with a criminal, but with a chastened and awakened adult."

"Thank you, Dr. Steele."

Gordon turned to address the judge.

"Your Honor, I have been representing health care providers since 1964. In that span of time, I have represented thousands of physicians, and I have utilized the services of consultants and outside experts throughout the United States. I find Dr. Steele's testimony to be some of the most compelling commentary on a fellow human being."

The judge nodded.

"Thank you, Mr. Fanning. Mr. Arnold, do you have any questions of Dr. Steele?"

"Yes, your Honor."

Mr. Arnold remained seated at the table.

"Dr. Steele, you have been Dr. Kepler's psychiatrist for five years. Is that correct?"

"Yes."

"And is it safe to say that over that period of time, you have developed a relationship with him?"

"I think we have a healthy patient-doctor relationship, yes."

"But as your role as his therapist, you are obligated to help him."

"That is my role."

"And as such, you probably are unable to be completely objective when speaking of him. Would that be fair to say?"

Rick stiffened in the chair.

"It is true that since Max is my patient, I have a special affinity for him. But in terms of my evaluation of him and the process that he has gone through over the past three years, I consider that objective."

"I think we'll allow the court to decide that," Mr. Arnold said with a hint of disdain. "No further questions, your Honor."

"Mr. Fanning, you may proceed," the judge said.

"I would like to now call Dr. Max Kepler."

I walked to the witness chair, giving the judge a half-smile as I did.

"Please introduce yourself," Gordon instructed.

"My name is Max Kepler."

"Dr. Kepler, do you acknowledge what you have done was wrong?"

"Absolutely."

"Do you feel bad about it?"

"I am truly sorry for my past misconduct, a fact I cannot emphasize enough to the Board. I have tried my hardest over the past two-plus years to atone for my wrongdoing."

"What has the time since your arrest been like for you?"

"I have suffered sleepless nights, tremendous guilt, anxiety, loss of self-esteem and self-worth. I have been in some very difficult circumstances over the past twenty-six months, financially, emotionally, and spiritually. I know that fundamentally all of this has been self-inflicted, and I cannot express how sorry I am for that."

"Thank you, Dr. Kepler."

"Mr. Arnold, do you have questions for Dr. Kepler?" the judge asked.

"Yes, your Honor."

"Were you aware there was no off-label use of hGH?"

"No, I wasn't."

"So, you're telling me that despite the fact you have a Ph.D. in Pharmacology and a medical degree, you didn't know it was illegal to prescribe hGH off-label?"

"That is correct. I know it's hard to believe, but it's the absolute truth. And I told that to the investigator on the day I was arrested."

"Well, that's pretty irresponsible of you, don't you think?"

"Yes, and I am so sorry for it."

"Did you perform a physical examination or any blood tests prior to prescribing hGH?"

"No."

"Did you lie to the undercover agent about the source of hGH?"

"Yes."

"Did you exaggerate the benefits and minimize the risks of hGH?"

"Yes."

"Dr. Kepler, why should the Medical Board allow you to retain your license?"

"My record in my chosen specialty before, during and after the misconduct has been exemplary. I am a good physician who takes excellent care of his patients. I promise never to engage in illegal behavior or to practice aesthetic medicine again. I am appealing to the Board for leniency."

"That all sounds good, Dr. Kepler, but you've been shown to be a liar. How is the Board expected to believe you?"

"I realize all of this might seem disingenuous to the Board.  I don't know how to impress upon you that I truly mean these words."

"How can we be certain you have learned your lesson?"

"The moment I received my medical degree was the proudest of my life. In that instant, I became an important asset to society.  At times over the last three years, it feels like I've become a burden.  In an effort to make up for this, I have worked very hard to care for my patients at Cade County Hospital. Through weekly meetings with my psychiatrist, I have tried hard to better understand myself and how I could so recklessly endanger my patients and my many years of medical training."

"Is there anything else you would like to tell the Board?"

"I just want you to know that I believe that this process of self-examination and the difficulties I have experienced as a consequence of my actions will make it impossible for me to engage in unethical behavior in the future.  Being a physician is my life calling, and I feel blessed to have been given this remarkable privilege. I hope that the Board will see that as well."

I looked to the judge, and she nodded.

"Are there any more questions or other witnesses?"

Both Gordon and Mr. Fanning answered "no."

"In that case, this hearing is adjourned."

My legs felt too weak to carry me. I sat there until the judge had left. Gordon started talking with Mr. Arnold as Dr. Morgan slipped out.

I made my way over to them, and Mr. Arnold shook my hand.

"Good luck, Dr. Kepler."

"Thanks," I said, smiling weakly. We both knew I needed it.

# CHAPTER THIRTY-NINE

They would make me wait another two weeks.

If those were to be my last two weeks of being a doctor, I was going to be the best doctor on the planet. I didn't hurry out of the hospital, I didn't get irritated with annoying patients. I didn't worry about all the work I had the next day. I lived each day, rounded out, top to bottom.

With the end nearing, I began thinking more about Lance. It had been three years since I had last spoken with him, and I had never tried to discover his fate. On one quiet day, I spent an hour searching the internet, including criminal databases, for any information about him. Unsuccessful, I asked Ted for assistance. He also was unable to find anything, and so he called the assistant US attorney in Charlotte who had interrogated me that day, seemingly so long ago.

"I cannot discuss with you past, present or future investigations," she said.

The uncertainty bothered me. Although I harbored some resentment, I found that I still cared about what happened to him. Ted postulated that he was probably charged with a crime involving hGH and/or anabolic steroid distribution, but that the case was kept sealed, and thus would not be in the public domain. This was usually done to facilitate ongoing litigation in related cases, suggesting Lance was possibly assisting in those investigations. But it was all just speculation, and, to this day, I have never discovered what happened to my former partner.

As for Follicle Research, I still believed in the effectiveness of our original hair peptide. The patent was still valid, and I knew how to manufacture the drug. I could have had a protein synthesizer pumping out the product within six months. But there was still the unsettled issue of safety, and that would require a lot more work to parcel out. Regardless, I had absolutely no desire to try to resurrect the company, despite how rich or famous it could make me. To do so would mean I had not learned the lessons of the previous three years. Plus, it would be impossible without Lance, as he was also an owner of the patent, and I was not permitted to have contact with him, per the proffer agreement I signed. All of this was moot anyway, because all I really wanted to do was to get back to caring for patients. It was there that I truly belonged, and it was there that I would stay, if allowed.

Several days before I was scheduled to hear from the Board, I stopped by to visit Sang. His door was open and I stood to the side of the doorway, stuck my head around the corner, and knocked against the wall.

"Busy?"

"Of course not," he said, waving me in.

"Just wanted to swing by to thank you once again for everything."

"It was my pleasure, Max.   I mean that."

"You really took a chance for me.   Not many people would have done that."

"It was because I believed in you."

"I've tried my hardest to make you proud," I said.

"You're a good man, and the world owes you some consideration for that."

Suddenly I found myself unable to talk.   Sang walked over to me.

"You're a good man," he repeated.

"Uh huh."   I avoided eye contact.

"Max, I mean that."

My shoulders started to shake.   "Yeah," I said feebly.

Sang closed the distance between us and hugged me firmly.   I felt all the strength leave my body.   I broke away before the tears came.   In the previous three years, no one had told me directly that, specifically, I was a good person.   I knew it, of course, on some level, but it was hard for me to really internalize and believe it.   With a single sentence, Sang bandaged a very deep wound, one that is still healing.

"Thank you," I managed, breaking away.

"When do you expect to hear?"

I shrugged as I walked away.

"I guess whenever the letter comes."

Friday, September 5, 2008, was unfolding like any other day until I stopped by the mailroom after lunch.   There I found a large, white envelope from the California Medical

Board waiting for me. I stared at it for several minutes before taking it into my office, locking the door after me. Too anxious to sit down, I tossed the envelope on my desk and slowly rubbed my eyes. I breathed deeply and tried to recall the serenity Jessica playing in the waves had brought me.

A decision had been made, and I would be powerless to change it. I scooped the package off my desk and, with hands slightly shaking, opened it to find a ten-page packet of information. I immediately flipped to the end, to a section titled, "Legal Conclusions." My heart raced as I skimmed to the bottom. And there I found it:

Therefore, Physician and Surgeon's Certificate Number A656723 issued to Max Kepler, M.D., is hereby revoked.

"Oh, no," I whispered, as I put my head down.
*They took it away.*
I couldn't believe I had lost. My mind raced back to Mom's proud smile on medical school graduation day, and I could feel the humiliation returning again. But I quickly pushed the image out of my mind; I had spent far too much time grieving and feeling sorry for myself. This was my new reality, and I had to accept it. And now I needed to find a job. Gathering my strength, I opened my eyes and began reading the paper again. Suddenly, I realized there was more.

However, the revocation is stayed for a period of three (3) years upon the terms and conditions listed in the next section.

*Stayed? My license was safe?*
I quickly stood up and punched the air in triumph. I couldn't believe the Board had shown mercy. I took a deep breath and closed my eyes, squeezing the rolled-up papers tightly. It was finally, unequivocally, over. Suddenly, I felt...remarkably lucky. And I knew beyond any doubt that I never wanted to place myself in a similar position again. I was done with the unhealthy drama, the never-ending stress, the constant worry.
I unrolled the papers to continue reading.

Cause for disciplinary action exists pursuant to Business and Professions Code...violation of drug laws...protection of the public...rehabilitation of the licensee... respondent has demonstrated significant rehabilitation...safe to practice medicine...would not be against the public safety...adherence to ethical principles and proscribing practices...

Another section was filled with the judge's evaluation of me.

Respondent was credible and honest...genuine remorse for his actions...truly cognizant of the potential harm...clearly understands his responsibility...marginal medical activities...trained physician...

I stuffed the packet back in the envelope, dropped it in a file cabinet, and locked the drawer. Then I took my white coat off its hook, put it on, and straightened the name tag dangling from the front pocket.

"Marginal medical activities," echoed in my brain.

I grabbed my patient list and stared at it, but the words wouldn't go away.

After a while, I realized I had to focus. It was now one-thirty in the afternoon and I had ten people to see. That left me about twenty minutes to see each patient if I was going leave the hospital by five to pick up Jessica. I'd tell everyone the news later. I pushed myself back into the usual Kepler mode of moving forward, pressing on.

Although my evolution was surely not complete, I knew the future trajectory of my life had been inexorably altered by the experience. There would be no more blurring of ethical lines, no more untamed ambition, no more identification of self through ego or external labeling. I would understand my life was not only about overcoming challenges, that there was something deeper and much more meaningful. Something that required a more experiential approach to life, an appreciation of the moment, instead of an anticipation of what was next. I had learned how to find peace, even in the midst of complete chaos. And I knew that I was okay, just as I was.

Later that evening, while I was still on an emotional high, Jessica asked if we could play Jenga, a game she had received for her last birthday. We began after a brief explanation of the rules, but my concentration kept being interrupted by names and faces prominent in the previous three years. Of them all, Judge Natas threatened to stay the longest, but I managed to dispose of him with a swift mental backhand. Before long, I was surprised to find that I was entirely absorbed by my daughter and in the game I was playing with her, all distractions gone.

Now six, Jessica was starting to look less and less like a toddler. Her black hair, naturally streaked with auburn hues, was shoulder length, with bangs a bit too long. She swiped them out of her way as she concentrated intently on removing each block of wood and placing it on an increasingly taller and more unstable tower. I watched her focused eyes, so clearly her mom's and so clearly perfect, and smiled widely.

With each passing moment, the excitement and tension of the game grew, and then just as Jessica pulled out a block from near the bottom, the tower came down with a crash.

"Oh, no!" she exclaimed, raising her arms in frustration. "What do we do now?"

I held her shoulders, squeezed softly, and grinned.

"We can just build the tower again," I reassured her. "It never really ends."

16171876R00307

Made in the USA
Middletown, DE
23 November 2018